What others have said about

Becoming Whole

Becoming Whole by Linda Myers is a thoughtful and important book for people dealing with upheavals in their lives. In a fascinating mix of cutting edge research and ancient wisdom, Myers makes a compelling case for the power of words as a form of healing and growth. This is a smart and heartfelt book.

James W. Pennebaker
Professor of Psychology, The University of Texas at Austin

Becoming Whole will give you a new perspective on the personal journey that is your life and serve as a healing, empowering guide as you explore the depth and breadth of yourself.

Susan Albert, author of *Writing from Life: Telling Your Soul's Story*

That writing can help us explore and articulate our pain, losses, and perplexities is a widely accepted idea, but how to go about writing effective healing narratives is hardly self-explanatory. Linda Myers has provided a lively, most helpful guidebook for memoirists setting out on their journeys of recollection and recovery. The practical advice and exercises are accompanied by a wonderful range of anecdotes that serve not only to entertain but also to model the kind of writing her readers may hope to achieve. A valuable addition to the literature of self-exploration.

Marilyn Chandler, Ph.D., author, *A Healing Art*; board member, Center for Medicine, Humanities, and Law, UC Berkeley

This compelling and wise book shows you how to listen to your inner voice and use it to uncover the important stories in your life. Myers provides a process that leads you to transformation and healing. If you've ever had a notion about writing a memoir, read this book!

Lee Glickstein, author of Be Heard Now! and
founder of Transformational Speaking Circles

What a wonderful, well-written, engaging book. With its combination of practical information, engrossing stories, and focused writing exercises, it is an excellent adjunct to psychotherapy and EMDR. I will recommend *Becoming Whole: Writing Your Healing Story* to my clients and colleagues.

Laurel Parnell, Ph.D., author of Transforming Trauma: EMDR and
EMDR in the Treatment of Adults Abused as Children

Linda Myers draws upon her many roles and perspectives – as individual, as therapist, as writer, and as teacher – in creating *Becoming Whole*. Artfully weaving together these views, she has produced a work that should prove a gentle and helpful guide to those who wish to write their own stories.

Joshua Smyth, Ph.D.

Beautifully written and organized. Practical, inspired, accessible, and inclusive, Myers' book gives you excellent tools to make writing a healing experience. Your story matters and this book shows you why.

John Fox, author of Poetic Medicine: The Healing Art of Poem-making

Becoming Whole

Writing Your Healing Story

Linda Joy Myers, Ph.D.

Silver Threads
San Diego, California

Becoming Whole: Writing Your Healing Story

For information, contact Silver Threads, 3738 Carmel View Road, San Diego, California 92130 (858-794-1597)

Silver Threads is an imprint of Silvercat Publications®

Cover artwork by Linda Joy Myers

Cover photography by Cindy Pavlinac

Text editing by Lisa A. Smith <www.writingatwork.com>

Text and cover design and layout by Robert Goodman, Silvercat®, San Diego, California

Publishers Cataloging In Publication Data
(Provided by Quality Books, Inc.)

Myers, Linda Joy.
    Becoming whole : writing your healing story / Linda
Joy Myers. — 1st ed.
        p. cm.
    Includes bibliographical references and index.

    1. Authorship—Psychological aspects. 2. Diaries—
Authorship. 3. Healing 4. Spiritual biography—
Authorship.   I. Title.

PN171.P83M94 2002   808'.02'019
                                          QBI33-699

printed in the United States of America

Contents

Part 3   Writing the Memoir

Appendixes

Foreword

*T*here is a healing power in the very writing of our stories, whether they are read by others or not. In the years since I began doing life story workshops in 1988, I have witnessed many times how this writing brings peace and resolution to writers who have been tormented and undermined by stories they have kept within them.

I am not the only one to take stock of this. Many times, my workshop attendees have said to me, "This is like therapy, but it costs a lot less and It's a whole lot more fun."

"As I wrote my autobiography," one woman said, "it became obvious that something was happening to me. I was feeling a peace with my life that I had not felt prior to writing. As I continued to write, I felt more and more acceptance and consolation."

As Linda Joy Myers explains so clearly in the following pages, the writing of a life story creates an observer self whose empathetic listening presence brings validation and acceptance to the writer. And as James Pennebaker has demonstrated over the years with various study groups, it is in the writing of the story even more than in the speaking that this healing occurs.

I have always felt that this was so because in the speaking the story remains evanescent, easily lost, enduring somehow only as long as the memory of the hearer endures. As such, speaking a memory offers little consolation to the speaker that his or her memory will last as a witness to what was lived. When a story is written, however, its memory has the promise of survival that is as long as the writing itself.

Healing is a process of becoming whole. And people cannot become whole until they know how and where their existence fits into the human experience. Otherwise they are left with the question, "Why?" Writing life stories is an important personal experience because it can answer the "why?" In the past, people sat with their families and told them stories, perhaps sitting in their kitchen rockers around the fireplace or woodstove. There the old people told stories of their youth and their parents' lives, and the children took the stories in even if sometimes only by osmosis, sometimes without even listening carefully. And the stories became part of the way families thought about themselves and interpreted their experience.

Now, however, with families scattered all around the country and the world, it has become increasingly difficult to tell these stories because too often there is no one to hear them. The storyteller who now wishes to tell the family stories has to put them in writing and disseminate them to the family in printed form. A different way of telling a story but an effective way. And one that brings healing.

Today, more than ever before, people are writing their stories to celebrate their lives and to create a way to break through the silence that envelops us all.

Now, Linda Joy Myers has written a readable book in which she brings to the topic of life writing as a healing art her years of psychotherapeutic experience coupled with her training and experience as a writer and teacher.

I am proud to say that she has been part of our Soleil Lifestory Network since 1998, teaching people to write personal and family stories. During that time, I have talked with her often about her work and have witnessed her dedication and commitment to bringing the art of life writing not only to the therapeutic community but to the average person who may never have thought of himself or herself as a writer.

The beauty of this book is that it not only explains why the process works but shows the reader how to make the process work in his or her life.

This book deserves to have a wide readership and to know a long success. It offers an important access to healing.

Denis Ledoux
Soleil Lifestory Network
Lisbon Falls, Maine

Acknowledgments

For their support, encouragement, and generous giving of time to talk about ideas and read drafts, I thank Doreen Hamilton and Terry Basile. To my teacher and mentor Ron Kane, who has shown me a healing path for twenty-five years, heartfelt thanks for his vision, his steadfast compassion, and, most of all, for his fierce belief in healing and transformation.

Denis Ledoux has encouraged my memoir teaching and writing for several years; his passion and love for memoir has been an inspiration and a guiding light. This book has come to life with the superb editing and mentoring by Lisa A. Smith, who spent hours listening deep into the intent of the book, as well as shaping its paragraphs.

Thank you to Cindy Pavlinac for her photographic and literary eyes and ears, and her passion for healing. Thank you to Barb Truax for protecting my time and relieving me of responsibilities, and to the other members of the California Writers Club, Marin Branch for their encouragement. I am grateful to James Pennebaker, Joshua Smyth, Susan Albert, John Fox, and Marilyn Chandler for their help, and for their work and belief in the healing power of writing.

My children, Theron, Amanda, and Shannon, have shown me that change and healing can pass to the next generation. My deep gratitude goes to them for their love and support.

And I thank all my students and workshop participants; they have shown me how writing is healing to them and how it transforms lives.

Introduction

I began learning about autobiography lying in a featherbed with my great-grandmother Blanche when I was seven years old. We nestled in the soft down and watched the lights from the highway flicker across the ceiling. Silver moonlight fell on white cotton sheets that smelled of the sun. A mile to the east, the Mississippi River flowed by, creating The Island, formed by the river and a slough, land where our family had lived for five generations.

Blanche was in her eighties and seemed an ancient relic, with great folds and wrinkles, deeply etched eyes, and a sharp nose. These nights in the featherbed, her teeth in a jelly jar by the bed, she lisped the stories of her life—how she was already grown up before telephone and radio were invented, how everyone lived before refrigerators or cars. She delivered milk, eggs, and butter by horse and wagon to the neighbors and to town seven miles away. On one of these trips, the horse fell down and died, and it was a walk of several miles to get another horse. She was a proud woman, though poor by most standards. "We always had enough to eat," she'd say with a lift of her chin.

During the day she'd fiercely hoe the weeds that threatened her beloved garden and shoved strawberries flecked with dirt into my mouth. She used a wood cookstove for all her cooking and taught me how to fill the stove with paper and kindling, how to listen to the roar of the fire to know when it was hot enough to bake our apple pie.

I lived with her daughter, my grandmother, rather than my own mother. By age seven I'd witnessed many intense conflicts between them that scared and confused me. Blanche was the mother of the mother of my mother, aware of the history that trailed behind all of them like smoke. I'd ask Blanche the questions I couldn't ask my mother or grandmother. She told me why they fought so much. "That girl," she said about my grandmother, "she went off and left your mama with a neighbor. She's my daughter, but that don't make it right, and ya see what happened . . ." Blanche waved her hand to encompass the fight going on right then behind us—sharp voices carried on the plains wind, making stabs in my heart.

Over time, as we lay in that featherbed, Blanche told the stories about generations of our family. One hot summer night, she told me how she had married her first husband, Lewis, on New Year's Day in 1894, and that two months later he had died of pneumonia. He was my grandmother's father, and his death was still mourned by both of them. The tears they both shed sixty years later told me of the power of history and that stories can explain how things came to be the way they were.

Blanche, my grandmother, and my mother are all dead now. The focus of my adult life has been to heal the wounds and patterns that were passed through the generations—my grandmother was raised most of the time by her grandmother, Blanche's mother; my grandmother and mother abandoned their daughters. For three generations these patterns of rejection and loss had caused heartache, tears, and terrible conflicts that were not forgiven or resolved. After growing up with so many power struggles and grudges, I was determined to break this pattern. I always wondered how people came to healing and forgiveness, how they found their way back to love even when there were deep injuries. These questions about love and healing became the focus of a lifelong quest.

I got a master's degree and became a therapist in my thirties, and worked to understand and break the generational pattern with my own children. Through my healing process I used writing—a journal, diaries, and stories—to tell and retell the family story of abuse, abandonment, and what I came to find out was mental illness in our family, a factor in the behavior of these women. I had always wanted to really write, to go beyond the journal and write our story so that I as well as others could be healed by it. So in 1993 I stopped teaching family therapy and joined the Mills College Creative Writing Program, where I received my M.F.A. In this process I encountered the skills and techniques I would need to shape my story into a book, into the larger story that had always called me.

I explored the ideas of body healing, emotional healing, and healing in the deepest layers of the soul. Eventually I came upon the research on writing as healing by James Pennebaker, Ph.D., and his colleagues. Finally there were studies to prove what many of us have known intuitively—that writing helps to heal the body and the mind, and perhaps even the soul. I went to the University of California library to gather more of this research and eventually met Pennebaker in February 2002, when we spoke of the most recent studies and the future of the research. His books and research, and a new generation of studies that appear in *The Writing Cure*, edited by Stephen Lepore and Joshua Smyth, prove how much writing the true, deep story of emotions can heal on many levels. We only have to take the time and make room in our lives to sit down and do it.

Through teaching memoir writing in Berkeley, California, I have become aware of the healing my students experience when they write the stories of their lives. Most of them come to me with doubts and worries about whether to write their memoir or how to accomplish what seems like an impossible task. Week by week the stories are created and then quilted together into what becomes a whole, healing story. They come to writing with humility, curiosity, and determination, and as with all creative processes, they have to make their way through the hard times when the writing doesn't flow. Through their writing they confront their feelings as well as their family history as they build new layers of determination to keep going. It has been a joy to teach these students and to receive their stories, some of which appear in this book.

In this book you will learn how writing can be used to heal your own pain, both physical and emotional. Exercises at the end of each chapter will help you to ponder the issues presented and to begin your own story. The second part of the book gives you a way to understand the psychological complexities involved in writing a memoir. Inevitably, writing stories about the past, about childhood and the family brings up various conflicts and issues that need to be sorted out and understood on a new level. In Part 2 you will explore family dynamics, childhood developmental stages, and how to address the ethics of writing and revealing family stories. In Part 3 you will be guided through a series of themes and suggestions that help you to use writing as a healing tool and to build your memoir. There are so many different ways that writing can penetrate the heart of a life story. In addition to the patterns, themes, and story ideas presented here, you may create others based on your own needs.

Students frequently ask me, "Where do I begin? How do I figure out what stories to write?" Techniques such as the genogram and the timeline will help identify family patterns and help you structure your memoir. This book can be used in conjunction with therapy to help clients deepen the therapeutic process. A note to therapists explains how to adapt the exercises and principles to help clients use writing as a healing process.

You can start your memoir today by writing about the memories you have and how you were shaped into who you are. Explore the thoughts, feelings, and events that are a part of your journey. Write your healing story.

Part 1
Healing with Memoirs

We shall not cease from exploration
And the end of all our exploring
Will be to arrive where we started
And know the place for the first time.

—T. S. Eliot

The Courage to be a "Real Writer"

. . . the same immense energies that create the symptoms of trauma, when properly engaged and mobilized, can transform the trauma and propel us into new heights of healing, mastery, and even wisdom.

—Peter Levine, WAKING THE TIGER: HEALING TRAUMA

*I*n the course of my work, I meet people who have a passion to write and others who want to write but are afraid. Many people do battle with the internal critic who marks their paper with a red pencil—at least in their mind's eye. Most of us are subject to family rules and a society that warns us not to expose the family's dirty laundry, warns us away from talking about our families.

An internal teacher shakes her finger at us, admonishing us to use perfect grammar and eloquent language at all times. That critical voice says that if we were real writers, all our phrases and images would be perfect, the writing would flow and be easy. But when we begin to write we discover that the beautiful images in our head don't just spill onto the paper, though we are occasionally blessed with prose or poetry that flows. If we want to accomplish our writing goals, we must return to the page to wrestle with words and phrases as we search for our own voice and rhythm.

Then there is the matter of giving ourselves permission to tell the truth in a story. Most often we tell only part of the story, glossing over the painful part and presenting everyone, including ourselves, in the best light. This is not necessarily wrong. In fact for people who tend to focus on the negative, this "best light" method is quite healing and right. But for those who are ashamed or who are obeying the old family rules of silence, it is wrong not to tell the true, dark, ragged story. The critic-censor taps into our fear, shame, and doubt to keep us silent, to prevent us from telling a negative story.

In my "Autobiography and Therapeutic Healing" workshops, I have seen amazing breakthroughs happen almost by accident. Perhaps the protection and support of the group catch the critic-censor unaware. Perhaps the intense passion of the person who is finally writing allows such amazing stories to emerge.

Patsy Phillips, a psychotherapist, attended one of my workshops in Oakland one bright winter day. As we did the go-around and introductions, she described herself as "not a real writer." We all talked about what a real writer was—published, well known, a person who writes every day. During that day Patsy wrote two stories. "My first writing other than journaling," she told us. Excitement rippled through the room as she read the story that appears at the end of this chapter. When she finished, there was applause and bright eyes all around the room. Patsy seemed stunned by our reactions. She looked at the group, her eyes shining and her hands shaking, and listened as others supported her writing and saw her as a writer. It was a magic moment.

"Just little old me?" she said.

The people who attend my workshops often gasp at the beauty and courage of vignettes written in a few short minutes. These snapshots of a much larger story can surprise us because they carry the yearning and core struggles of generations.

One woman wrote a character sketch about her young son, a beautiful golden boy of eight, who is the center of her life. As she wrote and read about him, the energy of the group embraced and held her. Kleenex was passed silently from hand to hand to her, as everyone received her story and her, and her son. In the silence after she read, the room was filled with compassion and support. She looked at us and wiped her eyes.

"Wow. I guess I took up a lot of time. I'm sorry."

Everyone began murmuring, telling her how deeply the story had affected them, reflecting back to her what she had written and lived. As she was witnessed, she began to relax and smile. She said, "I've never told anyone all this. I have never had the space to do this before."

The healing she experienced was not only in the writing of the story but in the witnessing, the sharing of what had been private. Afterwards she wrote: "Attending this workshop was my gift to myself. It gave me the opportunity to reach deep inside myself, draw a circle of words around my heart, and share my deepest feelings with a group of fellow writers who were there waiting to receive me and hold me with compassion and acceptance. I left the workshop feeling fuller and more whole."

The National Association for Poetry Therapy, a group dedicated to using writing and literature for healing, stresses the importance of groups for writers. The association describes the healing process as threefold:

- Writing
- Reading your writing to yourself
- Sharing the work with others and being witnessed

The title "writer" can be intimidating; it has the flavor of fame or excessive responsibility. I have met many people whose writing is poetic and wonderful, but they wouldn't call themselves writers. "I don't identify with 'writer.' It isn't really me." We get caught up in identity and labels. Writing is an activity. Writing is self-expression and a creative act. If you write, you are a writer. Invite yourself to dip into the flow of words in your head and write down what you hear.

You will be amazed at what you have to say, at the wisdom that resides within you waiting for a listener, a witness to your own story.

❧

If you want to write, think about how you can create space for writing in your life, a time and a place where you can encourage this spark into flame. Everyone, yes everyone, even famous writers, has to struggle with the internal critical voices, but for those who have been wounded or shamed as children, and for those who have a "writing wound" caused by having their creative efforts minimized or ridiculed, trying to write is a battle, often a ferocious battle, fought between the part that wants to write and the part that criticizes. The critical voice may suggest that you are boring or that your words and ideas will be a burden to the world. That voice says such things as, "Why bother, who cares, what makes you think that anything you have to say is important?" So it takes extra effort to encourage creativity, to invite it to come out of hiding.

Brenda Ueland, in her wonderful classic *If You Want to Write*, says that everyone is talented and original. All of us need to share our ideas with the world; it is part of our right as human beings to express ourselves. Ueland says that criticism destroys creativity (1987). So-called helpful criticism is often the worst kind.

Whenever I got discouraged about writing I would read and reread her book. It is full of wisdom and a positive spirit about our deep, inner creativity. She says we must write freely, as if to friends who appreciate us and our ability to be interesting. We should write as if they are saying to us, "Tell me more, tell me all you can. I want to understand more about everything you feel and know and all the changes inside and out of you. Let more come out." (1987, 8)

As you write, think of yourself as a listener, a translator. Focus on listening to the stories that whisper to you in a low key; tune into your desire to capture your grandmothers' history, your mother's face, or your father's character. The creative spark lives in everyone—all you need to do is feed the flame.

A Student's Voice

This story was written during a twenty-minute exercise in one of my all-day workshops. Remember that the author had said she was "not a real writer."

The Prayer Man

By Patsy Pinkney Phillips
Dedicated to Wayne Narvis Phillips, Sr.,
my loving husband

"Pray about it. Just pray about it." That is what Mother always said. I was a young woman of 22. I was finally very comfortable with myself. For once in my life I felt fast and fine. Of course, I was still cautious and very conservative. But in Atlanta in 1973, the Bible Belt of the USA, I was fast and fine. After all, I just graduated from UC Berkeley. Everyone in the world would expect me to be fast. Berkeley was known the world over for its drug culture, flower children, orgies, pot-smoking lectures, and hippies on every corner.

Of course all I had to do was say, "I'm from Berkeley," and folks would think of me as "fast, cool, on the cutting edge." So, in Atlanta I felt different, sophisticated, even a fashion statement. Well, I knew that I could keep them guessing. One day I would wear a miniskirt, knee-high suede boots, and Afro puffs. The next day a maxi, no bra, and a head rag. Dangling earrings, bright red and orange. What a fashion statement. I was sure no one would call me conservative or cautious. After all, I was miles away from family and friends. I was really on my own. Finding my own way.

It didn't take me long to realize that I was lonely. I was like a fish out of water, charting new territory. Finally sailing on my own, but too cautious to venture far from the shoreline.

I wanted a family like Mother's. I wanted a husband, a nice Christian man to marry. I could have a family and a career, but central to my desires was finding the "right man."

Mother was always there for me to talk to about this concern. But no matter where we started talking, she would always end up by saying, "Just pray about it." Then, as if I had never heard the story before, she would tell me again how she met Daddy. Mother would start off telling me how she was raised with her mother, sister, and a very mean stepfather. She shared how she longed to marry a good Christian man to take her away from all of that. She would pray and pray for this man. Then, every night she would dream and see this man, but she would never see his face. One day she prayed that the Lord would let her see his face. Mother would make a point to let me know that she only asked to see his face. For some reason, Mother wanted to make sure I understood that her desire for this man was holy and pure. Mother would emphasize each time she told the story that she saw him only above the waist.

After emphasizing the purity of her desire, she would continue to share how Aunt Earlene, a high school classmate, shared with her how she thought Mother and her brother would be perfect for each other. As the story goes, Aunt Earlene showed Mother a picture of my father, and to Mother's amazement the photo was a portrait of the man in her dreams. Mother wrote to this man. Mother and Daddy wrote to each other, dated, and got married.

So, according to Mother, I only had to pray and the Lord would send me the right man for me to marry. "Pray about it, just pray about it!" she would say. I would always respectfully assure Mother that I would pray about it, and then I would hang up the phone.

I would hopelessly, quietly review my inventory of past dates and future prospects of available single men. My list wasn't that long. After five minutes, I would call my girlfriends and we would go out on the town.

Back at work, as secretary for the university's African-American department, I was the first person to receive student requests for registration information. I spent a lot of time arranging the registration of new students.

Now, finally, on the first day of classes, I was able to put faces to the names of the students who had written for information all year long. I purposely wore my lime green head rag, halter top, green and orange platform shoes, and maxi with orange ear-boobs. I expected to be noticed. I don't remember much about that day except for this one student who came in.

It seemed that every student wore horn-rimmed glasses, a white pressed shirt, a black tie, and a suit jacket. In my five-inch platforms, I towered over all of the students. Since I was their first stop in the registration process, I quickly sent them on their way.

There was only one student who stood out above the rest. He was taller than me, wore a dashiki and a large Afro, and had a huge mustache. I remembered this student. I looked up and gave him a very long smile. I said, "May I help you?" Of course I could help him: I was the first stop. I gave him his papers and told him to go next door to see Dr. Long. I also told him to come right back after talking to Dr. Long. I was waiting for him. I waited and waited, and he did not come back. I sure hoped I'd see him again.

Mother would say, "You only have to mumble to say a little prayer." Well, I guess that was one little prayer, because that afternoon when I had to deliver the mail and stop by financial aid, guess who I saw? Yes, as I stood in the financial aid line this tall, fine man from registration walked toward me. He had a very serious look on his face. I thought, He doesn't scare me. So boldly I said, "How're you doing?" He looked around, as if not knowing who I was talking to. I kept staring at him with a smile. He stopped, smiled, and said, "Do I know you?" I smiled back at him. "You don't remember me. I guess you thought I just worked here. I am the secretary from registration this morning."

I told him I was also a student working on my master's degree. And then he asked me where I was from.

"I'm from Berkeley." From the smile on his face I could tell exactly what he was thinking. Oh yes, he thought I was fast and fine.

The next thing I knew, Wayne Phillips came by my office regularly. We dated and spent hours just talking. We had similar backgrounds, with similar values and family rules. I felt as if I had known him all my life.

What made things perfect for me was the next Thanksgiving. I didn't have enough money to go home, so I was just planning on having a very lonely holiday all by myself. Wayne wasn't planning on going home for Thanksgiving either, so we decided to celebrate together. We shopped for our food together and prepared our meal together. So far away from home, I felt at home with this man. I didn't have to spend Thanksgiving alone.

Four months later Wayne asked me to marry him. We got married in the little chapel on campus. Two years ago, after twenty-five years of marriage, three children, and two grandchildren, we renewed our vows. This was the man of my prayers.

Exercises

1. Name five reasons you want to write your stories.
2. Write about what being a "real writer" means to you.
3. What support do you have in your life to write?
4. What stories do you like to read? Have any of these helped to heal you?
5. Describe the town, city, landscape you grew up in. Include buildings, weather, your favorite things about this place.
6. How did the place where you grew up shape you into the person you are today?
7. What family story that you heard as a child excites you, captures your interest? Write that story.

Writing and Healing

One can enjoy the health benefits of writing without the emotional costs associated with writing about trauma The physical benefits of writing about one's best possible self were equal to or better than writing about trauma.

—Laurie King

Writing your true story heals both physically and emotionally. Expressive writing, writing true feelings integrated with events, improves the immune system and has a positive effect on diseases such as chronic fatigue syndrome, arthritis, and asthma.

Disclosure and confession play a role in relieving stress and promoting health. As an ancient church sacrament, confession ritualizes the unburdening of shame and guilt, which enables the person to move forward in a positive way. In the confessional, the person finds words to say the unsayable—halting sentences woven with threads of shame and guilt, grief and regret. Confessional words pierce through the darkness, opening out into the light of hope and forgiveness. Through confession and unburdening, forgiveness begins. We must learn to forgive ourselves before we can accept forgiveness from others.

Psychotherapy has been called the modern day confessional. Mimicking the priest in a darkened, closed confessional, Freud positioned himself in the shadows of a dimly lit room, a sacred, private space in which clients could reveal secrets and hidden truths. His treatment rule was that they were to speak freely about whatever arose in their minds. This was a revolutionary, even dangerous, idea in Victorian times, when repression and suppression of thoughts and desires were the order of the day. In therapy, as in the confessional, feelings, worries, and the secrets of the soul are whispered and formed into words.

James Pennebaker, a psychologist at the University of Texas, wondered if writing would offer the same relief as spoken disclosures. For a decade, he and his colleagues investigated writing in various settings and with a large range of populations, including prisoners and crime victims, arthritis and chronic-pain sufferers, new mothers, and people with various physical illnesses, across different social classes and demographics. They found that it is indeed healing to translate experiences into words, to put events and feelings into perspective through written language.

During the experiments, the control group wrote lists or plans for the day. The expressive writing group received the following directions:

> For the next four days, I would like you to write about your very deepest thoughts and feelings about the most traumatic experience of your entire life. In your writing, I'd like you to really let go and explore your very deepest emotions and thoughts. You might tie your topic to your relationships with others, including parents, lovers, friends, or relatives; to your past, your present, or your future; or to who you have been, who you would like to be, or who you are now. You may write about the same general issues or experiences on all days of writing or on different traumas each day. All of your writing will be completely confidential. (Pennebaker and Seagal 1999, 1244)

Both groups wrote for fifteen minutes on each of the four days of the study.

Even though Pennebaker is a psychologist, the intensity and depth of the trauma expressed in the subjects' stories impressed and surprised him (1990). Middle- and upper-middle-class students wrote about tragic and traumatic events, such as depression, rape, suicide attempts, child sexual and physical abuse, drug use, and family violence. Participants often expressed powerful emotions associated with these stories, and even cried, but almost all of them were willing to participate in the study again. Consistently it has been found that writing a deeply true emotional story has a positive effect on health.

In *Opening Up: The Healing Power of Expressing Emotions*, Pennebaker (1990) discusses how writing about emotional events that had previously been kept secret promotes the release of stress and the integration of a more complete understanding of events. He concludes that simple catharsis, or explosive release of emotions, is not enough. Feelings and thoughts and a new understanding need to be integrated with what happened to create a new perspective.

Pennebaker compares the effects of writing to psychotherapy, where emotional disclosure and the release of inhibition are part of the healing process. Psychologists from as far back as Wilhelm Reich (1897–1957) posit that repression and suppression of emotion contribute to stress and emotional and physical imbalance.

In a primitive fight-or-flight system, powerful chemicals surge through the body to protect the organism against perceived threat during stress. When the stressor has passed, the body may retain the pattern of tension and vigilance, especially if there has been ongoing or severe trauma. When stress is released, the immune system responds in a positive direction, toward balance and ultimate health.

Stephen Lepore and Joshua Smyth (2002) present a new generation of writing studies. An article by Smyth et al. (1999) about the effects of expressive writing on arthritis and asthma made a rousing splash in the writing and psychological community. Lepore and Smyth (2002) present other recent studies in which researchers investigated the necessity of writing about painful subjects. Writing about trauma and negative emotions causes emotional pain and distress for a short period, though both mood and physical health improve after some time has passed. The researchers questioned whether writing about positive emotions and other topics could also produce a health benefit. The results showed that writing about positive emotions and a positive future, and writing about a best possible future self all led to improvement in physical health.

The personality of the writer may affect the outcome of different kinds of writing. For instance, if a person tends to withhold emotionally, writing about negative experiences will likely have a positive effect on that person's health. If a person focuses strongly on negative feelings, writing about a positive experience or a happier life event may have a beneficial effect. There is no single "right" way to use writing as a healing tool. The research about the healing aspects of writing continues to guide us as writers and offers greater choices of how we might use writing as a healing tool. Here is what one of my students, Clare Cooper Marcus, wrote about her experience:

> I'm lucky—writing comes easily to me. Between the ages of five and eleven, I attended a small, country school run by five eccentric women who insisted that we all write at least one essay a week. It was assumed that we all could write, and we did.
>
> Fifty years later, my body and emotions thrown into turmoil by a diagnosis of breast cancer, it seemed the most natural thing in the world to record my feelings in a journal. I wrote while sitting, wracked with anxiety, in the hospital waiting room. I wrote about my fear of death, of pain, of not-knowing. I wrote sitting up in bed after my mastectomy, I wrote in the hospital garden, drinking in nurturance from the hundred-year-old Valley Oak tree, the squirrels running up its rotted trunk. I was writing myself into hope.
>
> Writing was for me a form of Zen practice. It helped me stay in the present moment, aware of each feeling and insight arising, then falling away like leaves drifting by on a stream of consciousness. Writing at such a time was an exercise in

mindfulness. Although I also spoke my feelings out loud, to friends, to a therapist, to members of a support group, it was writing that enabled me to go deeper, to give my soul a voice. I believe it was writing as much as medical treatment that enabled me to heal.

Healing Words

Pennebaker studied how the use of specific language affected outcome (Pennebaker and Seagal 1999). He found that a greater number of positive words (happy, good, laugh) along with a moderate number of negative words (angry, hurt, ugly) predicted health improvements. Cognitive or thinking words (because, reason, effect) and words of self-reflection (I understand, realize, know) created the most resolution.

So if you want your writing to be healing, pay attention to the emotional content of your words. Keep writing until you have causally linked events and feelings. Your first efforts may be filled with negative or unintegrated emotions and confusion. Write an emotionally difficult story several times in different ways. After a while you may find yourself writing from a positive perspective—such as what you learned from the event, or how a negative experience made you change your life in a positive way—thereby continuing the process of self-understanding and healing.

Writing true, emotionally integrated stories

- Makes thoughts and events more concrete
- Leads to greater self-knowledge
- Releases emotional constriction and stress
- Strengthens the immune system
- Leads to short-term changes in the autonomic nervous system
- Provides a template for the writer's future story

Causality

Causality occurs when an action or stimulus leads to an outcome: This happened because that happened first. There is no causal linkage between the two events in the following sentences:

The queen died. The king died.

But in the next example, you can see a connection:

The queen died. The king died of grief.

Think about the stories in your life that connect into a meaningful whole. What do you need to do now to bring together the frayed threads of your life? What secret stories could you tell that would free you from the trap of silence? Give yourself permission to begin writing your healing stories. Write for twenty minutes several times a week, and see what emerges from your pen. Visualize a creative friend to write to, who listens and asks for more. Write into acceptance, support, and encouragement. Write into a warm listening space, and let your voice be heard.

A Student's Voice

Nutmeg

By Nancy Grimley Carleton

I didn't want Nutmeg to be my rabbit, but she insisted.

I was taking care of her for a friend who was having some construction done on her house and didn't want her new rabbit terrified by the noise.

I gave Nutmeg food and water every day and was amused by the way she claimed her territory in the room where she was staying. But all my focus was on my beloved Willow, a gray Netherland dwarf rabbit like Nutmeg, whom I had been nursing through an illness.

Nutmeg lived with us during the last month of Willow's life, and when Willow died during surgery, Nutmeg set out on a mission to claim the rabbit position in my household.

I wasn't interested.

I was grieving the loss of Willow, who had had such a special quality about him that even his battle-hardened veterinarian wept when he died.

I thought it would be a long time before I'd be ready to get another rabbit. But Nutmeg had other ideas and set about winning me over with more determination than the most ardent lover. She ignored my partner, Susan, and focused on me, since I was clearly the rabbit person in the house. Day by day, this small three-pound rabbit pursued me, hopping over full of bunny kisses whenever I entered the room.

I resisted for almost a month, but then, when the construction at my friend's home was finally complete, I started to realize that I didn't really want Nutmeg to go. And when Diane arrived to pick her up, Nutmeg absolutely refused to get in the carrier. She ran away from Diane and jumped onto my lap. "Well, it looks like she plans to stay here," Diane said, gracefully accepting reality. And from that point on, Nutmeg was my rabbit and I was her person.

Nutmeg continued to show that she knew what she wanted and exactly how to get it. Her next mission was to become a mother. She needed a mate to achieve her goal, and she was determined to let me know.

By now she was living in my bedroom and, since there was no other rabbit around, Nutmeg began to court me, rabbit style. At night, when I crawled under the comforter, Nutmeg would jump up on the bed and hop back and forth over my head for hours on end while making a humming sound. After several sleepless nights, I set up a barrier of cushions to keep her away, but she managed to push them aside and continue her nightly hopping. The humming was hypnotic; it felt as if she were casting a spell over me.

I can't really say whether it was the spell or just that I was getting more and more exhausted, but after a week of this sleep deprivation I found myself purchasing a black male Netherland dwarf bunny with white highlights. Although he was only seven weeks old, Nutmeg began making her desires aggressively known the moment Blackberry appeared. The hopping back and forth over the head while humming was indeed a rabbit courtship ritual, and I watched as Nutmeg now directed it toward Blackberry. I had to appreciate her discernment, however, for she had spared me what I learned was the final component of the ritual: urine spraying.

Although at seven weeks Blackberry wasn't quite mature enough to father a litter, in five more weeks he was, and Nutmeg was soon pregnant. She pulled out her soft gray fur to make a nest in preparation, and a month later gave birth to four babies.

Once the babies were born, Nutmeg showed me that the person who coined the phrase "fierce as a mother lion" must not have known about rabbits. I'd never known that rabbits could growl, but Nutmeg would growl and lunge at the legs of any stranger who got too close to her litter. If she knew she weighed only three pounds, she wasn't letting on.

Nutmeg made it clear that once I'd named the four babies—Parsley, Juniper, Hazel, and Shasta—I could never give them away, and she presided as matriarch over my rabbit family of six for the next eight years.

Toward the end of 1998, when Nutmeg was eight years old, I noticed that her eyes had started to bulge and her breathing was getting harder. X-rays revealed that she had an inoperable tumor near her heart, the result of a genetic anomaly that I would eventually learn all her children shared. Prednisone could slow the process, but no cure was possible.

Nutmeg would never be one to suffer and decline slowly to a state of incapacity. She was too strong-willed and far too dignified for that.

I talked to Nutmeg every day and let her know that while I wanted her to stay with me as long as she could, I didn't want her to suffer, and I knew she'd know when to leave. But I had one request: I wanted to be with her when she died.

In the wild, rabbits usually go off by themselves to die, or let down their guard so a predator can take care of it for them. And house rabbits often go off by themselves too, dying when there's no one around. Because I hadn't been able to be with Willow when he died, it felt especially important to me to be with Nutmeg. Intuitively I knew that she did not need any assistance dying, and that a trip to the vet for euthanasia would not be necessary.

One afternoon in January, I came into my bedroom, where Nutmeg and Blackberry still lived. The midwinter sun shone weakly through the window. Nutmeg was lying on her side in an uncharacteristic position, but otherwise seemed fine, and hopped over to greet me as usual.

I sensed her telling me that she was ready to go, and that all I needed to do was hold her.

I got into bed with Nutmeg in my arms, and she lay on my chest as the winter light faded. Her heart beat strongly against my own, and her warm, alfalfa-scented bunny breath caressed my cheek. I stroked her soft gray fur, and she kissed my chin. As the minutes passed, I felt her body slowly softening as her legs started to go limp and then stiffen. Her breathing began to come in quick gasps, but she kept kissing my face, her tongue like a whispering feather. As the tears streamed down, I told her what a wonderful bunny she had been, what a good mommy to her babies. For two hours, I told her how grateful I was for all she'd given me, and I felt her love and gratitude flowing back.

Then the image came to me of her spirit leaping out of her body, and at that very moment, her body leapt in my arms, from my chest to my shoulder, and she died.

Although I was crying, I experienced an incredible sense of joy at the same time. I breathed deeply, and the air entered my lungs like an embrace. Nutmeg sent me an image of herself leaping in a beautiful meadow filled with the fresh green grass of springtime.

By allowing me to be with her and by dying naturally in my arms, Nutmeg taught me that death is nothing to fear. It is just a leap from here to there, a simple movement toward the realm of spirit. This was a greater gift than I could ever have imagined, and it served me in good stead when I faced a diagnosis of a rare and potentially life-threatening disease of my own later that same year.

Never again would I see a need to take a rabbit to be euthanized. They know perfectly well how and when to let go. And between that January, when Nutmeg died, and the end of the year when I received my diagnosis, three more of my rabbits would die naturally in my arms—Parsley, Juniper, and finally Nutmeg's mate, Blackberry—all cheered on by Nutmeg, fearlessly showing them the way home.

Exercises

1. Think about an important event in your life that was a direct precursor for another important event or person to come into your life. For instance, if you hadn't gone to the game that January night, you wouldn't have met John, whom you dated and fell in love with. Write about what led up to this turning point in your life—the causal factors in this story.

2. Set your timer and write for ten minutes about a traumatic event; look for an understanding, a causal linkage to that event, that doesn't create self-blame. If you think you were raped because you wore a short skirt, that is self-blame. But if you realize that your intuition was talking to you and for whatever reason you didn't listen to yourself, that is an insight that can lead you to take better care of yourself in the future. Perhaps you didn't hear footsteps behind you because you were upset, you just had a fight with a friend, or you were sick. What is important is to integrate what happened into your understanding so you can move on to your current life with more freedom and happiness.

3. Write about your best future self: Who will you be in one year? Five years? Imagine yourself living as you want to, but based on some aspect of reality and real possibilities that emerge from who you are now.

4. Make a list of positive, healing words that make you feel good.

5. Write about an unexpected way in which you were blessed with healing, such as an experience with an animal or a garden.

Journals, Diaries, and Poetry

The diarist writes from an ever-moving present.
Autobiographic writing is written from a later point in time, in retrospect.

—Tristine Rainer

Some of you may have started writing in diaries or journals as very young children. Then, as now, you poured out your most private thoughts and feelings. Perhaps as a child you had no privacy or perhaps your family believed that putting feelings or thoughts into words was dangerous or threatening. Perhaps you were lucky enough to have a secret place where you could hide your diary away from prying eyes.

When I was thirteen I received a diary with a little key, but I knew the key would not protect me. I found that diary recently, and I had to translate the words—jottings about events—to what I remembered was really going on beneath them. I had to keep my real thoughts and feelings secret even in my diary because my ever intrusive grandmother would have too much of me if she read it—and I knew she would read it. I knew that the written word could cause lots of problems.

With a background like that, how did I ever become a writer?

I loved stories and books, letters, and all kinds of writing. As I mentioned before, it was Blanche and her stories, as well as my curiosity about our family history, that brought me to writing. Despite an inauspicious beginning with diary writing, I found that later in life I clung to my journal as if it were a raft about to take me over Niagara Falls. Well, a raft might not help under those circumstances, but the journal helped me sort out confusion about my family, being rejected by my mother, and my grandmother's anger. Though these events happened when I was a child, their effect did not go away in adulthood. My journal provided me with a place to use my voice when I didn't have one in the world.

Because reality was an issue in my family, I became obsessed about what was real and what was not, so I used the journal to record what *really* happened. I wrote about my hopes for a better life and my dreams about the future. I kept track of my night dreams, which showed me my unconscious thoughts, desires, and traumas. This tracking of my unconscious helped in my long-term healing process.

One exercise in the first major therapy group I attended included writing hundreds of pages of painful and negative stories from the past. We had to structure our writing into a story. We had to write what happened (events) and our reactions (feelings) about what happened. We were taught visualization so we could see how we looked and what we felt in younger versions of ourselves. These techniques helped bring back memories, including specific words and dialogue to make the past real. Writing as if in a trance forced us to encounter mental and emotional states that we had tried, unsuccessfully, to bury in the depths of our unconscious. We had found ourselves caught up in repeating our past despite every prayer that we would not. That repetition is what brought us humbly to this therapy process. Writing woke us up.

Kathleen Adams, president of the National Association for Poetry Therapy, has written several books about journal writing: *The Way of the Journal*, *The Write Way to Wellness*, and *Journal to the Self*. Throughout her life she has been dedicated to the process of healing through journal writing. As a counselor and experienced journal writer, she learned various techniques, such as Ira Progoff's Intensive Journal method, that bring structure and logic to the process of journal writing. Through her training as well as her own experience, she realized that people bring different needs to their journal writing. She developed structured exercises to help create a safe and measured way to enter into potentially painful material. She suggests that the writer be careful when writing about very traumatic experiences because the writing itself can be overwhelming and cause more stress. During stress, relaxation, nurturing, and containment help bring a person back to balance.

If you want to know more about her suggestions for journal writing and healing, read her books and visit her Web site at www.journaltherapy.com.

Many kinds of journal-writing techniques are healing. A daily diary keeps us in the present and allows us to track our activities, feelings, and tasks. This is a way to stay in the here and now, and to structure time, feelings, and goals through writing. Adams and others suggest a technique called unsent letters. Writing letters that will never be sent is a way to express your feelings to particular people without blasting them in real life with the force of your emotions. The unsent letter may be written to anyone, dead or alive; it is a way to express perhaps forbidden or secret thoughts and feelings. Writing about your present and future self and dialoguing with past selves—the person you were in earlier decades of your life—allow you to explore your identity: who you were, who you are, and who you are becoming.

A freewrite is a style of journal writing in which the pen does not come off the page for fifteen or twenty minutes. The unconscious is invited to give full rein, to ignore boundaries or interference by logic or a critic. In *Becoming a Writer,* Dorothea Brande says that "to have the full benefit of the richness of the unconscious you must learn to write easily and smoothly when the unconscious is in the ascendant." (1981, 72) She suggests that you should write the minute you wake up.

In my memoir classes we often do a freewrite. In this way new stories and thoughts arise, and what comes out of the freewrite is often a surprise. New ideas seem to come from nowhere to find their way onto the page. Sometimes a certain problem with a scene or memory is solved during the freewrite. It is a time to let go, a time to put the intellect aside and just write.

Inspiring books about journal writing include *Life's Companion* by Christina Baldwin, *The Artist's Way* by Julia Cameron, *Writing for Your Life* by Deena Metzger, *If You Want to Write* by Brenda Ueland, and, of course, *Becoming a Writer* by Dorothea Brande. These books feed my soul and help me keep writing when I hit a dry spot. Even as you craft stories for your memoir, journal writing and freewriting help you to heal and to keep your self-expression fluid and fresh.

Poetry as Autobiography

I began writing poetry as a child. My grandmother had introduced me to poetry by reading to me from the *Oxford Book of English Verse*. One autumn night when I was nine years old, I sat next to her on the floor while she read "Annabel Lee," the cadence of the words sweeping us up together into a world of tragedy and love. Other poems by Wordsworth, Longfellow, Carl Sandberg, and the Brownings were part of our English curriculum.

At age ten, in the heat of grief when a beloved cottonwood tree was cut down, I wrote my first poem. Into this poem I poured my sorrow about the tree's murder and my confusion about the adults' silence regarding this horrible event. I was the only witness to this injustice, capturing the beauty and meaning of the tree in words.

Throughout my life poetry lifted me from the depths of despair, especially e. e. cummings in my twenties. I wrote his poetry on cards and put them throughout the house, and sat on the campus lawn in spring reading poems that gave me joy and hope.

When times were dark, I read Adrienne Rich, Denise Levertov, and T. S Eliot as I searched for ways to make sense of my world and my feelings. At the first meeting of my poetry class at Mills College, I told my teacher, Marilyn Chandler, that poetry had saved my life, and she understood what I meant.

When I began to write my autobiography, I did it through poetry, painting a picture of my family, my great-grandmother, my mother, my grandmother's death, and the grief I always felt because my mother denied me. I took poetry workshops and studied with Galway Kinnell, Lucille Clifton, and other poets at the Squaw Valley Poetry Workshop. Finally I gathered my poems, self-published them in a chapbook, and read them at poetry readings. But after a while I felt I had to write my autobiography in prose. A narrative would connect all the dots and would allow me to comment at greater length about my feelings and experiences. So I began a fictionalized version and then turned to memoir.

Poetry allows us to capture fragments because it does not depend on whole sentences or complete thoughts. Poetry allows us to take a snapshot of a single moment, and in this moment all is contained within. In his book *Poetic Medicine*, John Fox says:

> Writing poetry is a way to bring your voice to life. Nourishing surprise deepens our contact with life, our capacity to heal ourselves and others. . . . Poetry provides guidance, revealing what you did not know you knew before you wrote the poem. This moment of surprising yourself with your own words or wisdom is at the heart of poetry as healer. (1997, 3)

Think about what surprises you in your life. What kind of relationship do you have with words, songs, and images? You can have fun with words and poetry—it does not have to be deadly serious. If you have let your journal go, buy a new one. Allow yourself to choose one that gives you pleasure with the color of its cover or the smell of its leather. How you choose to write—in pen or pencil, in wire-bound notebooks or leather-bound journals, or on the computer—does not matter. What is important is to listen to your inner voice and give yourself permission to say what you think. Play with words; create images and stories that give meaning and joy to your life. Pick up your pen and listen.

A Student's Voice

In my ongoing writing group we spend a lot of time discussing how to write and how to access various kinds of memories. One of my students, E. J. Koch, did most of her writing on the computer, and she had received feedback about how her writing sometimes didn't carry the emotion she hoped it would. Below is what she said about an experience writing without her computer.

On Writing
By E. J. Koch

As a licensed psychotherapist, I have read research which shows conclusively that trauma gets stuck in the body. This is attested to by such body therapists as Babette Rothchild, in her book *The Body Remembers*, and Peter Levine, Ph.D., in his book *Waking the Tiger.*

In my nonprofessional life, I have had my share of traumas: neglect and abuse from those I have trusted; rejections by primary partners, close friends, and employers for one reason or another; spousal abuse; and the deaths of loved ones.

One Friday, I attended the Autobiographical Healing group for writers, led by Linda Joy Myers. I had chosen not to take my laptop computer with me that day and had with me only my compact four-inch journal in which to write. Linda gave us the usual 15 minutes or so to freewrite. I opened my journal to a blank page and began. I noticed that the words seemed to flow from me more freely than usual. The experience of writing by hand felt vastly, inwardly, different from writing on my computer.

As we shared our writings at the end of the exercise, I thought about what the group had said about my work in previous sessions and realized that they were right: when I write directly on the computer, little of my inner experience—the traumas, my intense feelings—makes it onto the page. I wondered why.

Then I noticed that this piece in my journal was deeper and more engaging. To create this writing, I had moved my entire arm to put the ink onto the page. An important and integral aspect of the writing process had been to move a part of my body, which allowed the trauma to move through me. When I wrote by hand I released some of my traumatic experiences out of my body and into the world.

I left that writing session feeling lighter, and I have since taken my journal and written in it.

Exercises

1. Select a group of words at random and write spontaneous poetry sparked by the ideas they provoke.

2. Write about a troubling event for 15 minutes. Consider how this event may have helped you make changes in your life or how it created new opportunities for you. In this vignette, tell what happened as well as your feelings about the event.

3. How do you feel now, after writing about that event? If you are upset, write about those feelings until you feel better. Then do something to nurture yourself.

4. Write about a positive experience. Think about moments when you felt whole, ecstatic, spiritually moved, or deeply loved. Consider experiences with nature, gardens, and animals.

5. Write an unsent letter to a person with whom you have unfinished business, such as anger, grief, or regret. Set a timer and keep the writing short, 10 to15 minutes for this first letter. Do not send the letter, but keep it. Later in the week write another version of this letter, and put it aside. In a month read both letters, and write a third version. Notice if you feel better or different about the person, the situation, or yourself.

When the Past Is Painful

All sorrows can be borne if you put
them into a story or tell a story about them.

—Isak Dinesen

When the students in my classes begin to write their memoirs, they work with enthusiasm, energy, and optimism. As the memoir writing brings the past into focus, sometimes memories arise that had been forgotten or repressed. While some lost memories may be positive, others may point to unresolved childhood experiences. When this happens, the writer's energy may flag, and the feelings that come up need to be dealt with, either through writing or perhaps therapy. In a memoir group, feelings about the writing are discussed, but it is the writer's responsibility to pursue further emotional resolution.

As I mentioned earlier, when Pennebaker asked people to write about painful experiences, many of the stories that emerged related to traumas resulting from events in the outside world—acts of nature, car accidents, rape by a stranger, war. Many others had to do with trauma and abuse at home—intense stories of physical, emotional, and sexual abuse; alcoholism; battering; date rape—abuse and trauma inflicted within what is supposed to be a safe place, at home, within the fabric of family and friends. This kind of injury is all the more insidious because the victims, particularly when they are children, often do not realize that what is happening is wrong. It is simply the way mommy and daddy act; this is the way it is. Even mature adults feel that nothing can be done about the depression, the sense of life not being what it should be. A person in this situation learns to feel and think that change is not possible and that life has few options. This conditioning has been called learned helplessness, an unfortunate term that has been used derogatorily in reference to women. It is not helplessness that is learned but a pattern of fear and immobilization resulting from the reaction of body and brain to trauma. This complex physiological and psychological reaction to trauma renders the person unable to make changes or to take appropriate action.

Whether a trauma occurs at home or out in the world, it has a lasting effect on the body and psyche. Some therapies address the physiological effects—the body remembers as well as the mind—while other therapies focus on the mental or emotional scars that affect people throughout their lives. Such hidden wounds can lead to destructive repeating of the trauma, which Freud called repetition compulsion. In addition, trauma victims may develop various kinds of phobias that can cause them to severely restrict their life and activities out of fear.

In my work, I have seen people with both kinds of traumas—the in-the-world kind caused by an event such as an automobile accident or earthquake and the kind caused by long-term abuse and neglect. Both can result in depression, work problems, anger, and unstable relationships.

According to Judith Herman, author of *Trauma and Recovery*, "Traumatized people feel and act as though their nervous systems have been disconnected from the present." (1992, 35) This means that the effects of the trauma follow the person throughout life, causing problems such as a strong startle reaction, sensitivity to loud noises, fears, phobias, nightmares, and depression.

In the last few years a great deal of research has been done on the physiology and chemistry of the brain in relation to trauma and emotion. This research is complex, but what is important to know is that trauma can affect people without their realizing it. For instance, people who have been traumatized may have recurring dreams or tell stories that sound to the listener as if a terrible event is being replayed, as if a phonograph needle is stuck in the groove of the trauma. It is known from studying the brains of traumatized people that traumatic memories are stored differently from regular memories and that they are harder to get rid of or resolve.

Writing, along with other treatments, is a way to reprocess these memories. We need witnesses to our trauma, including our selves. Writing helps sort out what happened, when, and why, and gives us a way to think of ourselves not only as victims but also as people who have talents, passion, and much to offer the world. It is possible to heal trauma and live a fuller, more expressive, and freer life.

All humans live through painful experiences. Sometimes we have written about or processed these memories and put them in perspective, and sometimes we have not. When you start writing your family stories and the stories of your life, you may unearth upsetting memories and discover unresolved issues from the past. You may have hesitated to write your memoir because you think there might be ghosts in the closet. Let sleeping dogs lie, you say. Let the past stay the past, and move on. But you've tried that, decades have passed, and the old ghosts still whisper in your ear.

Writing your stories is an opportunity to put these old ghosts to rest. If need be, you can approach certain memories and issues indirectly rather than confront them head on. Pennebaker told his subjects that if a topic was too painful, they should write about something else.

Take care of yourself. Be your own best friend. There is so much to write about without taking on everything right away. But if you do decide to try writing about what's in the closet, the exercises at the end of this chapter can help you get started.

A Student's Voice

By Kara Jane Rollins

I came to regular, sustained writing after thirty years of wanting to tell my stories but being too afraid. During those years I spent much time being anxious about what it might mean to write, what was keeping me from it, and what would happen if I worked at it. I yearned to see my life on paper, wanting to find some answers and healing from the guilt and pain I carried about relinquishing my daughter for adoption. At first I thought the writing could explain more fully to her what had happened, about my turmoil and struggle. In the process of writing that story, I realized that my motives had more to do with explaining it to myself, healing myself, than helping her.

When writing began to be a part of my life after all that delay, I was feverishly impatient, stumbling over myself to discover the right words to illuminate, clarify, or put everything into perspective. I believed that I should plunge into the oceans of material headfirst and fearlessly, just as I had been taught to do in swimming class. I had no idea how to take care of myself in the writing process. I told myself I could dive straight into the most painful times. I did exactly that, in the beginning, delving into excruciating places, scraping crevasses for the smallest details of memory. Mounds of pain hung in my consciousness in those beginning days of writing like bats hanging upside down in front of my mind, their beady little eyes on me. I had no concept of timing for myself, or for the unfolding of such deeply emotional material.

I struggled for months, starting the "day of choice" story at least a dozen times, but no right words came. I was puzzled that the emotional material was so hard for me to get to even though I could remember my depression after I left the baby at the hospital. I couldn't access the rest of the story. When I sat down to write about that day, I went blank, unable to remember the details clearly. I surmised that I had forgotten to protect myself, which seemed selfish and unforgivable. I became frustrated and angry with myself.

I have always carried birth-mother guilt with me, but at that time in my writing process I began to have doubts about my self-worth in other ways. I questioned whether my lack of memories around the more difficult issues meant that I was just a self-centered, heartless young woman back then. I fought off fears that I had never been a good mother to my other child, the one I kept. Self-doubts began to come flying up around me like dust from an old carpet. It seemed that I could no longer hang on to the parts of my life that I felt genuinely proud of—my sense of humor, determination, passion for education, kindness, and my ability to find delight in small things.

I had difficulty seeing anything except those hanging bats and the necessity that I had to approach them in my life-story writing. I was convinced that I had to tell the most difficult part of the story first or no other writing would be justified or important.

I had written myself into a corner and felt trapped. I was irritable, selfish with others, and depressed, but I didn't recognize it, obsessed about what words were going on the page, and not aware enough of what was going on inside me. Almost accidentally, during an exercise on burnout at a professional weekend seminar, I realized how dismal I was feeling. It dawned on me that I needed to find ways to take care of myself during the writing process.

I have begun to do that. I approach the day of choice story from different angles and write pieces of it. Fragments are all that I can handle right now. I make sure to intersperse that writing with episodes of less painful writing, accounts of my triumphs or humorous stories or ones that demonstrate my strength. When I doubt if I have ever been a good mother I remember this scene:

> It is a June evening in 1988. My six-year-old son and my husband are flying back to San Francisco from New York. They have been gone for a week visiting relatives. I wait in the front seat of the car at the curb, scanning the United baggage claim area for some sign of them,

my heart alive in my chest. A tiny blond head peeks around the door and we see each other at the same moment. Daddy must have told our boy to carefully look out for Mom. He stands there frozen, ready to spring, waiting for me to indicate it's okay to come out. Our Nathan, "Natan" in Hebrew . . . "Gift of God."

His eyes are wide and Dresden blue, his features delicate. The bright golden hair curls around his face like the halo on a Botticelli angel. His tiny legs look thin and knobby in his shorts. I wonder if he is warm enough in the San Francisco fog. He looks so small, so vulnerable, but so filled with delight at seeing me. He smiles and shows the gap in front where he has lost another tooth. His face is round and full of joyful light, a glow that could light a thousand cities. I feel I am seeing his wonder for the first time. I jump out of the car on the driver's side, my eyes on him. He hesitates until something in my face says he can come toward me. Then he runs pell-mell, first to the front of the car and then to the back, not sure which way I'm coming. We laugh at the joyful confusion of this moment. I scoop him up and hold him to my heart as we turn in a slow circle, in our own private, contained dance of love.

As my writing life moves on, I work on whatever feels right. I develop the other links in the family stories about where we came from and who we are. I write about my father's warmth, my mother's beauty, their love of words, and my experiences as one of eight daughters. And I wait for the writing process to tell me when I'm ready to tackle painful stories. I am gentle with myself as I move through my memories, trusting that I will know when it is time to tell each story. I know time and patience will help me find the words to bring life to the difficult stories.

The bats are fading from my consciousness, slowly turning into soft-feathered birds, harbingers of hope.

Exercises

1. Write about what happened in the third person: "she" or "he" instead of "I." You don't need to own the experience right away, but after a while you will need to write the story using the "I" point of view.
2. Fictionalize the story; make up other names for the characters in your family. Make up the setting and other aspects of the incident. Look at it from a distance or through a long camera lens.
3. Write a scene about a difficult incident, but make it turn out the way you would have wanted it to. Change the incident so it ends more pleasantly and positively.
4. Tell what happened before and after a difficult incident. Get to it indirectly, if you need to.
5. Tell your story in a letter to a best friend, someone who is nurturing.
6. Make a list of what happened.
7. Write about everything using exact details, as a journalist would.
8. Write about what happened from the point of view of who you are now.
9. Write about what happened from the point of view of you as a child.
10. Write the story from the point of view of another adult who witnessed it.

Witnessing and Self-Nurturing

Struck by the way people's lives played out themes of their childhood,
Freud coined the term "repetition compulsion" to describe the behaviors,
relationships, emotions, and dreams that seemed to be replays of earlier trauma.

—Peter Levine, WAKING THE TIGER: HEALING TRAUMA

*I*n *Drama of the Gifted Child, For Your Own Good,* and *The Truth Will Set You Free,* Alice Miller, a psychiatrist in Germany, writes about the prevalence and denial of abuse in society, and the hidden wounds of child abuse. She believes that for victims to heal, the secret, shameful stories of childhood must be revealed and expressed to a compassionate, enlightened witness. She says that if we are not alone with our pain as children, if another person becomes aware of what has happened, we have more of a chance to see ourselves and our experience with compassion, and not become as trapped in the consequences of our childhood circumstances. She writes, "A *helping witness* is a person who stands by an abused child . . . offering support and acting as a balance against the cruelty otherwise dominant in the child's everyday life." (2001, x)

When we tell our story to a therapist or spiritual teacher, that person becomes an enlightened witness, someone trained to fully understand the story. The enlightened witness sees us as the whole beautiful being that we are. Miller says, "Therapists can qualify as enlightened witnesses, as can well-informed and open-minded teachers, lawyers, counselors, and writers." (2001, 133)

When we write our life story, we are at once a witness to it and its narrator and author. When we write the true story of our life, we witness what happened, and take a position about our thoughts and feelings as we put the past in perspective.

The idea of witnessing and being witnessed occurs in Speaking Circles®, a program created by Lee Glickstein. In his book *Be Heard Now*, Glickstein talks about how the support of a positive group of people changes lives and provides a healing environment:

> When people give us complete positive attention, we can let ourselves feel the old fears and know that nobody will criticize, interrupt, or psychoanalyze us. No one will take over the conversation . . . no one will imply that there's something wrong with anyone. We are honored for whatever we say, or don't say. It's our time and our space in which to be completely appreciated. *That* is the healing. (1999, 34)

When we have not been received in this way in our lives, we feel inadequate and empty, we feel that there isn't enough, and we feel despair at not having enough of ourselves to support our own healing work. We need to learn how to listen to ourselves as we are listened to by a good friend, a therapist, a minister. As writers we need to learn how to receive ourselves fully and unconditionally within our own skin.

Doreen Hamilton, director of training for Speaking Circles International and a colleague of Lee Glickstein and mine, offers programs that teach people how to create a positive listening environment and move into transformation. Hamilton and I provide a similar program in our *Writing Out Loud* groups, which are attended by writers who want to overcome their blocks and write the real story that yearns to come out. As we create the listening environment, the deeper self is heard and received by the group. The stories are "listened out" of each group member in an environment of complete acceptance and unconditional positive regard.

There are many ways to create healing and to use writing and self-expression to break out of the wounds and fears of the past, including Speaking Circles, Writing Out Loud groups, writing your healing memoir, processes suggested in the works of Pennebaker and Alice Miller, and countless others. All provide ways to tap into your true self.

Pennebaker's studies complement what Alice Miller has been saying for years—that emotional wounds are carried in the body and need to be released through talking, writing, and expressing emotions. This release helps us integrate our experiences and frees us from the cycle of repetition.

How to shape the story of your life and how much to put on paper about other family members, if you decide to publish your story, are discussed later in this book. When we write a healing story, our first attention needs to be on the stories and memories that we need to write for ourselves, stories that witness our memories, truths, and experiences—how we were shaped into who we are, with all our strengths and our weaknesses. We are a part of all that has happened to us, and it is all a part of us. Our task is to come to terms with the negative experiences in our lives and balance them with the life-enhancing, happy, and joyous events.

Taking Care of Yourself

If you have been abused or if memories haunt you, consider therapy along with writing about your past. If you are not ready to write about painful events, write about positive ones for now. But when you are ready, writing painful stories may be a key to your healing. On the page and in a safe place, you can find your voice and let go of the old roles. The important thing for you to understand is how your family's dynamics apply to you, so you can make new choices to free your voice and tell your story. Writing stories that hurt may give rise to emotional reactions that require you to take care of yourself and find support.

If you become upset or overwhelmed, be sure to seek the support of friends, colleagues, or professional helpers. It is important to feel secure and safe when telling personal stories and to alternate painful stories with those about happy, positive memories. Creating a balance makes it possible for us to keep writing and not become overwhelmed when trying to write a complex story. As we grew up we felt out of control and unable to create the kind of peace and balance we wanted in our lives. Now we can choose to give it to ourselves.

Self-nurturing

Nurturing, comfort, and emotional soothing are necessary to the human organism, but sometimes they are missing in situations of abuse or trauma. Children who grow up in that kind of environment learn that they must rely only on themselves. Independence can be healthy, but if it's carried too far, it becomes neglect. An arid wasteland without comfort or connection becomes internalized in the child, and it can be difficult for an adult from this kind of background to receive nurturing or to nurture herself. Lack of self-nurturing can be as seemingly minor as not drinking enough water or as major as self-destructive behavior.

Allowing the self to receive is a self-nurturing act when we have been taught not to need or receive. Trust needs to be established again, with the self as well as with others. If you have been abused, you need to make a transition from internal judgments and the arid wasteland to being able to create an environment in which you can give yourself what you need.

Soothing and nurturing, within balance, repair the tears in the fabric of our childhood. Although different people consider different behaviors to be nurturing, these behaviors have one thing in common: they bring a sense of peace and well-being. When I want to relax at the end of the day, my kitties give me some of the nurturing I need. I love stroking their soft fur and hearing them purr. My shoulders relax and I sit back, filled with a sense of peace. Some people are soothed by classical music, a warm bath, well-prepared and tasteful food, or a clean house. Gardening, exercise, and aromatherapy are other ways to create physical and emotional nurturance.

For interactive nurturing, find a listening partner and exchange two minutes of complete, full listening. Open your eyes, look at each other with softness and acceptance. Receive from each other and give each other your absolute attention. Tell the other person what you felt and saw in his or her deep essence—qualities of beauty, love, and aliveness. Be positive, and maintain a positive attitude for the rest of the day. These new ways of witnessing and nurturing will become part of your healing process and help you find your way to fullness and transformation.

An Accidental Witness

I am a part of all I have met.
—Alfred Lord Tennyson

I still remember the moment when I first heard that line by Tennyson. I was sitting in my high school journalism class listening to Miss Scott philosophize. She sat at the big wooden desk in the front of the room, her hands folded. She wore cotton dresses over a generous yet contained figure, and she had Betty Davis eyes that seemed to see everything. Officially, she taught journalism, but I remember being inspired and shocked mostly by what she brought to the classroom that had nothing to do with journalism.

At that time in my life, I was barely making it. A good friend had recently committed suicide, and my grandmother had changed from a kind caretaker into a screaming monster. I realized that the only way to survive was to get out of high school and out of town, but I often wondered if I would get away, if I would be able to escape. My despair came from watching the grandmother who had once rescued me and taken me to live with her when no one else would, the grandmother who used to call me Sugar Pie and stroke my hair, turn into someone I didn't recognize. I had many worries, and all of them were secrets because one didn't air the family's dirty laundry. Once I was a teenager, I began to try to make sense out of my life and the lives of my mother, father, and grandmother, all of which were senseless to me. How could I cope with the terrible secret of my crazy wild grandmother, who had no teeth and wouldn't leave the house, without going crazy myself?

That spring afternoon in journalism class the windows were open and the air smelled sweet. A girl named Cindy, I think, with a blonde ponytail, sat in front of me. I looked out the window at the fresh greening trees and the blue sky. Nature had always comforted me. Then I heard Miss Scott: "I am a part of all I have met."

The world stopped for a moment. I returned from the floating green leaves and the sky, I raised my hand, and I asked Miss Scott to repeat what she had said. She spoke the phrase again, and as she did, a window opened in my mind. She went on philosophizing, but at that moment something shifted inside me. The usual tight knot in my stomach loosened, and a sense of well-being came over me. Everything that had happened in my life—my mother's leaving me, my grandmother's going crazy, my friend dying—all of it knitted together into a fabric of meaning. Everything that had been painful and confusing was simply a part of my life, and I could receive it suddenly in a new way. I was a part of everything, and it all was a part of me.

Miss Scott brought a new idea into my life that day. I realized that literature was about the exploration of the deep truths that underlie our everyday reality. Miss Scott did not know what was wrong in my life, but it seemed as if she had witnessed me. Or was it Tennyson? My teacher, and literature, gave me something to hold onto.

Exercises

1. Write about a witness who saw the real you when you were a child. Who was this person? What was your relationship with him or her?

2. How did you know this person saw you? How did you feel about your witness(es)?

3. What positive aspects exist in your life thanks to those who witnessed you? Write stories about your witnesses. Show who, what, when, and where.

4. List five favorite ways that you nurture yourself. Write about five more for particularly stressful circumstances. Be specific. Describe time, place, and activity.

5. Rank nurturing behaviors in terms of what works best when you are emotionally stressed. Do the same for physical stress.

6. What activities made you feel comforted and secure when you were a child? What smells, sounds, and sights were soothing and nourishing?

7. Certain daily activities create a security blanket of routine and predictability. Write about your three favorite routines, daily actions that make you feel at home with yourself and pleased with your life.

8. How do you define listening?

9. How do you know you are being listened to? What people have listened well to you in your life?

Transforming Memories

After I've written about any experience, my memories—those elusive fragmentary patches of color and feeling—are gone; they've been replaced by the work.

—Annie Dillard

Memories are part of the fabric of our lives. They help us know who we are; they help define us. But if certain traumatic memories have too strong a grip on our psyche, then we may become stuck, repeatedly struggling with unresolved issues related to those remembered events.

The world tells us, "Get on with life; quit thinking about the past." But we can't simply will ourselves to forget. We may try to get away from our pain through drinking or other addictions or by living in a fantasy world. Memories of traumatic events can be as painful as the events themselves were. The trauma of abuse, loss, or accidents affects the brain. A series of powerful chemical-physiological and emotional reactions accompany such memories. Psychiatrists and other clinicians use the relatively recent diagnostic category Post-traumatic Stress Disorder to describe this condition. After World War I and II, men came home with diminished functioning, nightmares, and a terrible recurrence of traumatic memories. At the time this phenomenon was called shellshock. Often the men felt ashamed and humiliated by their disability. Now we know that trauma has a long-lasting effect on the body and mind. Without a healing process of disclosure, containment, and release of stress, the quality of life is greatly reduced.

For example, a woman who has been raped may begin to avoid men and may generalize her fear to all men. She may become unwilling to leave the house and, as a consequence, lose her job. Her trauma has been locked into her nervous system. For her to heal, the feelings about the trauma and the story of what happened need to be expressed. Part of the healing process for trauma involves reintegrating the event into the person's sense of her life and herself. Writing about what she can do to make her life progress in a positive direction would also be part of that healing process.

Victim, Survivor, Becoming Whole

In our society the word "victim" has many meanings. Most of us have heard admonitions telling us not to be victims, or we've read articles saying that we should always take charge, grab the power, and never be afraid. That sort of advice, those judgments, give the impression that something is wrong with you if you are a victim, and they result in a sense of shame.

While it is true that we want to grow and heal beyond the victim persona, many of us have genuine sadness and loss that yearns to be expressed. For a time, I was stuck in the sorrow and grief of childhood, but no amount of hurrying me or judging me was going to get me out of that state before I had worked through the reasons for my unhappiness. I found myself writing again and again the story of my mother's visits when I was a little girl.

The silver Texas Chief heaved and shuddered at the Perry train station in the middle of the Great Plains. All around me was the huge blue sky, and the wind, and my mother's face up close. She seemed to be a dream come true, almost too real as she appeared from the mists of my imagination. Her visits were a year apart, and during that time I had to suppress my feelings and try not to remember my longing for her. So my mother returned again and again on the page to visit me, even after she died. In my dreams we ride the train, together at last

I told and retold my story, I wrote several novel-length versions, uncomfortable about not being able to get away from my past. I felt ashamed when well-meaning friends told me, "Just get on with it, quit hanging onto the past." But I hadn't healed enough to be able to genuinely move on to another phase.

We have to honor the process. Because the goal of this writing is healing, give yourself permission to first listen to the stories that your hand and body lead you to. If you find that you can't stop writing the same story, it might be a traumatic one that needs more emotional work. Experiment with writing about another stage of your life, or enter into a new story, and let the earlier one rest. After a few days or weeks, take out the story that you wrote and rewrote to see if you have gained a new perspective about it.

Choosing different vignettes and times in the life cycle offers different points of view. As you write about yourself at different ages and in new voices, you will be writing and witnessing from multiple perspectives to weave a larger, more integrated story of your life.

Resolving a Trauma

Jerry kept finding herself going out with dangerous men, men who drank too much or drove too fast, men who would seduce and then abandon her. Once she started therapy she began to see that these men left her feeling the way she had as a child—lost, lonely, abandoned, and scared. She was instantly attracted to this type of "love" because it repeated the scenes of her childhood: a mother who drank, a father who left the home, and being raped. She thought she could control these dangerous men, but she began to realize that they made her anxious again, and lost and angry the way she felt as a helpless little girl. It took a long time for her to realize that her current choices were based on the old pattern, and it took more time for her to stop impulsively going after what she thought was her type of man. Once she made the connection between the old patterns and her identification with them, she began to create a new self, a person who cared about herself. She became unwilling to exchange peace and security for the thrill of a dangerous life.

Part of her new awareness came through writing. In the past, she did not look at her actions clearly and forgot her own behavior and that of others as soon as it ended. As a child, she had learned to "forget" all the bad things. She was a daydreamer and loved getting lost in imaginary worlds more pleasant than her own. Now she began to keep a journal to record her current life. She wrote down what happened, who said what, and when so she could become more conscious of how she behaved.

In her journal, she kept track of herself, reflecting on what she was doing now and on her past patterns. She made agreements with herself about how to live differently, and she poured out her tears, fears, and disappointments onto the page.

After a while, she was able to stand back and see herself and her life as a story—that her mother was a person who had her own story, as was her father. It didn't make what had happened right, but it put her parents in the context of their own past and limitations rather than letting them remain the out-of-control monsters who still frightened her. She learned to see her life and the lives of previous generations as stories and was able to witness their pain for them. At the end of her mother's life, Jerry was able to be kind with her and forgive her for what had happened, even though she remained fully aware of the wounds they had both suffered. Jerry was no longer a victim.

A trauma is resolved if:

- You are no longer troubled by it.
- Your life is relatively free of a negative reaction to the event.
- Your life is not circumscribed by your fears.
- You are not disturbed when you remember the traumatic event.
- You are able to put the trauma in perspective.

Memories That Sustain Us

Early childhood memories, in which we see ourselves looking out at the world with awe and wonder, can exist in a dreamlike place in our psyche. Some of our memories have a numinous quality, like spiritual experiences that remain suspended above the tough realities of the regular world.

Some of my special, numinous moments took place in a rose garden in summer in the town where I grew up. The doves who-whoed, the Oklahoma wind blew through my hair, a breeze warm and sensual wafted the scent of roses toward me as Uncle Maj lifted the head of each flower inviting me to bury my nose in its petals. I inhaled the sweetness of roses, and I heard the sounds of airplanes from the nearby air base and the buzzing of cicadas swirling around me. I inhaled too the sense of safety I felt at Uncle Maj's house, where he lived with his wife, Aunt Helen, my grandmother's best friend. Here there was no yelling, no sharp words, just home-baked bread and the scent of earth and roses.

This memory has lifted me from sorrow many times in my life. I wanted to capture it in words not only to share its beauty and its healing qualities but also to share the love I was given by these two special people. They were compassionate witnesses, to use Alice Miller's term, and without them, I might not have survived.

A Student's Voice

The story that follows describes a little girl's wondrous, almost spiritual experience—her pure physical pleasure and wonder at being alive. She feels this joy despite her awareness of her own shyness and of how others might judge her.

Champion of the World
By Kara Jane Rollins

Today, Miss Shyness of America was not so shy. I had a swing-jump contest with my cousin Ben and Timmy Kendall. The game was to swing as high as you could and then jump as far as you could out of the swing. The winner got to be Champion of the World. The losers had to go tell all the other kids who won the contest and then be the champion's slaves for a whole week. Those were the rules, and we picked a good swing set, the great big metal swing in the backyard of the Methodist Church. You can only do a good swing jump in places where there's a lot of grass around the swings, and that yard has soft grass and lilac bushes all around the edge.

Ben and Timmy had their turns, both of them showing off to beat the band. They had their turns and then had these big-shot looks on their faces. They thought they'd win because I'm a girl and small for my age. But I knew I'd win the contest because I am the Queen of the Swings. That's a proven fact. I know how to hang upside down on swings and stand on swings and do a one-legged swing. I know how to dip my head down so my hair sweeps the dirt. I know how to do an acrobatic swing with my legs up around the chains by my hands. I am a bird when I swing, an angel, or a queen. I like the feel of the air as it flies past me. I open my mouth and take in the world when I swing.

When it was my turn, I was showing off a little because Timmy Kendall likes me. On my jump, I flew like a bird. Something caught me, maybe a fairy, and carried me yards past those guys. I tried not to be too stuck up when I won and Ben and Timmy had to go tell every other kid in the neighborhood that I was Champion of the World. Those guys had these shocked looks on their faces when I flew out of that swing, but I wasn't surprised at all. I knew it was just one of the magic things that I can do when there's no school, no girls with ringlets, not so much worry, and the world smells like lilacs.

Exercises

1. Think about a compassionate witness who observed you well, who seemed to see and understand you. Tell the story of how you first met this person, how you felt about him or her, and when you realized that this person was paying special attention to you or witnessed you.
2. Write the same story three times. How does it change?
3. Write about how you have resolved traumatic events.
4. How have memories affected members of your family?

Discovering the Truth

Keep writing! Your little "Freudian slips" are your
subconscious mind's way of feeding you information.

—Kathleen Adams, JOURNAL TO THE SELF

*A*ll my life I have been interested in how people can heal. As a child I kept hoping that the adults around me would try to get along. I waited for them to find peace and happiness—it seemed so elusive, impossible to achieve. It is easy to understand why, with this kind of background, I became a therapist and healer later in life. For the last twenty years I have had a private therapy practice, and I have been blessed to work with wonderful people. I respect and learn from them, and as we work together I hear about their families and how they all came to be who they are. My clients arrive with a variety of woes, most commonly depression. Their childhoods may have included extreme dysfunctional behavior—alcoholism, abandonment, and emotional abuse. Severe childhood abuse may have caused some of them to suffer all their lives. Yet they function well, with a house, job, friends, and hobbies. They appear normal; their families are not obviously disturbed. When I first meet them, they breeze into the office acting the way people do in any social situation, polite and reasonably cheerful. But as the work deepens, the masks they usually wear are gradually stripped away, and I begin to see that they carry tremendous secret pain, which no one would ever suspect.

A therapy office is a sacred space. In a sacred space, there is safety, trust, openness, vulnerability, and truth. I urge my clients to speak the truths about their lives, especially those truths that have been too painful to think about. The therapeutic space becomes a place to lay down old burdens and open up new vistas of self-development, but sometimes a client is unaware of what happened because, unknowingly, she has repressed past pain.

When an event occurs that is too painful for us to absorb and understand, automatic reactions called defenses take over to protect us from psychic pain. We learn from our families certain rules that serve to keep the family together as a unit in society. These family defenses and habits are passed on from generation to generation, creating a web of confusion about the truth. These defenses help maintain the family's often erroneous or distorted view of itself, which is called the family myth.

It is my job as therapist to gently and gradually penetrate these webs of beliefs and myths that often deny a deeper, more painful story. By asking lots of nosy questions, I find out what really went on behind the closed doors of the childhood home. For some people the problems at home are easy to pinpoint. In a house with slammed doors, raised voices, and broken dishes, the problem is obvious. But in some families the volume is turned down, and there is an elaborate dance to protect the feelings of parents. In a normal-looking home it is more difficult to see any hidden problems because they are underground and invisible.

When I work to uncover new levels of truth, I stress to the client that the purpose is not to cast blame but to bring to light hidden wounds carried since childhood. I assume that parents have done their best. However, the client needs to come to terms with the whole truth of the family situation. Without discovering the real circumstances of childhood, it is impossible to resolve the pain it caused then and continues to cause. In the final analysis, it is not a confrontation with parents that leads to resolution but a confrontation with one's self. The therapeutic and healing goal is to free ourselves of the aspects of the past that hold us back and to release patterns that keep us from being all of who we are, patterns that keep us from being our best self.

So when you write about the years of your childhood, you will explore ever deepening layers of how you see yourself and your family. You will uncover forgotten layers of memory, and you may find yourself questioning your assumptions.

Writing can help you know

- Who you are
- How you think and feel
- What your life story is about
- The meaning and direction of your life
- How to heal

If the idea of writing about the effects of your traumatic emotional or physical experiences worries you, stop and ask yourself:

- How am I feeling right now?
- Am I in my body; do I have feelings?
- Do I feel safe and comfortable?
- Would writing help me to release stress?

If your answers to those questions are negative, then engage in nurturing activities that will comfort and renew you.

It is important to contain emotional expression of painful subjects when you are vulnerable. Practice containment by becoming involved in a positive activity that keeps you away from deep feelings for a while.

If you think that writing would be comforting and would help you to reduce stress, set a timer for five minutes and write. Or alternate short bursts of writing with a pleasant activity to balance things out.

Writer's Block

When exploring your past brings you too much emotional distress, or you find that writing in depth about difficult situations becomes overwhelming, you need to decide how much in-depth, exploratory writing would be healthy for you at that time. It is important that you take care of yourself and not create more stress. Consider talking to your therapist about emotional subjects that arise through your memoir writing. If you are not in therapy, then talk to your friends, support group, or supportive family members as you continue on your healing path. Remember, each person has different needs when it comes to emotionally expressive writing.

The purpose of this book is to help you understand the processes involved in using writing as a healing tool and to help you write at your own pace and in your own unique way. As you familiarize yourself with some of the information about trauma and abuse, you will be able to make considered decisions about how to write your memoir.

It is important to become aware of your emotional hot spots and still keep your passion to write your story. A childhood that may not have been as you wished and a concern about painful memories can be major blocks in memoir writing. I find that when my students and I confront these issues, the writing continues on a much smoother path, and the work moves more rapidly toward completion. Writer's block is an emotional state created by fear and anxiety. When you deal with what you fear and with the feelings that stand in the way of writing, writer's block disappears.

Writing as Exploration

A misconception about writing is that you have to know what you are going to say before you write it, that you have to chart a clear outline and plan before you start writing, and that if you don't, then you are not really a writer.

This is not true. Writing is a wonderful vehicle for exploration, a means of finding out *what* you think and *how* you feel. You can start out with an idea, and that idea will change and grow as you write. View writing as a tool to help you find out more about yourself and your memories, as a way to gain knowledge different from empirical knowledge. Writing of any kind—freewriting, keeping a journal, or writing a story—will help you on the path deeper into yourself. Each process helps reveal memories and resolve feelings.

We need to give ourselves permission to write, to begin somewhere, anywhere, with the idea of exploration, the way Lewis and Clark explored unknown lands in the West. We explore unknown places and ideas when we write, and we need to come to it with humbleness, openness, and a willingness for the writing to take us where we need to go.

A Student's Voice

What follows is a student's description of writing about her family's multi-generational pattern of child abandonment.

On Getting Stuck

By Denise Roessle

There's no way to tell a personal story without revisiting old wounds. Most of us have been there many times—in our minds, on paper, in therapy—before deciding to write our stories for publication. But this time is different for me; I realize there's no way to paint a clear and compelling picture for the reader without looking closely myself. Good writing is in the details, showing instead of telling, and in these details sometimes is the pain.

I knew writing my story wouldn't be easy. It was so rooted in loss. I had given up what would turn out to be my only child. I learned that my first two grandchildren had also been relinquished for adoption. I had grown up with an emotionally distant mother and without the aunts, uncles, and cousins that, I later learned, she had kept secret from us all those years.

But I was determined to write. At first it rolled along fairly smoothly. I realize now that it was probably because I was focused on the task of writing, editing as I went, constantly checking the thesaurus for the perfect word. For a while, I was more reporter than protagonist, recounting the facts but never going too deep. The only way I could describe traumatic moments—my boyfriend leaving me, giving birth and walking away from my baby, or seeing him again 26 years later—was to hold my emotions at arm's length.

About six months into writing this story, I hit a wall. Every word sickened me, every story sent me into an emotional nosedive. I found myself unable to write about how wonderful the early part of the reunion with my son had been because my relationship with him had hit a snag. Writing anything good about my mother seemed impossible when I considered how badly she had treated me during my pregnancy and after the birth. I tried to keep to my writing schedule and stay glued to the chair, but most days I would get so sleepy that I had to lie down, or I would turn to mindless chores and errands for distraction.

Telling my story made what had happened so unbearably real, dredging up the grief, anger, and guilt that I'd kept buried all those years. It was overwhelming. Sometimes it still is. But I believe that finally allowing those feelings to surface has enriched my writing and enhanced my healing process.

I had to learn not to beat myself up over what I was not accomplishing and have faith that I would go back to it. I learned to take the downtime when it comes, and go ahead and sleep or cry or whatever it was that my mind and body needed at that moment. I also learned how important it is to keep writing, even if it's just a sentence that has nothing to do with the book—even if it's only about why I'm not writing.

Exercises

1. What is the most significant story in your life? Write about it for twenty minutes.
2. Do you have several significant stories? List them in order of importance.
3. Write your life story in just three pages. Use this exercise to get an overview of your story.
4. Imagine you are looking into a window of your house at dinnertime when you were a child. Describe a typical scene. Try to use dialogue; describe the room, the food, and the action in the scene.
5. Answer the question: "Who am I?" Write about this in your journal for several days.
6. List five reasons you want to write your story.
7. Write five fears or worries you have about writing your story.
8. What past issues do you want to heal by writing? Make a list, and then write in your journal.

8

Writing with a Beginner's Mind

*One function of the imagination in autobiographical writing
is to allow the writer to try out different versions of the self.*

—Marilyn Chandler, WRITING AS A HEALING ART

*I*n his book *Zen Mind, Beginner's Mind,* Shunryu Suzuki writes about
freeing the mind through meditation, creating the possibility of a
fresh and open mind especially when approaching new things. He
says that we should look with curiosity and openness at everything,
and be willing to be vulnerable enough and strong enough not to
know, to withstand discomfort, to be humble.

When you write with a beginner's mind, you will see your family
story through new eyes. When you write your story the way you see
it, not the way it has always been told, you free yourself from the
strictures of a "right" way to view the world. Perhaps you are the one
in the family who doesn't agree with the point of view of other family
members. You may feel lonely or even crazy under such circumstances. But still, this is what you know, this is your truth. Using a beginner's mind gives us permission to write what we don't know and
to write what has never been written before. Use a beginner's mind
for a healthy, open approach to writing. Write from your heart, and
put the critical voices aside.

Writing and meditation have much in common: inner listening, quiet and isolation, openness. Sometimes we resist writing just as we resist being alone with ourselves. We stay busy and don't take time to escape from the demands of a noisy, outward-directed life. The Buddhists call a mind filled with these mental distractions a monkey mind. Like a monkey, it chatters away, distracting us from our true self, a deeper part of ourselves that might be called spiritual.

Meditation is about awareness without attachment to a particular idea or thought. When we meditate, our thoughts are allowed to pass across the mind like clouds. When we write, critical thoughts can get in the way as we judge and critique them, our writing, and ourselves. Part of our healing practice is to accept our inner creative voices, to hear the deeper truth of who we are. We need to write with openness.

Meditation to Relax

To encourage our inner listening process, we need to put aside the stresses of regular life and relax. We need to let go of our busy thoughts as we make room for other voices, feelings, and parts of ourselves. To help access our inner listening, we learn to relax and focus on our breath. Breathing well and deeply is the basis for all letting go of stress. When we focus on our breath and our relaxed muscles, we can feel ourselves getting pleasantly heavier and warmer. When we relax the tension in our muscles, a tense mind lets go as well, promoting the flow of creativity.

When you're ready to do this relaxation meditation, find a comfortable place to sit or lie down. Set a timer for twenty or thirty minutes. After you learn how to relax, you can obtain the same benefit in less time.

> Settle in a comfortable place, and take some deep breaths. Feel yourself becoming present and being with yourself. This will enhance listening to your inner voice, the positive one, the one that nurtures you, the one that supports all your efforts to write and to speak.

Bring to mind an image of a living being that makes you happy. Some people think of a loved one, a mother, father, aunt, uncle, friend, or a favorite pet. Feel the feelings you have when you are being hugged or touched lovingly by this person or being. As you think of this, bring golden light down from the top of your head into your shoulders, and let it spill down your body, breathing deeply without forcing, just gentle breaths. Allow yourself to feel the warmth that this visualization brings, as you imagine warmth filling your body with well-being.

Feel the warmth in your wrists and hands, your fingers, your arms. Let your muscles relax, the muscles of your body and mind that sometimes keep you tight. Ask them to allow you write, to express yourself. Think of being encouraged by your pet or favorite person. Have fun with this; don't be too serious. Imagine being gently massaged or comforted. Breathe these feelings into your body. If you have a favorite, safe place, either in real life or in your imagination, bring it to mind now.

When you are relaxed, when the mind and body are in harmony and your thoughts are flowing freely like a stream, write for five minutes.

Meditation to Your Past Self

Now you will be guided into remembering earlier parts of your life. Follow the exercise as far as you like. If you become uncomfortable, stop, and return to the present.

See yourself at the age you are now. Picture how you look, what you are wearing, the shape of your life. See yourself in your mind's eye: your body, your clothes in your favorite colors, your hair, face, and skin. See the people you spend time with, the things you are most proud of. What do you need to heal or change?

Now imagine the calendar flying back to ten years ago. What did you look like then, what style of clothes were you wearing? Where were your favorite restaurants or clubs? What did you do in your leisure time? See if you can remember who you spent time with and what you did. What were your hopes and dreams?

Go back another ten years and ask yourself these same questions. Decade by decade revisit who you were, what you were doing, what you were feeling, wanting, and dreaming.

Notice—but don't dwell on—any issues and problems that you faced during these decades. What were you trying to heal or avoid? How did that work for you? Think about your hopes and dreams. What was the best part about your life? How did you feel about yourself during each period of your life? What was your favorite color? Food? Vacation? Who were your friends, pets? What books influenced your life?

See yourself all the way back into your adolescence and then into childhood. See your body, feel how it felt to be twenty, fifteen, ten, five. See yourself in your clothes, inside your room, in your house. Who are the people in your family back then? What did they look like, sound like? Notice the memories that have formed you and are a part of you.

Pick up your pen and write about one of the scenes you just pictured. Write a vignette; sketch out what you remember without anchoring it to a story. This memory exercise can help you bring the past into focus and help you picture important scenes in your life that may have receded into your unconscious mind.

A Student's Voice

Small sketches can say so much about how life is lived and the meaning we give it. The following vignettes, set in Iran, are small jewels. Strung together, they weave a tapestry of images and memories from a different place and time. Roya Sakhai, a psychotherapist in Berkeley, California, teaches at New College.

Madarjun and Her Opium

By Roya Sakhai

My madarjun, my grandmother, was a very strong woman. She was a large woman with beautiful black hair and tiny red-black lips, thick black eyebrows, and big brown eyes.

My most vivid memory of her is the daily opium smoking. The ritual of putting all kinds of nuts and pastries and teas on different dishes, and of course the little tea pot with small tea glasses. She smoked opium four or five times a day. It seems like those four or five times of smoking, her sweet ritual, was all she had to live for. I can not exactly remember what she wore. I have this image of pale yellow flannel cotton, something between a nightgown and a housedress.

Morning would start with her slow move to the downstairs room to set up all she needed to start the ritual. She would put chucks on a *manghal*, a special tray for the opium, fire the chucks, and start the opium. She'd have a puff of opium and a sip of tea, then eat some biscuits to cut the bitter opium taste.

She would start in a very bad mood, then switch to a better mood through the day as the opium started to work on her body and mind. When she started to get high, she would call us, my brother and me, to come to the room and sit by her manghal to listen to her stories . . .

Madarjun's Co-Wives

By Roya Sakhai

You could see the passage of time in Madarjun's life from being a co-wife to divorcing two times and being a modern woman.

One of Madarjun's most interesting stories was about her first marriage. She married three times, but none of the marriages were as interesting as the first one. She always kept the elegant frame with Grandpa's photo in the cupboard in her room. Once in a while she would bring the photo out. She would kiss it, and cry some, and then put the frame back in the cupboard. Every time the photo came out, I would hear a new piece of her life.

She was twelve years old when she became the youngest wife of my grandpa. He was from Afghanistan, a diplomat. He'd travel to Iran, India, and Pakistan, and would marry a new wife each time he went on a new trip. Grandma said she was his last wife, and, according to her, he adored her.

Madarjun told me that Grandpa, arriving in Ahwaz, a city in the south of Iran, had asked for the most beautiful girl in the town, and everyone recommended Madarjun. This was how she became his last wife. He sent for her hand with lots of jewelry and silk, and her father agreed to the marriage.

Grandpa had many, many other wives whom he had married during his other trips. The fun part of this story was that Grandma was still best friends with many of these co-wives decades after Grandpa's death. My brother and I would call them "aunts" and listen to their memories.

Grandma would tell us how much fun she had with her co-wives. How much they loved each other. She said, "Grandpa would bring lots of silk from India, and we would share the silk." She had a sweet laugh, and a shine would come to her eyes as she said, "Of course being the youngest and the most favorite wife, I would get most of the silk, but I was not selfish. I would share the silk with all of your aunts."

Exercises

1. Write about what "Beginner's Mind" means to you.
2. Find photos for each decade of your life. Write about these topics for each decade:
   a. What was most important during these years?
   b. What was the best part of your life; the worst?
   c. Write about your hopes and dreams.
   d. Describe your favorite clothes; activities.
   e. What were your mother and father like during this time?
   f. How about brothers, sisters, or other family members?
3. Describe your grandmother; your grandfather.
4. What life lessons did you learn from them?
5. What legacy did they pass on to you?

Beyond the Journal

If he wrote it he could get rid of it. He had gotten rid of many things by writing them.

—Ernest Hemingway, "Fathers and Sons"

*C*reating a memoir requires at least two levels of writing. A first draft arises from a fragmented and chaotic mélange of memories and experiences. Thoughts come in a stream of consciousness, in free association, and in dreamlike imagery, without structure or logical sense. As the writing evolves into later drafts, these fragments coalesce, and a structured and logical story develops. If you try to focus your writing into a story prematurely, you may lose the deep, inner, unself-conscious flow.

In his studies of writing, Pennebaker found that catharsis alone does not create healing, although expressing strong feelings may relieve emotional pressure briefly (1990, 37). In his early studies, Pennebaker discovered that incoherent and fragmented narratives changed to stories with a structure—a clear beginning, middle, and end—after several days of the writing experiment.

Pennebaker and Seagal say that "constructing stories . . . helps individuals to understand their experiences and themselves." (1999, 1243) One reason story writing is so important is that it gives an event structure and meaning, and provides a way to contain and organize emotions. "Constructing stories facilitates a sense of resolution, which results in less rumination and eventually allows disturbing experiences to subside gradually from conscious thought."

Linda Kitahara has attended my workshops for three years. She is a shy, quiet person who has kept a journal all her life. She didn't see herself as a writer. She said, "I'm just a journaler." But she stayed in my class and learned about story writing, story structure, and ways to make scenes come alive on the page. Her goal is not necessarily to publish her story, but she does want to finish it, for herself and for the sake of her own accomplishment. She realizes now that her story and her life are significant and worth capturing in story form.

"Writing my story has been healing for me," she said. "I needed to keep going, and try to understand myself in a new way."

Elements of Story

A story moves toward a goal, the denouement or climax—the reason the story was written, the resolution of the story. Important events relating to that story goal are put in order by the narrator. In an autobiography, the narrator is both the writer and a character in the story. The observant self, a part of you, stands back and sees the story from a distance. When you do this, you become your own witness. This is healing.

A narrative is a constructed story. Pennebaker and Seagal call a narrative a "type of knowledge." (1999, 1249) This expression of knowledge is not only intellectual but emotional. As we select certain events from the many in our lives and put them together, we process information, making decisions about what is important and less important to present in our story. We don't include all the small details that don't pertain to the main idea or the point we want to make in the story. We choose what to put in and what to leave out, and slant the story to show how we feel and what we think about the themes we are writing about.

A narrative requires integration: the observant self watches the part of us that was a child and comments on that child, describing the child and events in her life from a distance. The observant part of us witnesses the child that we once were, giving us the opportunity to have a new experience or perhaps to discover a new perspective about ourselves.

Pennebaker says that writing a story organizes life events and allows the person to go on with a new understanding of these events. He told me, "Language organizes trauma in a way that images can't." (2002) Writing about traumatic events allows them to be processed differently. Writing helps the person let go of the experience and quit obsessing about it.

Four Aspects of Story Writing

- A story has a beginning, middle, and end—a created structure.
- There is causality in plot development.
- Themes weave throughout the text.
- A story is shaped into a narrative that can be understood by a reader.

Reclaiming Your Voice

In school we learned academic writing, a style that traditionally left out the first person "I." The use of the first person is considered too personal and informal for much writing. Our society encourages us to distance ourselves from our emotions, which are viewed as too revealing and too personal. In school and on the job, objectivity in writing is expected. But the autobiographer is allowed to be subjective and writes from the center of the soul.

When you write to heal, it is important for you to reclaim your voice, to state your world view from the point of view of the "I." When you first write for the purpose of healing, it may be too painful to own your experience fully. It is all right to distance yourself as you come to terms with the subject of your writing, and it is important to take care of yourself during the healing process. If your memories are too close and painful, write in the third person—"he" or "she" experienced this, and this is the way "he" or "she" reacted. Once you have written stories using the third person and distanced yourself from the pain, you can gradually try using "I," your first person voice, to tell the story.

Even when my students are focused on their memoirs, I encourage them to keep a journal about the writing process. A writer needs a place where she is not thinking about the narrative voice or thinking about how to create a story. You need a place to download the raw material of your life and even new memories as they come up. You need a private, secret place where there is no audience and no judge.

Write in your journal when:

- You don't want an audience.
- You get stuck.
- You don't want to worry about plot and structure.
- You want to listen to your inner voice.

Gradually, you move from raw writing in your journal to writing structured stories. Exercises in this book will help you think about and learn about story construction.

Making Time for Writing

There is no one right way to write, or even a correct or proper time of day to write. Sometimes we try to freewrite but are unable to keep the flow going. Or the writing does not come regularly. Each of us may reflect and write best at a different time. If your best writing time is at midnight, then writing in the night stillness and silence can bring your day to a peaceful and centered close. If morning works for you, great. Enjoy the first fruits of the day at your journal, perhaps over a cup of steaming coffee or tea. Some women like to write at a café or coffeehouse so that household chores and interruptions don't keep them from writing. If you leave the house to write, don't take your cell phone.

Using Sensual Details

We live in a world full of sensations. When we write, we need to allow ourselves to feel this sensual world and bring it to the page. Writing our sensations means that the words and associations we choose create a world that stimulates sight, sound, smell, and touch.

Sight Use color, shape, texture, and other specific details to describe how things look. Specificity helps us remember better.

Sound Traumatic memories can be associated with intense sounds, such as loud noises, screaming, storms, anything that overwhelms our senses. Even small sounds—a clock ticking, keys jiggling, a cat mewing—may evoke memories. Most noticeable of all may be the sound of silence. Of course sounds may evoke happy memories as well—the ticking of a grandfather clock, a rushing stream, the ocean, and music.

Taste Our taste buds are particularly sensitive during childhood. Some of our best memories involve food and spice: the first time we ate a particular food, our favorite meal or dessert.

Smell Our olfactory sense may be the most powerful of all. Memory is easily evoked through experiencing a smell or scent connected with a particular person or event—the smell of someone's perfume; the way a person's clothes smell like no one else's; the smell of lilacs, oranges, the sea.

Feel Our skin can apparently retain memory of a particular touch, of the texture of rough or smooth surfaces, such as leather, sand, or a cat's fur. Our bodies remember how we felt when we saw our first sunset or when something significant happened—a thrill coursing through the blood, or a hollow ache.

When you write, allow your mind to slip into the memories of these sensuous experiences, to feel, smell, and sense the details that you remember. Keep in mind that the use of sensual descriptions and language creates a feeling in the reader similar to your own experience. This is what you want; you want the reader to feel your world, to enter into your body and mind, and to journey with you into the past of your imagination and memory.

A Student's Voice

Johanna has been in my classes for two years, but this piece was the first one she wrote during an all-day workshop. In this vignette written in thirty minutes, she paints a picture of grief, of silence. She presents such a vivid world of color and sensual detail that we feel we are standing behind her, watching, feeling the family's grief and loneliness that will haunt this young girl for years.

Bim

By Johanna Clark

It was in 1942 that my mother received the telegram. These were the war years. My father and two of my brothers were in the navy. Life on the home front seemed to revolve around the war effort, food rationing, and victory gardens, and around news from the Atlantic or Pacific fronts.

I had just turned four. My father had by now, as they said, "lost all the money." The family had moved to a smaller house on what was called the wrong side of town. My mother's and father's marriage, the second for my mother, was strained. Her central attachment was to her first-born, the boy called Bim. Bim was her golden child. He was a handsome blond fighter pilot who had been her hope and protector during her earlier years of single motherhood.

When the telegram was delivered to our door, my mother clutched it and sank to her knees. This might otherwise have been an ordinary morning. Sunlight streamed through the living room window and dappled the faded oriental carpet. My mother was in a housedress, her light blond hair swept up in the style of the '40s. She was a small woman, with a plumpness she would lose later, when she became sick. I stood on the side of the room, a scraggly little blond girl, hair in pigtails, wearing overalls that were too small for me.

I moved toward her instant grief. She tightened and was at that moment pulled further into a world apart from me. The morning light was the same, and the rug still bathed in its radiance, and she was moving away.

The telegram said that Bim, Rufus Campion Clark, was reported missing in action. His plane probably went down somewhere in the South Pacific. His body was never recovered.

After the day of the telegram, my mother hung a special memorial cloth in the front window, as was the custom, the gold star indicating that a young man was not to return.

In time, my father and my brother Neal did return. My sister, Lee, married her boyfriend who was back from the army. And we moved again, my parents, my brother Smitty and I, back to a rented house on the West Side.

My mother commissioned a neighbor to paint a large portrait of Bim from photographs. The portrait showed a smiling and handsome Bim in naval uniform, against a blue sky. It was put in a gold frame and hung over the fireplace mantle. Brass candlesticks were placed on either side. And my mother had all the downstairs rooms painted blue, to go with the blues of the portrait. Upstairs, all the wallpapers were in blues.

By 1945 the war was over and my parents' marriage went through a final couple of years of breakdown before it dissolved, before my father disappeared in defeat and my mother went back to work to support Smitty and me, her late-in-life children.

We didn't talk much about Bim at the dinner table, Mother, Smitty, and I. In fact, I don't recall Mother ever mentioning him. I do remember the bottom drawer of her oak desk, stuffed with carefully wrapped letters, her correspondence with Bim throughout his college and war years. My mother's letters were neatly typed on her old Royal. Respecting her privacy, I never read the letters.

My mother stayed behind her veil of sadness and sorrow. Sometimes she would sit and read or listen to music on Sunday afternoons in the living room near the painting. But mostly she was occupied with her six-day-a-week job at the store, and Smitty and I constructed our own lives, separate from our mother and separate from each other as well.

After a few years, when I was eleven and Smitty fourteen, our mother became sick and had the first of several surgeries for cancer. She lived for another three years.

When she died, there was still the painting of Bim. My sister had returned from her home in California to clear out the house. She destroyed Bim's and my mother's correspondence, but she took the painting back to California and hung it over her own mantle and painted her walls blue. She lives in another state now, and Bim's portrait is still over her mantle.

A few years ago her younger brother, Neal, told Lee that he'd resolved so many of his conflicted feelings toward Bim and wanted to borrow the painting. Lee said that she couldn't part with it, that she spoke with Bim every day. She sent Neal a Xerox® copy.

I often think about the Bim shrine that my mother erected and that my sister perpetuated. And I think of how the Bim painting froze a real young man into eternal glory, a prince forever. But mostly I think of that ordinary, brilliant morning when my mother sank to her knees into a life of grief and disconnection and of how, even as a four year old, I knew that it was one of those moments that would change the lives of everyone in the family.

Exercises

1. Set a timer and write in your journal for 15 minutes about a significant childhood memory. Don't worry about structure or if it makes sense. Write it as you would any journal entry.

2. Now, using that same memory, write a story scene from the third person point of view. Watch the scene as if through a camera lens, and write down what you see. Use sensual details to describe the way people and things sound, look, smell, and feel. Include internal perceptions: how your body feels and how you know what you know. Style and polish don't matter. Just write.

3. Reflect on the differences between the journal form and the third-person story. Did you worry more about the second piece? If so, what were your worries? Did a critical inner voice come out and hassle you? Write down what that voice said, and put it aside.

4. Make a list of ten positive memories.

5. Choose one of these memories and freewrite about it. Don't worry about grammar and spelling; just write what comes to mind freely, without trying to make it perfect.

6. When you are ready, choose another memory, and write another vignette.

Part 2
The Psychology of
Memoir Writing

Those who cannot remember the past
are condemned to repeat it.
—George Santayana

How the Past Shapes the Present

Time present and time past are all present in time future.

—T. S. Eliot

While you write your memoir, you re-encounter your family and relive your childhood as your early years come to life on the page. As the narrator, you will tell the story of the significant things that shaped you and your life through your own eyes and your own point of view. Memoir requires reflection, thought about the "how" and the "why" things happened the way they did, as well as the "who, what, when, and where" of a typical story.

When students read their family stories aloud in my class, they are often surprised by their classmates' reactions: they receive unexpected insights and comments about their families and themselves. The reactions of the class reflect views of family dynamics that are different from those the student holds. Most of us grow up perceiving our family and childhood as "just the way it is," unaware at the time of the many different ways families live, raise children, and cope with stressful events, needs, and disappointments. We begin our writing from this internalized, even naïve, perspective, only to find ourselves surprised by how other people react to our story. I have found that when writing a memoir, it helps students to learn how the family crucible shapes a child and how child-rearing practices from past generations affect them. When students understand how tragedy, trauma, or stressful events alter the family, the critic is stilled, and the writer is able to confront difficult and painful material with greater insight and compassion. The progress of writing a healing story is aided by this knowledge of family psychology as well as of how to write such a story.

"Family" can be defined in many ways, and these definitions seem to be expanding as the world changes and gets smaller through technology. Ordinarily, "family" refers to a group of people who have a common ancestor or are related by marriage. The nuclear family includes parents and children; the extended family includes a collection of grandparents, aunts, uncles, and cousins, great aunts and uncles, great-grandparents, and people added to the family through marriage. The extended family may also include intimate friends and life partners who are unmarried.

People who were orphaned or grew up in an atypical family will have a more complex history and perhaps more questions to ask as they consider writing their memoirs. Some experience a persistent heartache that accompanies the early death of a parent, abandonment, divorce, or any early loss. Children can feel abandoned even when they live in the same house with their parents if those adults are so dysfunctional or in such pain themselves that they can't be present for the children. Mental or physical illness creates a situation of abandonment for children because the afflicted parent can't really do what is needed for them. It can be difficult to sort out this kind of family history because of struggles with guilt: unacceptable, negative feelings vie with feelings of empathy for the ill person. You may think of yourself as selfish if you feel angry about your own unfulfilled needs when your parent is ill. Nonetheless, it is natural to experience those conflicting feelings. And of course it is important to remember that not all atypical families are dysfunctional. Each family is unique, with strengths that balance some of the more negative traits. In some families, it is difficult to see these points of light, at least early in the healing process, because of the emotional pain that gets in the way of finding compassion. It is important to help your authentic voice to speak and tell the dark stories that will help you go to the next stage of healing.

For me, growing up with a grandmother and living far away from my divorced parents, I always felt that I was odd, different, and of a lower status than other people. But my grandmother acted as if she was better than everyone, so there was no way to talk about how I felt. I hated filling out those forms where we had to write our mother's and father's names. I had to fill in "guardian" and then endure the questioning looks I thought that word implied: "What happened, what's wrong with your family, why aren't you normal?"

In addition, my mother and grandmother acted bizarrely—screaming, throwing dishes, rushing dramatically to and from trains, and crying during each visit. During my early years, I didn't realize that my grandmother had left my mother when she was young. I could see their pain, but I just wanted us to be like everyone else. (Of course that's a common childhood wish that rarely comes true.) It wasn't until my mother was on her deathbed that I received an official diagnosis for her and my grandmother: manic-depression. Finally I had a name and an explanation for behaviors that had caused pain for so many people in our family for generations.

Whether we like it or not, family is the training ground for our adult lives, where we discover who we are and who we are not, and where we form the habits and beliefs that we carry with us into adulthood. Theories abound about whether this early learning process is primarily emotional, cognitive, spiritual, or some combination of these. In 1975, I was drawn to the Fischer-Hoffman Process, my first therapy experience, because of its philosophy: that we are all whole human beings, with physical, mental, emotional, and spiritual aspects. According to Bob Hoffman, founder of the Quadrinity Process and author of *Getting Divorced from Mom and Dad*, we strive to become like our parents, adopting their positive and negative traits to try to please them and gain their unconditional love. We focus on the outside, on getting that love, which can leave us vulnerable and unable to learn how to love ourselves. The therapy experience taught me that in order to find myself, first I had to confront all the repressed "bad" feelings I'd carried through the years, trying to be "good" and likeable. Only then would I be able to see the past clearly and to understand who I am, and who my parents and grandmother were. The idea that, deep down, we are loveable, perfect beings gave me the freedom to search for peace and healing through the years, and provided me with a way to break the pattern that had passed through the generations of my family—three generations of mothers who had emotionally and physically abandoned their daughters. One of the most significant tools used in this therapy was writing. We wrote for hundreds of hours. During the three months I was involved in the Fischer-Hoffman Process, I wrote autobiographical material for the first time—a negative, emotional version that tore the veils from my eyes.

Writing helps us to see family patterns and dynamics more clearly, and helps us to create a transformed view of ourselves, our identity, and how we feel about our family. Through this refashioned view we can heal old wounds and find the freedom to be ourselves, be more of who we truly are, at a deep and satisfying level.

A Student's Voice

In this story of heartrending family separation, the author sets the scene and uses the senses to show how the children experienced this traumatic moment.

The Departure

By Geraldine Messina Smith

My sisters and I watched from the front window of our house on Josephine Street as a black car pulled up in front and stopped. A woman wearing a dark coat and carrying a black handbag and black notebook got out and walked to our door.

I hoped this wasn't the social worker Daddy said would come for us. She had gray hair, wore glasses but no lipstick, and had on old-fashioned shoes with thick heels. Her thin lips made her look stern. Maybe she was expecting to have a fight with Daddy. I knew he did not want us taken away from him. Daddy bent his head down as he came to the door. The lady stood with her coat on and refused his invitation to sit down. She said, "Are the girls ready? They do not need to take anything with them. They will be getting clothes and shoes at the orphanage."

I was twelve years old, and I had heard about this orphanage. I thought only children with no parents were orphans, and I could not understand how we could be taken to an orphanage when we had parents, but I was afraid to ask questions. My little sisters clustered around me, and I tried to be strong for them.

The lady ushered the four of us down the stairs. Daddy hung his head and followed us. Why didn't he say anything? He was still in his dirty work clothes, with cement still sticking to his khaki-colored shirt and pants. I looked up at him—he had always seemed so tall and strong, I knew he was proud of his strength. He had to be strong for his work at Mondo Construction Company, paving streets, sidewalks, and driveways, digging ditches for sewer pipes, and laying bricks for foundations. I was surprised to see tears streaming down his ruddy, weather-beaten face. This was the first time we had seen him cry. He was still a handsome man with his black curly hair and rugged face, but today his shoulders were hunched. Today he did not seem strong. He was sad, broken down, and upset. Our family was being broken up just because Momma had been taken to the state mental hospital, and he could not prevent it.

Charlotte was just three, and Doris was five. They began crying, too. I was stoic and kept myself from crying by clenching my teeth and tightening my lips. I needed to take care of my sisters as I was used to doing. Rosalie, aged ten, had a very frightened look on her face, but she did not cry until Daddy hugged and kissed her as he in turn hugged each of us. He stroked Rosalie's curly auburn hair, and then she began to cry.

He leaned down to hug and kiss Doris and gently tug her pigtails. She began sobbing, "Daddy, I want to stay home with you." Charlotte picked up the refrain and cried louder, "Me too, Daddy." He picked up Charlotte and hugged her, stroking her light brown, kinky hair.

He said, "You gotta go with Jerry, Rosalie, and Doris to the orphanage. I'll come see you. You are my 'piccialidda,'" my little girl.

Doris clung to one leg and Charlotte hung on the other, but Daddy released their grips, took their hands, and walked the four of us to the social worker's car. Charlotte was carrying the doll Mom had made for her out of some rags. There had never been enough money to buy dolls or other toys, so this doll was special.

The social worker said, "Okay girls, climb in. It's time to go."

One by one we crawled into the back seat. Charlotte and Doris were still crying as I helped them step up into the car. All four of us huddled together in the back seat, clinging to each other. Rosalie was drying her tears on her dress, trying to act very grown up by not crying. My eyes were watering, but I fought back my tears. We worried about Daddy being left all alone. He came and stood next to the car, took his red handkerchief from his back pocket, and dried his tears.

He leaned over and said, "Stata tenda." Take care. He was always telling us to do that. The social worker slammed the door, and we all jumped. Before she got into the driver's seat, he asked, "You sure I visit my children? Promesa, they come home some Sundays?" When he was upset and tried to speak in English, he would mix up his English and Italian.

She reassured him in a voice that sounded annoyed. "Yes, Mr. Messina, you can visit some evenings and every weekend, and you can even take them home sometimes." He shook his head as if he was unsure of whether he could trust her words.

As we drove away, I realized that none of the neighbors had come to say good-bye, though they were probably watching us from behind the curtains in their front rooms. I wondered if we would ever see them again or if we'd be able to come home.

Exercises

1. Write about the history of connections, abandonment, and losses in your family.
2. Were there behaviors in your family that you did not understand? Make a list of them, and then freewrite some scenes that come to mind.
3. How did you feel during family conflicts? In your body? In your mind?
4. What behaviors and beliefs did you learn from your family?
5. What generational patterns in your family concern you?
6. What positive traits have you adopted from your family?
7. What negative traits do you have that you'd like to change?

How Families Work

Nothing has a stronger influence psychologically on their environment and especially on their children than the unlived lives of the parents.

—C. G. Jung

Family stories are a combination of grief, joy, love, hate, and loss. When the writing touches on abuse, alcoholism, rigid political beliefs, separation, or injustice, the writer worries about the family's reactions, and these worries can get in the way of the writing. In my work over the years, I have observed that an understanding of how families work helps resolve some of these writing conflicts.

Family Dynamics

Family dynamics are a potent and powerful force. They bind the family together in its need to protect itself and stay safe as a unit. Memoir writing goes to the heart of a family's vulnerability. Love and concern for the feelings of others, positive or negative, can silence a writer's voice. The goal of memoir writing is not to blame parents or anyone else for how you feel and what you think. We all know how powerful family alliances and a family's unwritten rules can be. Even as adults we feel a powerful pull, like the moon tugging the earth, to be silent, to put on a happy face, and to brush aside our need to tell our stories.

It's important to remember these facts about families:

- Each member is doing the best he or she can.
- Most people do not intend to hurt anyone.
- Each person in the family is trying to get needs met, to survive, and to grow into his or her unique birthright: to be a full human being.
- Every person sees the family, his or her place in it, and the roles of other family members from a different perspective.

One important aspect of family dynamics is the jockeying for power and control. Who is the boss? Who makes the important decisions? Normally, in a nuclear family, the parents are at the top of the hierarchy, and they maintain boundaries to protect the marital relationship. The children, although governed by the parents, have their own subsystem and sibling dynamics. When the parent and child systems are balanced, the family functions normally, with everyone's needs taken care of. When the systems are out of balance, symptoms may develop, such as school problems, illness, and interpersonal conflicts.

Homeostasis is the tendency to maintain balance. When something happens to disturb this balance, members pull together to prevent change, which feels like a threat to the family. Families maintain homeostasis by using techniques such as shame and guilt to keep the members in line. If the family's defenses are broken, the pain it has been harboring will be brought to the surface.

When writing a memoir, we may disturb these precarious balances, and we will almost certainly break the rules of secrecy and protection. Deciding how much to break the rules and how to proceed in the writing are issues that most memoir writers must confront. You were shaped by your family and want to respect them, but it is important to consider your own autonomy and your role in the family. Understanding something about how families work and how children develop in the context of family may help you decide what to include in your memoir.

Family Roles

Family members take on roles that can become ingrained as part of the family dynamics. According to Claudia Black, author of *It Can't Happen to Me*, the children in a dysfunctional family develop roles to handle the imbalance created when parents are not in charge. Often the oldest child becomes the responsible one who makes sure all the homework is done, the food is on the table, and the other members of the family get to school and work. The placater, the peacemaker, tries to stop conflict from erupting, calms things down after a fight, and convinces people to kiss and make up. The scapegoat, the black sheep of the family, gets in trouble to distract the family from what is really wrong. The mascot keeps the family laughing by cracking jokes and clowning.

For the most part, we function in these roles unconsciously, beneath our own awareness and that of the other family members. In a dysfunctional family system or in a family under stress, the family business—emotional and physical nurturing—does not get taken care of adequately.

Family members unconsciously slip into different roles in the family to maintain homeostasis. Most of us take on different roles for a period of time, but in a dysfunctional family the roles become rigidified. When this happens, it may be difficult to change the pattern or to get away from the powerful family energy system.

There are many potential roles in a family. One role is that of martyr. The martyr gives up his own needs to meet the needs of others, sacrificing his own happiness for that of others, often unnecessarily. The payoff is gratitude and a way to control the behavior of other family members. Another family role is that of victim, who plays the injured party. Though a legitimate injury may have occurred, the person takes on a role, which helps get his needs met, such as appreciation and acknowledgment of his worth. The passive ruler may appear to be the weakest person in the family, but he wields the strength to control other family members. We've all read novels in which Aunt Sissy stays in bed all the time yet wields considerable power from her reign between the covers.

The hero/rescuer role is one we all identify with in movies and stories. The hero/rescuer takes care of everyone, does everything, only to find that there is no time for her own needs to be met; she may suffer illness or psychological stress trying to keep everyone happy.

Family Rules

Unwritten rules govern families, and these rules help to preserve the family's functioning. To be accepted by the family, you must obey the rules. If you don't, the family's balance is disturbed. Some typical family rules include:

- Don't embarrass the family.
- Don't be more successful than we are.
- Don't be happier than your [fill in the blank: mother, father, grandfather . . .].
- Be successful and make us proud, no matter what it costs you.
- Don't expose us by telling the truth.
- Keep our secrets.
- Don't rock the boat.

Family Myths

Family myths control how the family interacts with its members and with the outside world. These myths are unconsciously held beliefs about the family that help to protect it. They are the equivalent of the psychological defenses used by individuals to protect themselves. Some typical family myths include:

- We are better than other people.
- We are more intelligent.
- We are poor but proud.
- We are perfect.
- We always get along.
- We don't get sick.
- Uncle Jake is our hero; he can do no wrong.

The Real Self

Running like a deep stream within us throughout our lives is our real self—the part of us that was there before we were born, the part of us that is balanced and wise and able to love. The real self is both a psychological and a spiritual aspect of our selves. James Masterson, a psychologist and the author of *The Real Self*, posits that the real self gets covered up as we form protective defenses. These defenses protect us from emotional pain that would be too great for us to bear. They include processes such as denial (It didn't happen), projection (It's your fault, not mine), and rationalization (I didn't really want that new job anyway).

Masterson (1981) says that when the real self is beleaguered by severe, ongoing psychological stress, another mechanism, the false self, is established to protect the fragile real self from disintegration. The false self denies our true feelings and creates a false front, or persona, that faces the world.

Writing memoir can shift the balance of all these family and individual forces. It invites the other parts of us—our creativity, our vulnerability, and the love in our hearts—to return to our consciousness. As this happens, we come back to our real selves, and we heal.

Child Development

According to developmental psychologists, character and personality are significantly shaped before the age of five. We do not stop growing at that time, nor are we necessarily stuck with who we were at that young age. Opportunities for growth and healing appear in all seasons of a person's life. As we pass through each stage of development, we encounter opportunities to evolve new strengths, heal old wounds, enhance our creativity and spirituality, and remake ourselves into the best person we can be.

When we write memoir, we come face to face with our former selves, the child we once were, the teenager, the young adult. Through the years we may have forgotten these shadowy parts of ourselves; writing brings them back to us as we listen intently to a voice within. A brief review of the early developmental stages will help us to better understand our younger selves and to draw on them later as we write the memoir. A developmental approach allows us to see ourselves as whole beings. After all, our behavior is the result of many forces: psychological, social, biological, and spiritual.

For the first few months of life, an infant is merged with his mother, unaware of his own body and without a separate sense of self. According to Margaret Mahler, author of *The Psychological Birth of the Human Infant*, the infant needs to feel secure enough with his mother or mother figure (caregiver) in order to separate from her in a healthy way. When the mother figure meets the child's need appropriately, the child proceeds smoothly to the next level of development, but if there is stress or if the developmental stages are disturbed by physical separation or some other trauma, the child will be vulnerable to psychological problems later in life. The earlier the wound, the more vulnerable the child will be. One of the cornerstones of human development is the infant's need for secure attachment to a caregiver. The child goes through several stages of separation and differentiation during which, ideally, the caregiver supports the child's exploration of the world and provides unconditional love.

Two-year-olds typically struggle with individuation—the process of becoming individuals in their own right, separate from their primary caregivers. The two-year-old's imperious "No" really means, "This is me; I am not you." Through this stormy period, caregivers need to show the child she is loved, and must provide limits and boundaries with compassion. Two-year-olds may see the world and themselves as all bad or all good; they may be unable to integrate conflicting images and feelings.

By age three, the normally developing child feels secure even when parents come and go. He is now able to integrate conflicting images into a smooth sense of self and others. Physical growth, the acquisition of certain social skills, and cognitive development all help the child understand and interact with his world.

In adolescence the young person repeats certain aspects of earlier developmental stages to integrate them at a new level; this is why teenagers are so passionate about "no" and "yes."

When adolescents leave home, families undergo a major transition. At such times, families show signs of stress and conflict; they must gain balance again in a new form. In dysfunctional families, the necessary adjustments may not be made, leading to further stress and to crisis.

In Chinese, the word for "crisis" and the word for "opportunity" are the same. Family therapists agree that a crisis in the family provides an opportunity for new patterns to develop. Every one of us strives to find balance, love, and acceptance as a unique and wonderful being. Healthy family patterns help us meet those needs.

Events and conditions that create stress in the family, such as the physical or mental illness of a family member, alcoholism, frequent moves, poverty, emigration, and war, may disrupt the developmental timetable and force children to grow up too soon.

Certain developmental patterns may also differ from family to family because of differing ethnic and cultural customs. For example, child-rearing patterns in rural Iowa may differ significantly from those in urban New York. First-generation Chinese-Americans may raise their children differently from third-generation Irish-Americans.

All of the factors that affect child development and the workings of families need to be considered when writing a memoir to heal.

A Student's Voice

When Thomas joined my group, he wanted to write several memoirs. He decided to begin at the beginning and develop a chronological story. By capturing his early years, he hoped that his later years would make sense, both to himself and to the reader. Below is one of the vignettes he wrote. Notice how he uses full scenes, dialogue, and emotion to convey a sense of family dynamics and roles, with both humor and a hint at what's to come.

The Move

By Thomas Markham

When I was six years old my family embarked on a major move from Wayne to Park Forest, Illinois, a suburb south of Chicago. We left in mid-August so that we could settle in to our new home before school started. I was going into first grade and my brother Jimmy, eighteen months my junior, was going into kindergarten, an event that our beleaguered mom anxiously anticipated with a dual sense of loss and relief.

The summer sun searing its way above the horizon climbed to a dizzying height. It was a Midwestern scorcher, the kind that sucked out all of our bodily fluids through our pores and slapped them back at us, leaving us limp and listless, with our saturated clothing stuck to our flushed skin. The movers arrived at dawn, in their bright yellow truck with its deep, tunnel-like trailer, to load our stacks of cardboard boxes of various shapes and sizes that had been filched by Dad from the back room of the grocery store where he worked part time. All were filled to the point of bursting, sealed with multiple applications of packing tape, and neatly labeled with a black Magic Marker® by Mom. Along with the boxes, the movers loaded our frayed furnishings, beginning with the threadbare olive-and-brown tweed sofa and matching easy chair. The blistered walnut-veneered coffee table and end tables had been acquired separately from those who could afford better. Along with the living room furniture went our distressed kitchen table with its black-and-white-flecked Formica top and chrome edging. The matching chrome legs were dimpled from the glancing blows of us rambunctious boys wielding toys as weapons in our continuous assaults on each other. The black vinyl chairs that completed the ensemble would absorb the heat from the sun pouring in our kitchen window, which made them very uncomfortable to sit in, especially when wearing shorts. Our bare legs used to stick to the vinyl, leaving red marks on the backs of our thighs when we got up.

I watched as Mom finished arranging the boxes and suitcases to create an uneven platform in the back of the car. She spread out several layers of blankets and a comforter, and covered it all with one of our white bed sheets, telling us it would be cooler to lie on in the sun. She threw in all of our bed pillows to make it even more comfortable. My brother Bobby crawled in first, Jimmy scooted in next to him, and I followed. We had a view out the back windshield. The space was so small that we slightly overlapped, like sardines in a tin.

Dad's full-time day job was the reason for our move. We were being transferred. I don't think Mom really wanted to move away. It was upsetting for her to leave behind the community of people they had started to know at the local Baptist church we had been attending since their tearful and heartfelt conversion through a televised Billy Graham crusade. She and Dad were going to counseling with the pastor, and Mom was afraid that whatever progress they had made toward potential salvage of their marriage would fall by the wayside in the face of starting over in a new place where they knew no one and had no network of support. I heard them fighting about it late at night. Dad had illusions of climbing the corporate ladder to success from the basement up. This meant, to his way of thinking, that this savvy career move was essential if he was ever going to get anywhere with the company. Mom told me years later that she would have left him rather than move away from everything and everyone she knew, but where would we have lived, and how could she have survived on her own with four small children?

Dad maneuvered through the rush hour traffic on the way to the main highway. All of the car windows were rolled down so the hot flow of air gave some relief as we cut through the exhaust and humidity. Jimmy and Bobby were tickling and poking at each other and squealing and wiggling around. I was trying to ignore them, which was next to impossible in those cramped quarters. It helped me to keep busy watching the trucks coming up behind us on the highway. I waved to the drivers in their big rigs, and some of them waved back, blowing their ear-piercing horns as they changed lanes and rolled past. I felt excited about moving to a new state and was happy to be traveling down the highway toward a mysterious unknown.

Dad was yelling from the driver's seat. "You kids better stop horsing around or I'll stop this car and blister your behinds." Looking over his right shoulder with his all-too-familiar screwed-up expression, tongue clenched between his teeth, he reached back with his hairy paw of a hand to swat at us. Suddenly the car swerved onto the shoulder of the road. My brothers and I screamed, the baby wailed, and my stomach jumped into my throat.

"Jesus jumped up Christ! Are you trying to get us all killed?" Mom yelled above the commotion.

"It's these goddamned kids that are going to get us killed with all of their horsing around back there," Dad shot back, regaining control of the little car as it skidded in the dust. He managed to return all four tires onto the asphalt, shouting insults at other drivers as they leaned on their horns.

"How do you expect these kids to ever listen to a word you say, George, when you're hardly ever around, and, when you are, you're always threatening them and never doing a goddamned thing." She bounced the baby up and down, his tiny face all red and wet with tears, his big gray eyes wide with uncertainty.

"Just shut the hell up. I'm sick and tired of your nagging! If you're so goddamned smart, then you do something with them so that I can concentrate on driving and getting us there in one piece!"

"You always leave disciplining these kids up to me. You're next to useless," Mom said as she turned her head to glare back at my brothers. "Tommy! You scoot over and change places with Jimmy, and make sure those two keep their hands off each other!"

My face burned with resentment as I climbed between my sparring brothers and repositioned myself sullenly in the middle. Of course, my brothers continued to reach across me to poke at each other, alternately whining and giggling. My parents ragged on up front, while my brothers continued to squeal and whine on either side of me, the fussing of the baby lost in the pervasive cacophony of my contentious family. Jimmy reached past me to pinch Bobby, who then let loose a howl of pain and protest loud enough to break through the steady din of my parent's arguing.

"I thought I told you to make those two keep their hands off of each other." Why was she yelling at me, I thought. They're the ones who are acting up, not me! My brothers momentarily paused at the dangerous tone of Mom's voice. She soon got back to where she had left off with my dad, and Jimmy went back to his harassment of Bobby.

Jimmy reached over me again and Bobby tried to slap his hand away when I, without warning, jabbed my elbow into Jimmy's ribs. He yelped like a wounded cur. "Mommy, Tommy hit me!"

"It was an accident," I lied. "There's not enough room back here."

"It was not! He did it on purpose."

"That's what you get for horsing around. Now shut up and settle down, before I really give you something to cry about," came one of Mom's standard replies.

Jimmy flipped over onto his side, facing away from me, and pulled a pillow over his head.

"I hate all of you. I'm going to smother myself," came his muffled voice from under the pillow.

"Go ahead," I said. "See if I care. You're just a trouble maker anyway."

Exercises

Let the following questions guide you as you reflect on developmental patterns in your family and write about them in your journal. Apply the questions to both your own experience growing up in your family and to what you know about the lives of your parents, grandparents, and great-grandparents. You may find patterns that continue through the generations. When you are ready to write your memoir, you can draw from these journal entries to build the stories about your life. Looking at your early years in terms of developmental stages can prevent you from feeling overwhelmed by the many stories you may have to tell. For more developmental questions, see the appendix.

1. What stories do you know about the early years in the lives of your parents or grandparents? Were they secure, or did they suffer early separation due to illness, moving, immigration, or abandonment?

2. Did your family encourage autonomy and separation, or were children kept at home or taught to cling to parents to meet the adults' needs?

3. How did parents give attention to developing children or show that they were loved and important members of the family?

4. Were children forced to grow up too soon because of family stressors? What were some of these stressors? Write about them first from your point of view and then, if you can, from your mother's and father's points of view.

5. What ethnic and cultural contexts may have affected development in your family?

6. How was punishment used during childhood? What was the manner of discipline, and who delivered it?

7. Were caretakers reliable or did children have to move from family member to family member?

8. Were real selves encouraged? How?

The Genogram

I ought to be able to remember the family ties, since all my cells are alive with reminders.

—Lewis Thomas

The genogram, a map of the family, helps sort out family traits and history. With this map, you can track family characteristics, relationships, and behaviors that are repeated through the generations.

The genogram reveals relationships and repeated family patterns, which can give insight into your stories. The genogram can be created before you write, or you can write a summary of the story you're going to put in memoir form first and then map the relationships to see the patterns more easily.

Linda's Story Summary and Genogram

The Dickersons and the Stinemans settled in Iowa in the mid-nineteenth century and became farmers in the rich soil near the Mississippi. German and English, they were hard workers, tied to the land, strict with children, and proud of what they could do for themselves. They were proud even when there was no money.

As a young girl, Lulu, my grandmother, noticed that women wore themselves down with housework and too many children. She saw that poverty made for a depressing life, and perhaps she intuitively knew that if she remained a lower class, barefoot, farm girl, the fate of these women would be her own. In 1911, she eloped with Blaine, a middle-class man whose family owned the newspaper in the small town of Wapello twenty-five miles away. Blaine's father and grandfather were involved in Iowa politics, and his grandfather was an attorney. I can't imagine his family being very happy about the farm girl who eloped with their son. Out of this union came a stillborn boy, and then my mother, Josephine Elizabeth, was born.

The marriage suffered from various stresses and strains, and from my grandfather's interest in alcohol. All the men in that family drank, and drank to excess. Blaine's youngest sister once told me there never was a gathering in her family when Blaine and his father didn't have a horrible fight—about politics, about who was right and who was wrong. About the weather.

According to Blanche, Lulu left the family when my mother was a baby. I have always tried to imagine the story Blanche told me about Lulu leaving my mother with a neighbor. The story of how my mother had been abandoned when she was a baby helped me to have empathy for her when she would scream and rage at my grandmother, when they'd erupt into dish-throwing tantrums. As the story goes, Josephine, a little girl without a home, lived with various family members, including Blanche's mother, Josephine, for whom she was named. At age twelve or thirteen, she came to Chicago to live with her mother, who had divorced Blaine and remarried. It was then, I believe, that the battle between mother and daughter began in earnest and continued until Lulu's death.

When she was twenty-nine, my mother married my father, and I was born nine months later. He lived with us until I was eight months old. He left—so the story goes—to fight in the war. Later I found out that he worked for the railroad during the war, an acceptable way for him to escape my mother's irrational behavior.

As I grew up, I heard stories about fights between my mother and grandmother before I was born. When I was five, Lulu, whom I called

Gram, bought a house for Mother and me to live in, and we all lived together for a few short months until my mother decided to leave. It was during another screaming fight that I watched our lives together dissolve. My mother declared, "I'm going back to Chicago." My stomach flipped and my breath stopped. My body knew without a doubt that this was the end of us as mother and daughter, and I was right.

I stayed with my grandmother, whom I soon discovered had a huge agenda in raising me. It took years for me to understand it: her tight control and unyielding will resulted from her need to force me into a way of life she had wanted for my mother and for herself. She finally had someone on whom she could impose her unlived life.

The family feud, which included my father, finally ended with the death of my grandmother and father within eleven days of each other in 1971. When I was twenty, I discovered that my mother did not want, or was not able, to face the reality that she indeed had a daughter. When I visited her in Chicago, she would deny me, refusing to introduce me to those she knew. I grew wavery and ashamed. Did I exist? The struggle to get my mother to accept and love first me and then my children forms the basis of my memoir and ends with a resolution of sorts at her deathbed.

The pattern of abandoned daughters and grandmothers—the fights and rejections—seemed destined to go on forever, but I was determined to break it. Through therapy, writing, and learning to love my children in a way that is different from the previous generations in my family, I have been able to break the chain of abandonment and begin new connections based on respect and love.

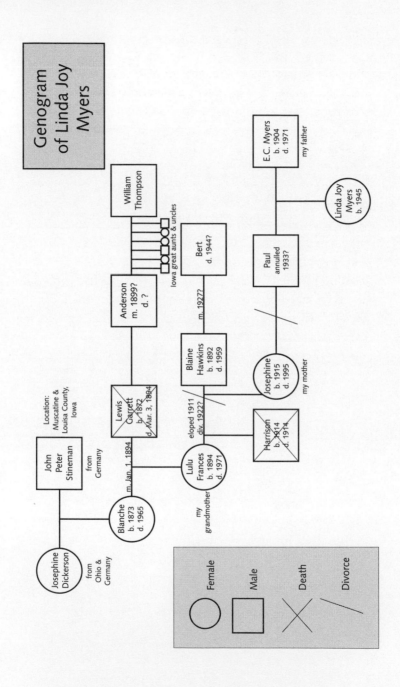

Genogram of Linda Joy Myers

Exercises

1. If you have information about your maternal grandparents, start your genogram with their generation. Draw a long horizontal line to make room for succeeding generations. Use vertical lines to connect your mother and her siblings beneath your grandparents. Do the same for your father's side of the family. On the line connecting husband and wife, write the marriage date and the date of divorce or separation if applicable.
2. Then connect your mother and father with a horizontal line, and use vertical lines to connect to yourself and your siblings.
3. Fill in whatever names and dates you know. If family members have done genealogical research, perhaps you can use their material. But you don't have to do genealogical research to create a genogram.
4. Write a brief summary of your family story. Try to keep it under three pages.

The Critic-Censor

The life which is unexamined is not worth living.

—Plato

When we write stories that are not part of the "happy family" myth, a voice starts chattering in our heads, trying to convince us not to write. It whispers that we are no good, what is the point—making us doubt our writing. Most people hear this voice, but it gets in the way of writing a memoir. From my students, I have heard about the voices of the critic-censor on a continuum from extremely negative and critical to seductively soothing. The soothing voice may whisper, "This is so hard on you. Why don't you just stop; life will be easier. Focus on something you know how to do. Your family will hate you."

When you hear this voice, you know that the critic-censor has arrived. Pay attention to what it says so you can learn how to release its power over you.

On the next page are more of the critic-censor's favorite phrases. How many of them sound familiar to you?

Critic-censor Phrases

- The past is the past.
- Quit whining.
- You're having a pity party.
- You should be ashamed.
- Don't air dirty laundry.
- Writing about yourself is narcissistic.
- You're just navel gazing.
- It didn't happen that way.
- You always did have a bad memory.
- Uncle Jake will just die if you say that.

- Your mother (father, grandmother) will die if you publish this, and it will be your fault.
- Your writing is terrible.
- Why do you even try.
- You are bad to tell the secret stories.
- You don't make any sense.
- What will people think?
- Get on with your life.
- Just get back to scrubbing the kitchen floor.

The critic-censor is tenacious. You probably already know how strong this voice can be, how strident and intrusive. My students always ask how they can get rid of it. But the good and bad news is that the critical voice is a part of you. But because it is within you, you can understand where it comes from and learn how to cope with it and manage it. The critic-censor reflects the natural aspects of being a vulnerable human being: doubts, fears, and worries. I ask my students to speak the critic-censor's voice. By speaking aloud, the writer shares the shameful secrets of this voice and becomes more free of it. Silence feeds shame. The antidote to this is to speak, to state your truth out loud and in writing.

We all need to create a safe place to write, both physically—at home or in a workshop or café—and inside our hearts, where the stories live.

Self-witnessing

Earlier I talked about the need to be witnessed as an important part of the healing process. We need both kinds of witnesses—internal and external. We accomplish internal healing when we listen deeply to ourselves and give ourselves compassion, forgiveness, and comfort. By not allowing the critic-censor to shame you and by talking back to it, you learn to refuse abuse, and learn not to shrink and crumble in the face of negative, critical statements. If you received this kind of treatment during childhood—and most of us did in varying degrees, if not from family, then from the world—it was impossible to talk back. To do so was either against the rules or dangerous.

Now, even with the new perspective of adulthood, we still hold back, afraid. Because we have learned this behavior, we can unlearn it. Dealing with your critic-censor to claim your own voice can be extremely healing. As you do so, you learn to be your own witness, and you build creative muscles.

Some phrases die hard. I have noticed that people who have been abused can be stricken with a very harsh critic-censor. If this applies to you, then

- Be patient.
- Have compassion for yourself.
- Keep writing.
- Work with the exercises at the end of this chapter, and try to heal past conditioning.

A Student's Voice

Although Amy Peele's stories about spending the summer at her Aunt Mary's house were delightful and well grounded in time and place, I felt that something was missing. Being polite to Amy, not wanting to delve into what might be painful secrets or memories that perhaps she didn't know she had, I gently questioned her about why those summers were so wonderful. Then she told me that she began writing her memoir with the idea that she would just write "the good stuff" and leave out the abuse and tension. The "dark side" was missing from her stories. We discussed what she wanted to do. Did she want to examine those stories? Did she feel that they were really part of her story? She decided to integrate some of the darker moments into the positive stories. Here is what she said about silencing the critic-censor:

I find it difficult to write my memoir with all my critical siblings sitting on my shoulder constantly telling me I'm not accurate with my descriptions. Once I learned how to muffle or silence them, when the family audience was no longer in my head, I found the courage to write what I remembered and how I felt. It took me a while to do that.

Part of the challenge is describing how and what I felt without worrying about whose feelings I might hurt. Sometimes I wonder if certain family members should be dead before I submit my manuscript for publication. The writing stirs up some wonderful feelings and some sad, uncomfortable, and angry feelings that had been frozen inside and unavailable to me. After writing several stories, I learned to just see what feelings came up and deal with them as they thawed out. I do feel lighter after writing some stories. It's as if the story in my head held me hostage, but once I wrote it, it wasn't as big on paper as it was in my mind. I'm not sure that I will use all the stories I wrote, but I'm glad I wrote them. I'm also thankful for the psychological support of Linda Myers's memoir group and the encouragement to go for the hard stuff.

Goldblatts

By Amy Peele

It was a cool fall Saturday morning in Park Forest, Illinois. The leaves had just started to turn from green into hints of red and orange with tips of yellow. I was ten and my sister Lorna was three years older. Lorna usually took me with her on her capers since our sister Charlene, the oldest girl, would never consider doing those kinds of things. I would go along with whatever Lorna said. I had to or else she would beat me up.

I finished my work, which was the bathroom. I scrubbed the tub, sink, and toilet with generic cleanser. I hated to wash the toilet because we only had one bathroom that all six of us and my mom had to use. It was always pretty dirty, especially with two boys. But, in order to pass inspection, that's what had to be done. The chrome at the sink and tub was polished and shining. I was always especially proud of that. The brown tile floor was washed by hand and dried with a towel. The mirror was sparking clean, and fresh towels hung on the bar on the wall.

I called for Char. "I'm ready for you to check the bathroom." She headed around the corner from the kitchen and down the hall to the first room on the right, the bathroom. I watched her eyes as she looked from the toilet to the sink and then the tub. She even picked up the white cap that laid beside the toilet to make sure I had washed under and around it.

"Looks good. You can go out now. Where are you going?"

Before I could answer her, I noticed Lorna looking around her shoulder, and she interrupted.

"Amy and I are going down to the Plaza."

That's all the information Lorna would give. She never was much for words, and she thought everyone should mind their own goddamn business. Charlene looked her square in the eye. "You two don't have any money to go shopping. What are you going to do there?"

Lorna walked down the hall to our bedroom. "We can window shop, and you can't stop us!" Charlene just shook her head and walked back towards the kitchen. I guess she was going to ignore Lorna. Sometimes they would get into knock-down-drag-out fights, with hair pulling and lots of swear words. Lorna had been really angry since my dad left, and she was mean most of the time.

We walked out the screen door and crossed the front lawn that our brother John had just mowed. Blades of fresh-cut grass stuck to the sides of our sandals. The Plaza was two long blocks from our house, a huge collection of stores that circled a big white tower with a clock on top of it.

I looked at Lorna. "Which store are we going to, Marshall Fields?" I loved their Barbie Doll clothes collection.

"You know we 're too poor to walk into that place. We're going to Kresge's for some fries, and then I want to go over to Goldblatts to look around." Sounded just fine to me.

Kresge's was our five-and-dime and had the second-best soda counter at the Plaza; the first one was the Grill. We slid into the red booth, and the waitress with her frilly white apron and black short dress came up. "What do you girls want?"

Lorna took her baby-sitting money out of her pocket. "We'll have a large order of fries and a cherry coke."

"You both have to order something or you can't sit in a booth."

Lorna gave her one of her mean looks with her eyebrow up. "Then give her a cherry coke too."

"I want a vanilla coke."

The lady turned around and went to order. Lorna gave out a loud sigh, "What a bitch." I just cringed, hoping the lady didn't hear her and wouldn't throw us out. I wondered if she knew how poor we were. After we enjoyed every last crunchy fry with a dip of catsup, Lorna got up and nodded for me to follow her.

We went up and down different aisles and looked at hair products, empty photo albums, cheap clothes, make-up, and then headed down to my favorite aisle, the candy aisle. Lorna turned around and grabbed my blouse. She whispered, "Look, just pick one or two candy bars you want and quickly shove them down your shorts. Then we're getting the hell out of here."

I was scared, but I didn't have any money and I wanted some candy so I grabbed a five-cent Butterfinger and a few Reese's peanut butter cups and shoved them in my shorts. My heart was racing and my eyes were darting all over the place. I knew I was doing something wrong, but it was also exciting.

Lorna grabbed my arm. "Just look normal and slowly walk towards the door, stop and look at something right by the door, then slowly walk out like you got all the time in the world."

Good thing she told me that or I would have run out the door and surely given myself away. A few stores past Kresge's, I went to take the candy from my pants, but Lorna said, "Not yet. Wait till we turn the corner, in case anyone's looking."

I had put the candy in the middle of the elastic band of my shorts. "They' re digging into my skin."

"Shut up, you big baby, we're almost out of sight."

A few minutes later I was enjoying my Butterfinger. I opened the Reese's peanut butter cups and gave her one. We strolled past Fannie May Candies—that was for the really rich people. We passed the Holiday theater, and then walked into Goldblatts, the candy and wrappers long gone. I followed Lorna to the record area, and she started looking through the forty-fives. I knew she didn't have any money left, but I figured she was just browsing. Next thing I know she took a stack of forty-fives and shoved them down the front of her pants, grabbed my arm, and started for the door. I shook my arm free and kept pace with her until we got right in front of the double doors to leave. I stopped.

Lorna looked at me with her gritted teeth. "Amy, come on now, we have to go!"

I looked at her. "You got to look around. I want to look at these wallets." I started picking up a black leather one. It was soft, with lots of room for pictures and a little clip coin purse attached to it.

Lorna's voice got louder, "We're leaving now!" I looked at her red face, put down the wallet, and followed her outside.

As we started to walk towards Sears, a lady called after us, "Excuse me girls, could you please wait a minute?"

It was Marie, the store detective. Everyone knew her. She was a running joke. She was five foot two and wore a tan raincoat even when it wasn't raining. She wore old-lady black shoes and carried a black handbag that was almost as big as she was. You could spot her a mile away, but we hadn't.

She walked up to Lorna. "Young lady, do you have something that doesn't belong to you?" Lorna was quick to reply, "No!"

"I think you do. Now follow me back into the store, and I won't call the police. We can keep this as store business."

I looked at Lorna, who started to follow Marie back into the store. I followed. My heart was pounding so loud I thought everyone could hear it. Marie took us behind a curtain marked "Employees Only" and into a small room with a gray metal desk. She closed the door.

"Now, what's under your shirt?"

Lorna took the records out and threw them on the desk. I couldn't believe she was acting like this. We were in serious trouble. Marie looked Lorna straight in the face. "How often do you two girls steal here?"

Lorna let out a huff. "We've never stolen anything here before."

"How can I believe you? If you steal, you probably lie too."

"Believe anything you want. I don't give a damn."

Marie was angry now. "That's it. I'm calling your parents, and I may even call the police. What's your name?"

Lorna calmly looked at Marie. "Carol Wright." I couldn't believe she was lying to Marie. We were getting in deeper by the minute.

"What's your phone number?"

"PI 8-7864."

Marie picked up the phone and dialed. A man's voice answered.

"Hello, this Marie from down at Goldblatts. I'm sorry to tell you we have your daughter Carol here for shoplifting." A pause.

Marie slammed down the phone. "He doesn't have a daughter!" She looked over at me. "Now you better tell me your real names or I'm calling the police to come pick you both up, and we'll see you in court."

Lorna was giving me the "don't spill it" look. I was only ten, and I wasn't good at lying or stealing yet. I blurted out, "My name is Amy Peele and this is my sister Lorna, and our number is PI 8-2434."

I could feel Lorna's eyes burning a hole through the side of my head. "Nice job, asshole."

Marie dialed our number, and my mom answered the phone. We were screwed.

"Mrs. Peele, this is Marie from Goldblatts. I'm sorry to have to call you like this, but we have your two daughters Lorna and Amy here. They've been caught shoplifting. I'd rather not call the police. Could you come down here so we can settle this matter here at the store?"

Marie put the receiver down, a look of confusion on her face. "I'm sorry, girls. Your mother wants me to go ahead and call the police."

I was shocked and scared as I watched Marie call the Park Forest police department. I looked over at Lorna for some comfort, but she was acting as if nothing was wrong. I think she had watched too many prison movies. It seemed like a long time until a uniformed police-man knocked on the door. Marie stepped outside and closed the door behind her. I could hear them talking. Lorna leaned over and gave me a knuckle sandwich punch in my left arm, hard. She always made her middle finger knuckle stick out so it stung when she hit, and it always left a bruise on my arm.

"You stupid bitch, if you hadn't told her our name she might have let us go. Now we're really dead, thanks to you. Mom's gonna beat us."

The officer opened the door and gestured for us to follow him. I looked down at the floor as we walked out to the police car, hoping no one who knew us was in the store. It was already dark out, which meant it was dinnertime at our house. Our brothers and sisters would know about our crime.

The police station was a couple of blocks from the Plaza. We were taken into a big room with a wooden desk and chairs. A short, fat, balding officer with glasses sat across from us. His badge said "Officer Milky."

"Hello, Lorna and Amy. It seems we have a problem here."

How did he know our names already? Neither of us had said a thing.

"You want to tell me what happened over at Goldblatts?"

I wasn't going to speak. I didn't want a bruise on my other arm. I nodded to Lorna.

"I stole a few forty-fives, big deal."

Officer Milky pulled his chair up to the table and leaned toward us. "It's a very big deal because both of you have a police record now. I've called your mother three times, and she has hung up on me each time. She says you got yourselves into this mess, you should get yourselves out. She wants me to keep you here. She doesn't want thieves in her house. I can't say I blame her."

He looked over at me. Tears were rolling down my face. This was the most terrible trouble I had ever gotten into in my life. "Amy, you're a little young to be in jail overnight, don't you think?" I nodded my head and then burst into a full-blown cry. Lorna sat there not reacting to Office Milky. He handed me the Kleenex box.

"I'll try your mother one more time, but if she doesn't come, then we're going to have to ship you to Juvenile Hall in Chicago Heights, and you'll spend the night there." He got up and went out of the room. I looked at Lorna, tears streaming down my face. "This is just great!"

She glanced at me, "Just shut up. They can't send us to Juvenile Hall. Our crime isn't that big."

Officer Milky came in shaking his head. "You two ladies are lucky. Your Mom's on her way, but I wouldn't want to be you two when you get home. She is very angry and tired. Too bad she has to work all day and then come home to this kind of news. Shame on both of you! Follow me."

We went to the front lobby where Officer Milky motioned for us to sit on the black vinyl chairs. "Stay there. Your mother will be here in a minute, and don't even think about moving." I watched him go back into the dispatcher's room. As I turned my head I saw my mother, still dressed in her white nurse's uniform, walking into the police station. She walked right by us as if we didn't exist and around to speak to Officer Milky. She seemed to know her way around the station. I think my brother had gotten in trouble once or twice before.

She came back into where Lorna and I were sitting. "Get in the car."

We got up and she followed us. As soon as we left the parking lot she started in. "So, Lorna. You're not content getting into trouble alone. You have to bring your little sister along for the ride now. Amy, where is your common sense? You know better. Shame on both of you for disgracing yourself and our family. It's bad enough your father leaves me with six kids, debt, and no money, but then this shit. I work seven days a week, ten hours a day just to keep a roof over your heads and food on the table, and this is how you show me respect. Well, I've had it! Lorna, I've grounded you, taken away every privilege you have, and you still defy me. This is the last straw!"

She pulled into our driveway, slammed the car into park. "Both of you get inside and go straight to the bathroom." My mother went into the kitchen, opened a drawer, took something out, and headed toward the bathroom.

I was trembling. I didn't know what was going to happen. Lorna had long since detached from my mother's threats and beatings. It seemed as if nothing could make her feel remorse. The rest of the house was silent. We both went into the bathroom. My mother followed and closed the door. She placed big silver scissors on the sink.

"Take off all your clothes. You want to act like criminals, I'm going to treat you that way!"

I was afraid. The rage I felt from my mother was intense. She was out of control.

She made my sister Lorna stand under the cold shower, and then she began to cut her long brown hair off in clumps. I screamed and screamed for her to stop. She kept cutting. I stood there shivering from fear and cold, scared that I was next and scared for my sister. Would my mother do something else even worse to her?

It took a long time. I stood there watching and hearing my sister scream and cry. My mother turned to me and said, "Next time you two think about stealing something, think of this. Now put your clothes back on, clean up this bathroom, and go to bed."

She left the bathroom. My expectations of what she was going to do to me lessened as I saw her enter her bedroom, but my fear of what might happen another day was still strong.

I don't remember exactly what happened next, but I know I cried myself to sleep that night. None of us kids talked about what happened that night, just like we never talked about Dad leaving.

Exercises

1. When you hear the critic-censor while you're writing, take a separate piece of paper and write down what it says to you. Listen to it carefully, and take dictation. Then put the paper aside and go back to your writing. If the critical voice starts again, write down what it says. Try not to judge or analyze it. Just write down what it says, and go back to your writing.

2. In a writing group or other safe place, talk about what the critic-censor says. Shame exists only in silence. Sharing the writing process is an important healing tool.

3. Write a letter to the critic about what it does to you. Talk to it directly about its power, its pain, and how it frustrates you.

4. Write a dialogue with the critic. When it says, "You're stupid, you can't write," ask, "Who taught me this? Where did this belief come from?" If the critical voice says, "You're stupid. What makes you think you can write such a long work," you answer back, "Well, it's true that I didn't know everything, and I was bad in [fill in the blank], but I have written some good things before, and even [fill in the name of a friend, editor, teacher, family member] liked it."

5. If you suffered humiliation when you expressed yourself in school or in front of family, write down those phrases. For example, "You always got the worst grade in spelling, and you always failed your essays."

6. Now write new phrases that contradict the old, critical voices. For example, "This is not about getting good grades, and I am no longer fourteen years old. I have learned to write well enough, and besides, I can hire an editor if I need to. Just shut up and let me write." Keep writing anyway. Have faith.

7. Keep a list of the negative phrases you hear for a few weeks. Read them over and decide how to counter each of them with positive, assertive statements. Some will simply melt away after being acknowledged. Often you can tell that the negative phrase is the voice of a parent or other family

member. For example, if the voice says, "Don't you dare tell," you can respond with, "I am not telling to embarrass you or to be mean. I just need to tell this story. It has bothered me for years." If the voice says, "You're going to kill me . . ." you can answer, "I know that you have used guilt to control me for years, but for now this is my private project, and I need to do it. I am exercising more autonomy by saying what I have to say."

Ethics

The experience of recollection can be extraordinarily powerful. The personal, internal strength of a moment of remembering is only matched in force by the interplay between people when they exchange memories.

—Susan Engel,
CONTEXT IS EVERYTHING: THE NATURE OF MEMORY

Writing a memoir inevitably brings up ethical dilemmas: how much to write about family secrets, how much truth to tell. Furthermore, each family member sees and remembers events differently. Many families live for years with a shaky truce about what "really" happened—a truce that is easily shattered when someone close to them decides to write and publish a memoir. There is nothing like the printed word to stir up family disagreements.

Blackbird and *Still Waters*, memoirs by Jennifer Lauck, were published to great critical acclaim. Lauck is the only remaining member of her original family. In *Blackbird*, the narrator is a seven-year-old child who presents her feelings about complex living arrangements and decisions that profoundly affect her life. In the story, she is very young when her mother dies, and her father remarries soon after. *Still Waters* continues her story into adolescence and adulthood, as she revisits childhood mysteries and fills in other layers of the story.

After publication of *Blackbird*, Lauck found herself embroiled in a disagreement with her stepmother and stepsiblings, who accused her of lying and presenting incidents that make them look bad. When and under what circumstances the relationship between Lauck's father and stepmother developed is one of the matters disputed by the stepfamily. Salon.com published an article about the conflict. Lauck defended her work, saying, ". . .this is the memory of a little girl, and I wrote it to the best of my ability, and I stand behind it 100 percent." (Salon 2001)

The issue of how much to write and whether it will please or anger family members lies at the heart of each memoir, striking at the memoir writer's critical inner voice and inner censor. Memoir writers may be haunted by questions such as:

- What will the family think?
- Will they still speak to me?
- Will my writing hurt anyone?
- Will I be written out of the will?

The memoirist worries about being accused of terrible things by the family—betrayal, disloyalty, and extreme selfishness. Some stories in the memoir may no longer be hot subjects for the writer, but other family members may not have resolved the issues involved.

Family disagreements bring up guilt and shame in the memoir writer. The writer may worry:

- How dare I think this or say that? I love my parents. They have changed; we've worked it out. I feel guilty writing about what really happened.
- I don't want to bring back up the past. I am afraid of those feelings.
- I have already talked about it endlessly in therapy. I don't understand why I can't just forget it, but the memories haunt me day and night in dreams.
- I feel guilty and ashamed.

Memory or Fact?

You can't prove a memory. You can never prove what happened or didn't happen. Several years ago a court case in California that involved memories made the front pages. A woman reported a flashback about her father killing one of her childhood friends. On the basis of this recovered memory, the father was tried and found guilty. He was freed upon appeal, however, on the basis that the memory was influenced by hypnosis and therapy.

Many families have been torn asunder by painful accusations made as a result of recovered memories. The person making the accusation asserts that the memory was recovered during the process of therapy and that it had been repressed for years. The judicial system does not want to send people to jail based on something that can't be proved. According to the law, a memory is not an objective fact.

As a therapist, I know that memories can suddenly appear and cause great psychic trauma for the client. What the client does about it becomes part of the therapy. Whether the memory is "true" or not isn't our focus; instead, we work on how to heal the wounds that are now part of the person's conscious experience.

So it is with memoir writing. Family members can object strenuously to certain stories in a memoir, insisting that they simply aren't true. "That never happened, you are making it up." Your justified defense is, "This is the way I see it. This is what happened to me." Some family members have borrowed memories. I've heard brothers and sisters insist that what one remembers actually happened to the other one.

To complete your memoir, you'll need to resolve what memory means to you. The simplest way is to write what you remember as clearly and as well as you can. As you write, your memory may shift, or more memories may arise from your unconscious. Keep a dream journal and an open mind. For the first few months, focus on writing your stories without getting the family involved. Concerns about family will not go away, but after you have worked for a while, you may have a better idea of what to say and what not to say to the family about the content of your writing. If you are writing about events and situations that you know will bring shame and guilt, it is important for your own healing that you complete the writing before confronting family members with it.

Secrets

It is safe to say that there are no families without secrets or conflicts. Some writers choose to go along with the family rules to keep the silence; others want to explore deeper truths, believing that exposure heals the wounds that secrets and lies create. No one can tell you what you should or should not reveal in your memoir. Perhaps you feel that, knowing your family as you do, there are some issues which should not be discussed.

As a memoir writer, you must ask yourself:

- Who will be injured if I write this?
- Is there a purpose to write this; will there be a healing?

As a memoir writer, you must come to terms with your own position. Remember: the first draft is for your own healing. Secrets hold danger, like the submerged part of an iceberg, and they have a profound effect on those who keep them. Energy is required to cover up secrets, and for that reason, they often feel like heavy burdens.

Telling secrets has always caused controversy in our society. For instance, victims are often afraid to speak out about harassment or sexual abuse by family members, priests, teachers, bosses, or anyone in a position of authority. A secret holds power; the person keeping it can completely change another person's life by revealing it. Often a great deal is at stake—reputations, jobs, economic well-being, family unity, and most of all, the way the family sees itself. As a result, the life of the person who tells the secret may also never be the same afterwards.

As a family therapist I have been privy to a huge array of secrets that families don't want revealed, that would cause them shame.

Some of these secrets may be of concern to you as you prepare to write your memoir:

- Illegitimacy, adoption
- Murder, criminal behavior, jail sentences
- Sexual crimes: rape and incest
- Lies about parentage: a "sister" who is really the mother
- Money: who has it, who doesn't; how it was acquired
- Death, natural or unnatural; wills; inheritances
- Sexuality, sexual identity
- Race, religion, or ethnicity: fear of persecution or rejection
- Mental health and developmental issues: the "slow" child kept at home, the grandfather everyone keeps an eye on
- Drugs, alcohol, and other addictions
- Physical illness or genetic problems
- Domestic violence

These supposedly hot subjects, possible secrets that might create shame and guilt, can crop up as the inner voice of your critic-censor. It may be difficult for you to decide if you should listen to the voice that says you are bad if you write that story, that it will surely kill your mother.

James Framo, a family therapist who invites the family of origin to therapy sessions to help resolve couple conflicts, teaches therapists how to confront unresolved family shame and guilt. During one of his training workshops that I attended in the 1980s, he said that every couple resisted having the family come in and peppered the therapist with reasons: "It will kill them. They'll never speak to me again. My dad will have a heart attack." In every case, none of these dire events occurred. The secret, the anger, the stuck place was gently discussed, opening up communication in the family for the first time in decades. Our worst fears may come from our child self; they are usually unfounded in current reality.

One writer I know had a positive attitude about his memoir. He believed that the information he told in it was already known and understood by his family—it wasn't a secret. He had omitted the worst details and secrets from his story so he wouldn't violate privacy rights or defame anyone's character. But suddenly, this writer, whose nuclear family was dead, was shunned by the extended family. A cousin told him that various family members were gossiping about him because of a few innocuous paragraphs that had gotten around. These paragraphs were combed for possible insults, and insults were found even where they were not intended. The family had become worried about what "sins" might be uncovered.

The writer was not able to get direct criticism of himself or his work even when he asked for it. The family pretended that everything was all right, thus depriving the writer of the opportunity to set the record straight, to reassure, even to have any discussion about the stories he had written. The writer came to understand that the family's reaction was part of a longstanding pattern of indirect communication, gossip, and power positioning—and that he could do nothing to stop it. He had to ask himself: What can I do to handle my family ethically? Should I publish this memoir if it causes so much trouble?

Even when we write what we think are positive things about family members, they may interpret our words as they wish and may still become angry or upset with us. Family problems that we thought had been resolved may erupt with dramatic flair once words appear on the page.

As I wrote and rewrote my own memoir, I decided that despite a negative reaction from my extended family, I had to continue. I did not disclose most of the family secrets because they weren't necessary to the story I chose to write. But the fact that I am a writer and have written a memoir created a kind of paranoia: "What is she saying? Is it about us?"

My concerns about what my family thinks took me back to my early years, when I learned I should not share my thoughts. My grandmother punished me when I spoke my mind. She kept me in line with shame, guilt, and physical punishment, so it was difficult for me to learn to say, or even to know, what I really thought much of my life.

I learned to hide, to lie, and to be a pleaser. When I was young I had learned to mirror my grandmother, to model myself after her, her taste in clothes, her style and flair. Some of this modeling was positive, but she had tried to live her unlived life through me: I was to be a musician and a good student, with a high school diploma and a college degree. When I began to turn against this program-ming—branching out in my interests from music to art and writing, trying to find myself—I felt like a bad person. I had let her down. I was ashamed.

When I found my way to therapy, I was able to come to terms with my grandmother's harsh and crazy-making expectations. I developed skills to figure out who I was and to recognize what I thought and felt. During this period of searching and confusion, I kept a journal, trying to make sense of an upside-down world. Later I would find out that my grandmother was manic-depressive, even psychotic at times. I was not "bad" all those years after all. I was simply the focus of her distorted projections.

When I began my memoir, I found that I still had to face the anger and pain I held about certain events in our lives. I faced my grand-mother as she screamed at me and abused me from inside my head. But as I wrote over a period of years, as I kept telling the truth the way I had experienced it, I gradually let go of layers of anger and sor-row, and especially the fear I had carried about her. Through the writing, I learned how to differentiate myself from her, and in the process I became more myself. To develop more compassion for her, I began writing the story of my grandmother as a young woman. I stood in the shoes of a sixteen-year-old girl who had eloped in 1911, a young woman who had given birth to a stillborn child in 1914, and who bore my mother in 1915. I imagined her pain and heartache as I wrote these stories through her eyes. I felt that I was healing not only myself but her as well. She had not been able to tell the truth; her fear, anxiety, and mental illness prevented that. By telling her stories,

I was able to free myself—and perhaps psychically, my grand-mother—from the past. This was an aspect of my ethics—to try to create more compassion, to attempt to heal decades of pain and rage. I could not do it directly, but I could do it in the writing.

Writing Ethically

After you have written a few drafts of your family stories, think about the issues that concern you. Did you reveal any family secrets or expose any subjects you fear you could be sued for? Could your writing cause a huge family uproar? What is most important, the family or the writing? Consider the ethical dilemmas that need to be resolved before your memoir is published.

Just because we *can* say certain things does not mean it is a good idea to say them. Just because we might not be sued or have legal action brought against us does not mean that we should put questionable or hot information into words. In the final stages of writing, you must decide whether or not to include potentially damaging or upsetting material in your memoir.

Revenge

Getting revenge is not the best motivation for writing a memoir. If you have been wounded, writing about your feelings is a good way to resolve them. Writing the stories about what happened can help you come to a new understanding. But writing to get back at others almost always backfires. I heard a published memoir writer describe his many complaints about what happened to him after his memoir came out: he was sued, and his family was shocked and hurt at what he wrote. He had not warned the people involved about the content of his work, however, and much of it was angry and highly judgmental. He said he had hoped they would never find out about it because he had changed his own name. He talked about how the memoir had created another level of conflict and hurt feelings, but he seemed to have no idea how this had happened.

You are the only one who can decide whether putting the "truth"—your version of it—out into the world will help create a healing experience for you and your family. Ask yourself if you have a fantasy that after your memoir is written, there will be an upsurge in family forgiveness or that longstanding grudges will suddenly dissolve once you present your point of view, which you believe is the correct one. It may be hard to predict how the memoir will affect family and friends. All you can do is to be as ethical and compassionate as possible when you present your work to the family and the public. Being ethical does not mean that you agree with what other members of the family think or that you have to be close or connected. Being ethical means that you protect yourself and your work, and that you maintain proper boundaries when sharing your opinion, which after all is what a memoir is, with the larger world. Here are some topics to consider and some suggestions that will help you to behave ethically in regard to your memoir:

- Are there serious grudges or emotional cutoffs with family and friends?
- Do you want to *ask permission* or do you want to *tell* your family what you are writing about?
- "Asking permission" means making a request that can be denied. This affects what you write about and how you write it. Be clear before you speak about your intentions or make your requests.
- Be prepared to negotiate sticky issues.
- If you mention real names, get permission to use them. After you write your piece, show it to the people named and obtain their written consent before putting it in print.
- If your piece reveals information about a town or any public figures or events, be sure that your facts are accurate before publishing.
- Make certain that you are not defaming anyone's character or invading his privacy. Check with a literary attorney to see what

these terms mean. If you have a publisher, the staff and attorneys will work with you on this, but if you publish independently, you need to take care of it yourself.

- Be sure that you do not express your opinions as facts. As you do your research, check as many facts as possible.
- If nonfamily members are included in the book, be willing to change names, physical descriptions, and the locations of towns or other public arenas.
- Fictionalizing, changing certain things to protect the guilty and the innocent, may be necessary when preparing for publication.

Publishing a memoir means considering it as a public literary endeavor. Publishing concerns should be put aside until you complete a full draft of the memoir. As with any public statement, ethical issues arise and must be solved. Ideally, the solutions will allow the work to be healing for everyone involved.

A Student's Voice

On Writing the Truth about Loved Ones

By Denise Roessle

I'm constantly wrestling with how much truth to reveal about family and friends who are still alive. During my pregnancy I lived with a woman who had an enormous heart and a huge drinking problem. I witnessed a lot over those seven months, and while it's not all relevant to my story, some of it is. We became friends and still are, 32 years later. I worry that portraying her honestly will hurt her, and I find myself going back over that part of the story, looking for ways to soften it without totally sacrificing the truth.

With my parents, who played a major role in what happened, it's even worse. A little voice in my head says: "These people aren't monsters. It couldn't have been that bad. They love you, and what you're doing is going to kill them." I envision them completely cutting me off once the book is out, and my sister and brother being angry with me for spilling my guts in public. Sometimes I catch myself wishing that they were already dead so I wouldn't have to worry about their reaction.

I don't want to hurt anybody, but I need to tell my story, to say the truth and be heard. For once, I'm making my needs more important than everyone else's. I'm going ahead with it, letting the chips fall where they may. That decision alone has been a major step toward healing.

Exercises

1. What emotional reactions are you concerned will occur when you present your memoir to family? What are your top five worries about what will happen when you talk with your family about your memoir? Write about those worries.

2. Think about revenge. Is there anyone you'd like to get back at? Do you imagine someone reading your memoir and feeling sorry or apologizing to you? Write about this in your journal.

3. Will your family think your work is fair and balanced?

4. List the ethical problems in your memoir that concern you.

5. How do you feel about taking your memoir into the public arena? Write about this as you go through the process of writing and publishing your memoir.

6. If you want your work published, research your rights and your legal and ethical responsibilities.

Forgiveness

'Tis the most tender part of love
Each other to forgive.

—John Sheffield, "The Reconcilement"

*U*nresolved issues may surface as you stimulate memories to write your memoir. Scenes from the past float into consciousness. You may realize that you have unfinished business with someone in your family or with a friend from the past. Looking at who you once were and at the kinds of relationships you had at different times in your life can stimulate a new awareness of injuries done to you, or wounds you may have inflicted on others intentionally or unintentionally. As you reflect, you may find that you need to bring certain relationships into balance through a process of forgiveness—either by asking for it or by forgiving someone else.

All families, all people, have their own vulnerabilities and emotional triggers. What would be an insult to one person is not to another. A family's vulnerabilities will most likely be connected with its dynamics. Consider your family rules and myths. If you or anyone else in the family breaks these rules, it can set off a reaction. The family's view of itself is shaken, and defenses go up. How dare you (or Aunt Josie) talk about Sara's abortion, Bob's drunken girlfriend, or great-grandma's secret second marriage. When the war starts, people take sides and create opposing factions, setting up dynamics that go on for years and even cross into the next generation, which is expected to continue the war out of loyalty. Walls get built that are hard to break through.

How, then, can forgiveness occur? The process involves two roles: the person requesting forgiveness and the person being asked for it. Forgiveness can be sought in person or through writing. Sometimes it can be accomplished only in absentia, as when the other party is deceased or out of reach. And there may be times when you would prefer to resolve your feelings without confronting the other person directly, times when you want to put your feelings aside, to forgive even if you don't forget, and move on.

Forgiving an action does not mean acknowledging it as acceptable or no longer considering it an injury or injustice. Forgiving does not necessarily mean forgetting. What has been done can't be undone; forgiveness does not mean that it didn't happen. It does not mean undoing any action.

Forgiveness means that you stop feeling resentment. Forgiveness means that your energy is freed up. When you let go of the resentment, you are free to move on with your life. If you desire forgiveness, it means that you are trying to bring balance to your life, realign your ethics, and let go of guilt and shame. All this considerably lightens emotional burdens and enables both parties to move on and live more positive lives.

Forgiveness Through Unsent Letters

If you have been injured by the behavior of another, write a letter stating directly and in exact detail the time, place, physical location—the entire scene—of what happened, how it happened, and your conclusions about the event. Tell how you felt about yourself and the other person. Be thorough and specific. State each event, each action, and each reaction as it appeared from your point of view.

Write this letter to the person you feel injured by, but do not send it. Put it aside in your journal or another private place. You may have to write several versions to get everything said the way you need to say it.

Then write a letter about your injury to a best friend, either someone you knew at the time, who was familiar with the situation, or to a current friend. When you focus your words toward a specific person, you focus your thoughts and emotions. Write this letter as many times as you need to.

Don't cut this process short. Continue to write different versions until you feel you have nothing more to say.

Now switch roles. Stand in the shoes of the person you feel injured by. First, write the response you expect he or she would give you in person. Next, write the response you want to receive from that person, whether or not you feel he or she will give it to you. Write what you want to hear; write what you need to hear. Write this response as often as you need to.

A Forgiveness Conversation

If you are the petitioner, the one asking for forgiveness from someone you have injured, it helps to:

- Acknowledge the other person's feelings with empathy, saying something like, "I understand it hurt your feelings when I . . ."
- Apologize and ask for forgiveness, but only if you are sincere about it. Clearly say, "I am sorry. Please forgive me." This needs to be a genuine response from your heart, and you must realize that the other person may not choose to respond positively. You are taking an emotional risk. Do not expect that the other person will grant forgiveness immediately. It may take time.
- Don't make excuses. Any explanation can slide into an excuse, which takes away from the apology.

If you are in the position of offering forgiveness:

- Express what hurt you, and be specific.
- If you are angry, choose words that state your anger clearly.
- Ask if the other person understands what you are saying; have the other person repeat your communication back to you.
- Consider your response carefully. If you can't genuinely forgive the person, don't pretend and don't be dishonest. Although the petitioner may have waited a long time to request forgiveness, don't feel pressured to forgive unless you really mean it.
- If you do feel that you can forgive, express yourself clearly. Communicate your understanding or empathy. Forgiveness is a great gift. By giving it, you bring balance back to the relationship.

What I Learned about Forgiveness

I have always felt passionately about the need for forgiveness, having grown up in a family whose members held grudges and hatred until their deathbed. My grandmother hated my father, for what exactly I never knew. I only knew the extent and depth of her hatred. It was so important to her that she spent sixteen years of her life teaching me to hate him, savoring her passionate hatred like so many poison chocolates. This hatred filled our small house as she ranted and raved. She spilled out the hatred and dictated it to me to write in my own hand. I was forced to write hate letters to my father for eight years, and it sickened me. I'd go to church and hear about the forgiveness of sins, I'd read about it in the Bible, and I'd wonder why my grandmother dedicated her life to hate.

She fought with my mother, her daughter, just as passionately. For years, they screamed and cried, neither one backing down. I always believed their conflict had to do with Gram's abandonment of my mother. I always hoped they'd reconcile; I'd urge both of them to talk to each other, to come to terms before it was too late.

On the last evening of my grandmother's conscious life, she was told that Mother was downstairs at the hospital. She looked up and murmured, "Oh my brown-eyed baby," her pet name for Mother when she was young. At the nurse's instruction, I went downstairs to occupy Mother for a time. She was known as a disrupter of the peace, and the nurse was concerned about what she might do to upset her patient. By the time Mother and I came upstairs, my grandmother had gone into a coma. She died two days later, without waking up. There was no forgiveness on either side.

I had heard a rumor that Gram had paid Mother off ten years earlier, that she had given my mother thousands of dollars never to visit or bother her again. I didn't find out for sure if this was true until 1993. All I knew when my grandmother died is that she and my mother had not seen or spoken to each other for ten years. Our neighbors Ken and Mary knew us all too well, having witnessed the screaming matches through the years. They told me this story: "Your mother came to visit, and it was terrible. We could hear them, you know, the fighting. Finally a Yellow Cab came and took your mother off. Ken went over to see your grandmother, and she was sobbing."

Ken took over the story: "Yeah, and I said, 'What's the matter, Mrs. Hurlbut?' She was pathetic, you know, no teeth, her hair . . . she looked up and said, 'I paid her off never to come back.' I asked her about it. She gave her several thousand dollars and told her never to ask for another thing, and never to come back."

I know that my mother carried that sorrow with her, and she never was able to resolve her relationship with her mother. I silently promised that this would never happen to me.

Before my grandmother went to the hospital for the last time, she summoned me to her bedside. I noticed the energy in the room was lighter, not heavy and dark as usual. Her voice lilted upward, and she seemed so small and authentic—nothing like the raving maniac I had learned to fear. She grasped my hands firmly in her own. "I have to tell you. I had the last rites. [She was not a Catholic, but had stayed in a Catholic hospital earlier.] The priest took pity on me. I'd been crying and crying, and couldn't stop. He blessed me and absolved me of all my sins. Now, please, will you forgive me for hating your father?"

I looked at her clear, brown eyes and touched her bony fingers. My heart tugged in different directions. My father was dying then too. It was all such a mess. I visualized a mound of unfinished business to sort out in years to come. But here she was, asking now. I had sweeping flashbacks about all the previous years; I saw her as she was when I was young; I remembered how she had rescued me when no one else wanted me. The good years and good times came flooding back, how she called me "Sugar Pie." My heart opened, and tears gathered behind my eyes. I said, "Yes, I forgive you." A breeze lifted the white curtain in the room, and she squeezed my hand.

Exercises

1. Write about an injury that you feel you can't forgive. Write very specifically—who, what, when, where, how. Use sensual detail. Write slowly and deliberately.
2. Write about why you can't forgive this injury or the person who committed it. Over a period of time, write several versions, first for ten minutes and then for twenty minutes, until you feel you have expressed all your feelings about it.
3. Think about how you hurt another person. Write a story giving details about that person, how you knew each other, what was good about the relationship, and the circumstances of the injustice or injury you caused. How do you understand yourself in that situation? Would you act differently now?
4. Write the story with a new plot. How could it turn out differently? What skills, understanding, or emotional knowledge do you have now that you did not have then? Have you asked for forgiveness from that person? Can you forgive yourself?
5. How did your family act when it came to grudges and forgiveness? Write family stories about forgiveness. Be sure to describe the "characters," your family members, using sensual details—color, sound, smell, and tactile sensations. Use action and dialogue to show what happened.

16

Love and Healing

What is love? All of us have different experiences that we associate with love, from great bear hugs to looking into the eyes of our beloved, from dark chocolate to unity with God and nature. Love is petting a cat or dog. Love is spring rain, snow on bare trees, exalting music. Love is the healing force in the universe. Love shines its light into dark corners. Love is expansive and empathic; it understands and gathers in the lost and lonely. Love is connection and beauty, acceptance and courage. Love is the opposite of fear; it is like a prism, each facet reflecting a different color of light. Love is . . . many things.

Thich Nhat Hanh, a Vietnamese Buddhist teacher, writes in his book *Teachings on Love*: "Happiness is only possible with true love. True love has the power to heal and transform situations around us and bring deep meaning to our lives." (1997, 2)

He says that we can learn to practice love by meditating on its qualities. "Love, compassion, joy, and equanimity are the . . . four aspects of true love within ourselves, and within everyone and everything." (1997, 3)

True Love

"True love is the intention and capacity to offer joy and happiness," Hanh writes. Love contains and encompasses all the other aspects: joy, equanimity, and compassion. To love unconditionally means to love with no expectations of return. This may be difficult, at times even impossible, but we can practice it by becoming aware of expectations or the need to "give to get." For Thich Nhat Hanh, love includes trees, animals, and spirits—the whole universe (1997).

Compassion

Hanh defines compassion as "the intention and capacity to relieve and transform suffering and lighten sorrow." (1997, 5) Compassion means to suffer with, but we don't need to suffer to help relieve suffering. We show concern when we are compassionate; we open our hearts to a deep understanding of the other person, his trials, needs, stuck places. We do not, and cannot, fix his problems, but by acceptance and our own full presence we can provide deep comfort.

"With compassion in our heart, every thought, word and deed can bring about a miracle," says Hanh (1997, 6).

Joy

Joy is the capacity to receive the beauty of the world, green trees, ocean spray, birdsong, the purr of a cat. Joy is peace and happiness and the beauty and love reflected in those around us. It is natural to feel joy and to receive it. Joy bubbles up like a stream; joy spills over, is contagious. Joy is within us and shines through us.

Equanimity

"If your love has attachments, discrimination, prejudice, or clinging in it, it is not true love." (Hanh, 1997, 8)

Equanimity means balance and presence, the awareness of self and other. Equanimity is love that gives without guilt or possession, admires without envy or greed, receives without demand for reciprocation.

When we practice equanimity, there is balance and empathy for others, and we feel peaceful with ourselves and our loved ones.

Love and the Eye of the Beholder

You must define for yourself what love means and decide how you will carry on family traditions and beliefs about love. Family members may agree or disagree about what love is. To one it might mean unselfish giving; to another it could mean mowing the lawn, baking a pie, or cutting someone's hair. Love can be physical, emotional, free, or extremely costly.

A negative family cycle can be broken by an extraordinary event, such as a natural disaster, the death of a family member, a birth, a marriage, or some other event so striking that it breaks through bitterness and grudges, roles and myths. Sometimes an innocent child unites a split family as they see through fresh eyes the patterns of the past. A single person can break through patterns and unconscious conditioning, creating a new form and destiny for the future. It is in our families that we test our skills, try out our developing personality; and it is to the enfolding family with its unconditional love that, if we are lucky, we can return.

The protective wings of the birth family may not be available to a child who has been abandoned, denied, or orphaned. Some children who have been raised by non-blood family or extended family feel that they have been cared for more truly than they would have been in their family of origin. If your family has been fragmented, writing stories about it can help unite the broken strands in yourself. As the narrator who observes with perspective, you can use this weaving to heal ancient deep wounds, to create an identity that holds and a matrix that can contain and comfort.

Most families, however defined, have a wealth of resources to balance problems and difficult issues. Human beings are capable of immense acts of generosity and kindness; altruistic love; and acts of beauty that transcend pain and hurt, that alter and transform it. Such acts are part of the natural healing process in our lives, changing anger and depression to hope and success.

When you examine your family's history, you may discover inspiring stories of courage, love, generosity, and strength. The positive qualities of our ancestors can be gifts for us to draw on. We can be inspired by a great-great aunt who walked behind a Conestoga wagon for three thousand miles, or a grandfather who managed to feed his family during the Great Depression, or acts of bravery and sacrifice during wartime. These kinds of stories galvanize our energy and make us want to carry on these traditions and qualities in our own lives.

In every family there are stories of spirituality, love, miracles, and blessings. We must remember that a necessary part of our healing is to discover and write our positive stories of happiness, joy, and love. It is in these stories that we find sparks of understanding to inspire us to live our lives fully and richly, with a feeling of blessing.

A Student's Voice

Kind to Animals

By Catherine Jones

I don't know when I began asking my mother why she'd married George. Or, for that matter, when I stopped. I asked in grade school and more urgently in junior high, but not so often later on.

"It's a mystery," Irene, my grandmother, told me once. "To tell the truth—it's a terrible thing to say—when June married him, my first thought was that she might have done it for the death bonus." Meaning a lump sum of government money paid to widows of men killed in action.

Whatever my grandmother felt about George as a son-in-law, she was a fatalist and good-natured as well. When he came back from the war—not an obvious outcome, a lot of his shipmates did not—my grandmother welcomed him into her home and set to work trying to fatten him up. "He was that thin," she used to insist, making her finger and thumb almost touch. "He looked just like a strip of bacon."

Irene, George often said, was like a mother to him. By which he meant kind and not like his own mother. Irene was cheerful. She wore bright lipstick, big button earrings, a starched apron with blue flowers. Widowed young, she worked as a bookkeeper, conscientiously but without ambition. She just got up every weekday, struggled into her girdle, dressed, cooked breakfast, and went off to the bus stop to do what, apparently, had to be done.

Irene held that bookkeeping job for thirty years, starting just before the crash of '29. She stayed in her old house, too, through the Depression and World War II, taking in boarders to keep up the payments. Not until 1950 did she finally make a move, swapping the house for a duplex and thus splitting a household of four adults, one dog, and one child into two semi-autonomous units.

I remember Irene best right after she retired. That would be around 1959, the year after my parents fled from Cupertino, fled from the whole suburban-ranch-house-low-down-payment dream, which hadn't ever been their dream anyway. In 1958 we moved back to San Francisco, or, as George always called it, the City. First, though, came months of fruitless search through the rental listings; even if we were welcome, our dog was not. Which is how we wound up moving back to where we'd started: the downstairs flat in my grandmother's duplex out in the fog belt on the avenues. Thus we gained the City but lost the sun and our independence, the very reasons we'd moved in the first place.

My grandmother welcomed us back, of course. And my parents insisted on paying the full market rent, double what our mortgage had been in Cupertino. So there was honor in this new situation, intermingled with defeat. Other living arrangements may have crossed my mother's mind, but by then she'd stopped discussing such things with me. I guess by then she saw no way to salvage her life, short of walking out on the whole lot of us. I would have forgiven her; I would have understood; but that's not the way this story goes.

So, there we all are in 1959. We've spent the last year in the city living under one roof: George, my mother, the dog, and me downstairs; my grandmother Irene and my Aunt Claire above. Irene has recently retired, and I'm in my first year of junior high. I see myself walking home from school, trudging up the stairs with an armful of books, and stopping at the first floor landing. There's not much light or beauty in that part of the stairwell: no plants, nothing personal, just a plain city door with a peephole and a deadbolt. The only clue to life behind the door is the place at dog-paw level where the paint has been scratched away. Leash law or no, our dog, Barney, runs free. He goes where he likes, barks when he pleases, and scratches on the door when he wants to go in or out. He's bitten people in the past and fought with other dogs; over the years George has done a lot of talking, getting Barney out of trouble.

By 1959, though, Barney is slowing down. When he's not out walking with George, he spends most of his time stretched out on the basement floor, nose against a grate facing the street. From this position he sniffs at passersby, scaring them, often, with a terrible bark worthy of an animal twice his size. Barney's a piece of George, really; Barney's more than a dog; George calls him my older brother. Still, he's a comfort, this lawless brother of mine. Anytime I cry, Barney's there, concerned and ready to lick away the tears.

I hear him snuffling impatiently behind the door as I search for the key. Barney doesn't bark at me; he knows the sounds I make. In his dog's mind he can see me, rummaging through the purse that's wedged between my skinny chest and my stack of books. Then I'm inside, running my hand through his fur, dumping my books onto the bed in my room, and heading out the back door and on up the back stairs. No one else is home downstairs; my parents both work days. It's not till the following year that George will take the foreman's exam, buy a clip-on tie, and start in as a boss on the midnight shift.

On the walls of the back stairwell, which is open to the sky, my grandmother has hung pots of geraniums. So there's a cheery display of red, pink, and green as you approach her back door. I walk in without knocking, and there she is, sitting in the breakfast nook on the red, fake leather bench that I nicknamed, many years ago, the Red Zucchini.

There's a stew with peppers and onions simmering on the stove and, mixing in with the steam from the stew, the smell of linseed oil and turpentine. In her right hand, my grandmother holds a brush; with her left, she steadies a canvas on the fold-away easel set up on the kitchen table. A pair of drugstore eyeglasses balances, just barely, on the tip of her nose.

I stand beside my grandmother and peer over her shoulder. A boy of about five is coming into focus in the center of the canvas. He looks like the photograph taped to the easel, but friendlier and better mannered. In the photograph I notice a slight jut of the lower jaw, something defiant or even mean, that hasn't survived the translation onto canvas. I wonder if my grandmother has noticed this too. It occurs to me that she hasn't, that Irene simply sees people as better than they are and then paints exactly what she sees.

"Have a cookie," she says, motioning with her brush toward a jar on the shelf above the Red Zucchini. I thank her but shake my head no. Grown-ups are always offering me cookies, but cookies—even the fresh-baked oatmeal-raisin kind—aren't really what I want. I want, maybe, not to be shy. I want to trade my saddle shoes for a pair of pointed-toe flats. I want to rat my hair, draw black lines around my eyes, shriek, chew noisy gum, and say sassy, forbidden things the way the bad girls do at school. Or, since that's beyond the reach of possibility, I want to grow up and be Madame Curie.

Meanwhile, though, I'm in my grandmother's kitchen, which is not a bad place to be. I borrow charcoal and paper from her, swipe my Aunt Claire's magazine from the coffee table, and settle in on the other end of the Red Zucchini to draw a portrait of my own. The magazine—Vogue (my Aunt Claire's a subscriber)—is full of models with dark-rimmed eyes. They look a little like the bad girls at school, but thinner, with shinier hair and dressier clothes.

I pick one with her face in three-quarter view and her hair pulled back so you can see her ear. I tell myself that this time I won't chicken out. I'll spend as long as it takes to get the ear down right, even though I'd rather be working on the eyes, which are sly, shadowed, and enticing. Then, for a while, everything's cozy and peaceful: my grandmother and me, side by side in the kitchen, with just the sound of the brush, the charcoal stick, and the bubbles in the stew.

Later I'll go back to the darker flat downstairs, where there aren't any potted plants, where George and my mother smoke cigarettes, where Barney sheds his black hair onto the light brown couch, and life feels more difficult and more real. I'll sit on the couch with Barney and read about Madame Curie.

Exercises

Reflect on each of the following, and write about your reflections.

1. Love: How did your family show or define love? Think about the small acts as well as the larger ones. What acts of love do you hold close to your heart?
2. Loyalty: How was loyalty defined in your family; how were you loyal? How much was loyalty valued in your family?
3. Generosity: How did your family demonstrate generosity? Through gifts, actions, words? Whose generosity did you admire? How do you show generosity?
4. Compassion: How do you define compassion? Who was the most compassionate member of your family?
5. Courage: Heart (*coeur*) is the root of courage, the ability to act in the face of danger or threat. How do you define courage? Write about courage in your life.
6. Tolerance: This is the ability to stretch emotional resources and accept differences. How has tolerance been shown or not shown in your family?
7. Creativity and creative expression: This includes gardening, sewing, building cars or houses, crafts, the arts, painting, knitting, and hobbies. In what ways do you and your family show creativity?

Part 3
Writing the Memoir

As we reveal ourselves in story, we become aware of the continuing core of our lives under the fragmented surface of our experience. . . . Most important, as we become aware of ourselves as storytellers, we realize that what we understand and imagine about ourselves is a story. And when we know all this, we can use our stories to heal and make ourselves whole.

—Susan Wittig Albert,
Writing from Life: Telling Your Soul's Story

The Process of Writing

The narrative is artificially shaped out of a chaos of memories.

—Marilyn Chandler

When you write a memoir, you invite reflections and dreams. When you are in reverie—the French word for dream—you are in a right-brain, nonlinear world, a poetic world of images and associations. To enhance creativity, it is important to allow the right brain to dream. This lets the creative mind unwind its secret processes. Many people say that after trying unsuccessfully to solve a problem, they engage in some unrelated activity—taking a shower, baking a pie, cleaning the house (writers tend to have some of the cleanest houses in the world), going for a long walk—and afterwards they find their problem solved. That is because the right brain works holistically and needs to be unburdened from directed thinking, which is linear and logical. Inspiration comes from the nonlinear part of our minds, and it requires room to perform its miracles.

Brenda Ueland (1987) suggests taking long meditative walks to allow the mind to wander, unfocused. Inspiration often comes in this way.

Stages of Creative Writing

Just as a flower evolves from a seed to green leafiness to a larger plant with mature blossoms, so your memoir will grow in stages.

Beginning: Follow your idea, your spark, an image that presents itself. Write in your journal. Don't censor your work. Do the writing exercises in this book. Create a folder of vignettes. Work on your timeline (see Chapter 18). Put questions about publishing aside until later. I have seen students get stuck writing their memoir by trying to sell the book before it is written. Most first-time authors need to finish their book before anyone will take a serious look at it, though surprises do happen. If you are working on your first book, you won't know how it will turn out until you have written at least a full first draft. So be patient and surrender to the writing process.

Developing: In this stage you make time to write. Create a schedule, setting aside several small segments of time each week to write. Write as often as you can, either in your journal or for your project. Attend readings to hear other writers' work, and attend writing conferences. You may want to join a writing group. This stage requires that you listen deeply to your story; it also requires the motivation to continue to write the painful stories. Keep your critic at bay. If it will help you, do the exercises about the critic-censor at the end of Chapter 13. Encourage an open, positive frame of mind.

Focusing: During this stage you track the stories that you know need to be included in your book; keep a record of the stories you have written and another record of the ones you intend to write. There is a synchronicity to this process. Someone else's story that you hear in your writing group may spark a memory for you. Reading published memoirs is a good way to learn about structure, writing style, and story, and it may stimulate ideas of your own. At this time you may also want to do genealogical research, visit relatives, and talk to siblings.

Quilting: In this stage the book begins to take shape. You can see a narrative line or theme that weaves through it. You organize the parts and make decisions about what goes in and what does not go in the book. You think about ethical issues, the questions about family and privacy. Quilting, organizing and reorganizing the parts, may continue throughout the writing of the first and second draft.

Smoothing: Now you can begin editing and rewriting. You look closely to see what the book really needs, what it is really about, and how to focus the themes. You will need to think again about your ideas and concepts, and then perhaps perform a heavy revision of your text. Michelangelo once described his work as releasing the sculpture from the marble. During the smoothing stage, you release one story from the multitude of possible stories you could include.

Presenting: Now you should engage the services of a professional editor to help smooth the text and prepare it for publication. At the same time, inform your family or friends that you have written about them, and ask them to read what you have said. Your role changes now from writer to marketer. You must decide whether to get an agent, whether you can find a publisher on your own, or whether you want to self-publish.

Writing Groups

A writing support group—along with patience, determination, and energy—helps you through the long process of writing a memoir. But joining a writing group helps only if it's the right group. An ideal group would be one that focuses on memoir. When my students have joined fiction groups, they have found themselves vulnerable because their personal story is exposed as real and authentic while other members are protected because the stories they read are supposedly not true. Unless the group you have joined focuses on writing as an act of healing, unless the group understands family dynamics and the vulnerability of writing about it, you may hear unhelpful comments and judgments, such as, "That can't be true; that could never happen; oh come on, you are exaggerating. That's crazy, how could you let that happen to you." One group I attended scathingly (and of course erroneously) talked about "stupid women who stayed in abusive relationships for the money." Be careful when you share stories about violence, mental illness, and other controversial social issues. People who have not been in therapy or who are unaware of the complex dynamics involved often find it difficult to understand these elements of the human story. They may be frightened by them or be reminded of their own buried issues.

Reading aloud to a supportive group helps you hear the rhythm and music of your sentences. You will catch awkward phrases, missed beats, incorrect words. Typing mistakes also stand out when you read aloud.

Women may find themselves struggling to find or maintain their point of view and voice in a writing group attended by men. Although their published work will be read by both sexes, during the sensitive, early, creative process women may prefer feedback and support from women only. In 1997, Susan Wittig Albert formed the Story Circle Network, which offers online groups, a quarterly journal, and ways that women can create a supportive local writing network. Please visit them online at www.storycircle.com.

A supportive writing group will provide more useful and objective information about your work than your friends and family can. Well-intentioned friends and family members frequently give non-objective feedback based on how they feel about you. Because spouses and friends do not want you to feel bad if you are writing painful stories, they may suggest that you give up the writing. The people who love you do not want you to cry, struggle, or feel pain. "Just let it go," the non-writer, trying to be helpful, says to the writer. And you may feel tempted to give up your project—moments of pain do occur along the way to healing; struggling with emotions is part of the memoir-writing process. That's why it is a good idea to protect your writing and yourself by joining a supportive writing group. The wrong feedback can kill your work in its infancy. Here's what one of my students, Robin Malby, wrote about her experience:

> Participating in a memoir-writing group has given me a great deal of healing and encouragement as a beginning writer. My stories center around my journey from a life of chronic pain and illness to a state of improved health and spiritual strength. They are not easy stories to write because they require that I call up unpleasant and often traumatic memories and put them into words. I have found that the process of revisiting those dark days of pain and illness and putting those experiences on paper allows an additional layer of sadness and trauma to be released, physically and emotionally. What is most healing for me is reading my stories aloud to the group, whose members have come to serve as a circle of supportive witnesses. What I discovered on my journey to wellness was that dynamic people and committed healers come in all different kinds of packages, some being not at all what one would expect. Being able to bring these individuals to life on the written page and receive feedback from my writing group has encouraged me to keep writing.

Keeping a Journal

Because healing is the purpose of writing your memoir, you will find it especially helpful to record your feelings about your memoir writing in a journal. You may record ideas, fears, worries about what your family will say about a particular story—anything that helps you keep the memoir writing alive.

As you visit the corridors of memory, and the past makes its way into your consciousness and even into your dreams, you may encounter raw emotions, deep feelings you may not have been aware of until now. For some writers, making the transition from present to past is as easy as closing their eyes; for others it is like standing on the edge of a pool deciding when to jump into cold water. Each individual has a different relationship to memory. Part of memoir writing is confronting the past and your various selves face to face. This is what makes writing healing. Because you are writing a healing memoir, it is important that you balance your entry into painful stories by alternating them with stories in which you feel strong and positive. These stories remind you of your strength and resilience, and help you face the next set of stories that are more painful. Keep writing in your journal as a way to listen to your inner voice and allow unstructured writing. The unconscious mind seems to need both musing time and structured time.

Making Room for Writing

Writing requires reflection, time, and a routine. When my students tell me, "I didn't have time to write this week. I was dreaming, and thinking, about the story, but I don't have anything to show for it," I tell them that they have already done some of their work. A memoir writer needs to spend time thinking, and will spend a great deal of time dreaming, musing, and keeping a journal. A story must live inside you, and you must learn to listen it out—listen deeply and with full presence—in order to bring it out of your body, like a birthing. Accepting your process and your self assists in this listening-out stage.

Because everyone's creative process works differently, you need to do what feels comfortable for you. Louise DeSalvo, in *Writing as a Way of Healing*, suggests setting a firm time by which you decide when the work will be complete, and then counting backwards from there. To use this method, you would need to figure out how long the project will take, how many hours a week you will write, how many hours a day, and how many pages per hour.

Most writers find that it's best to set a writing schedule. Even a book-length memoir can be completed with steady but brief bursts of writing. You will be amazed at what you can accomplish in just fifteen minutes. Some new writers set impossible goals for themselves: "I will write every day for two or three hours." Then they become unhappy with themselves when that impossible schedule can't be kept; they feel like a failure and want to give up. Most people are not supported by a prince, are not independently wealthy, and do not have two or three free hours a day in which to write.

Set realistic goals. If you have a job or have family to take care of, set aside just four twenty-minute blocks of time each week. After a while, when the writing begins to flow smoothly, you may increase the time you spend on it. But the creative process can't be rushed. You must follow your natural rhythm. As you work, you will discover a pattern. You will then be better able to schedule your writing, making time for creating and generating new work as well as time to rewrite, read, and muse.

At times you may feel stuck. When that happens you'll come up with all sorts of excuses:

I can't write unless I have a three- or four-hour block of time.
I can't write until I know what I am going to say.
I'm afraid I'll feel bad afterwards.
I'm depressed.
I don't see why I should bother doing it.

The solution to feeling stuck is to remind yourself that you have dedicated yourself to the process of healing through writing and to find ways to make it a priority. Remind yourself also to approach the writing with a beginner's mind: simply put your pen to the page and write. It doesn't matter what you say; just write. You can edit later. If you only write when you feel good, you miss the opportunity to allow the writing itself to help you feel better. Remember to balance writing about painful subjects with writing about the happy and successful times in your life; both are healing. And remember to nurture yourself.

Vignettes

The complexities of real life make it difficult to sort out the many threads; the multiple strands of action, conversation, and mood; the myriad emotional undertones that are part of our stories. To simplify the task, you can approach your memoir through writing vignettes. Vignettes are short, one- to five-page stories about a single event, person, place, or thing. Each vignette contains the heart of a story that you can flesh out later, in your first draft. Vignettes are the discreet pieces that, when quilted together, compose a memoir.

The Elements of Memoir Writing

- Remembering and reflecting on memory
- Visualizing specifics—houses, landscapes, cities and towns, people, states of mind and emotion, behaviors and interactions
- Choosing a narrator to tell the story
- Showing who, what, when, where, and—in memoir especially—how and why
- Telling the tale

A satisfying way to begin is to write vignettes about things that rouse your passion—memories that worry you or make you curious or angry. The energy of this "fire in the belly" method helps you start writing. Writing a vignette every few days makes you feel that you are making progress, and you are!

As you write the vignettes, don't listen to your worries or your critic-censor. You can always edit your work later. For now, just put the words down as they come out. Listen to the creative, hopeful voice inside you: *I need to write this. I need to heal . . . I have a story that needs to be told.*

Quilting Together the First Draft

In your first draft, you quilt your vignettes together to set the structure for your memoir. By quilting together several vignettes that tell a fuller story, you create a chapter. And so, vignette by vignette, chapter by chapter, you create a book-length draft, a tale with plot, characters, themes, and emotional insight.

Using the elements of fiction—scene, narration, dialogue, point of view, and description—helps you to build each chapter. Your great-aunt, grandmother, father, and best friend become characters in the book. Remember, these people are strangers to the reader. To make them familiar, you will use writing techniques that capture their essence, feeling, and character.

You must translate your poetic dreamworld into words and images. As you translate experience from your inner world to the outside, you will search for language to create a state of mind in the reader that matches the memory, sensation, and image within you. This is called creating verisimilitude, creating a believable world.

One of the foundations of a memoir is the storyteller's voice, the way the narrator—you—speak, think, feel, and express yourself. In a memoir, you are both the teller of the story and a character in the story, a split self. The narrator is a detached observer who tells the story. The narrator has a point of view, usually expressed by the first person "I," sometimes by the third person "she" or "he." You describe what happened and how you felt; you present your interpretation of events to the reader.

You may create a scene to show your grandmother's house and how the family gathered around at Christmas; you may show the smell of the fireplace, how people dressed, the food they ate. You will probably use dialogue and character portraits to show how people interacted. As narrator, you present a whole world, yours, to the reader. A detailed, structured narrative forces you to be fully present.

Just as some movies begin with long shots that pan the location or setting and then focus in a window or down a street searching for a person or some action, you may start your story by setting the broad scene, describing the geographic location, and then focusing on your childhood home and a main character. By what that character does or says, the reader becomes engaged with the story and wants to hear it all. Alternatively, you may choose to do just the opposite: start with a detail and move out.

When your words flow, it feels as if you're taking dictation—you place your pen on the page and write as fast as you can. When you are lucky and blessed, the writing flows, but this does not always happen, even with an oft-published author. Sometimes there are hard days, days when you stare at a blank page or a computer screen. Out dribbles a sentence, or a few words. But each of these hard-won sentences is work that needs to be done, work that will lead to another blessing from the stream of consciousness. It is said that we must do the hard work for the blessings to come.

Most of your first draft may sound and look terrible on the page. You may be tempted to tear it up and throw it away. In *Bird by Bird*, Anne Lamott says that everyone writes "shitty first drafts." Lamott's bald statement has given many writers permission to write that first awkward draft without feeling guilty. Instead, they read her amusing and cheery chapter and laugh at hanging participles and sloppy metaphors.

The critic-censor may try to shame you into getting rid of writing that could be improved or an idea that was interesting but needed time to be clarified. The critic can be particularly savage when you write about shameful things, or areas of your life that bring up insecurities or questions about yourself. No matter how bad you think your writing is, never, never erase what you have written. Download it into a file labeled "saved stuff." Remember, all writing leads to more writing, and the "bad" writing always leads to better writing. When in doubt, read writing that you hate to your group. It helps to let your group know how you feel, and see how they reflect your work back to you.

Have faith. Keep writing.

Organizing Your Work

Through dreams, the various dwelling-places in our lives retain the treasure of former days . . . we travel to the land of Motionless Childhood . . .

—Paul Bachelard, THE POETICS OF SPACE

There are so many stories. How do I begin?

That is the lament I hear from students as they being to write their memoirs. After thinking about your story for a long time, perhaps for years, you have started writing, or at least you've decided to "begin to start." But as you think about it, chapter one could be chapter ten; or you could start a hundred years ago and tell the story of a great-grandmother or grandfather. Or you could begin the story in the present and flash back. Where and with what story is the best way to begin the family saga? How do you separate the layers of stories? How do you speak about healing if you don't present what created the need for healing? Where did it all start? Organizing the memoir can be especially difficult when writers have to deal with generational patterns.

Beginners often feel daunted by the emotional responsibility of writing a memoir. This psychological burden can get in the way of figuring out how to begin and what to write first. It can be resolved by putting the emotional questions aside, working them through in a writing journal, or by doing the exercises in Parts 1 and 2 of this book.

Students frequently come to me overwhelmed by the immeasurable number of potential pages they might write. Two practical approaches to resolve that problem are described below.

The Card System

Keeping track of your vignettes and stories on large index cards (4 x 6 or 5 x 8) has several advantages. You can lay them out and arrange and rearrange them in various configurations as you decide on the order in which you want them to appear in your book. You can use cards of one color for vignettes and another color for stories. And you can use inks of different colors to make various distinctions, such as between painful and positive stories.

On each vignette or story card you might note the following:

- Date written; dates edited
- Subject or working title
- List of characters
- Setting and time
- A short summary telling how the subject is significant for you or your family and why it fascinates you or needs to be written

The Timeline

The timeline is another way to organize your life stories. When you see ideas, memories, themes, and patterns grounded in time and place—when you see the big picture, the arc of the story—it is easier to decide what you want to write and in what order you want to present your vignettes and stories.

Stories often flow best in chronological order, tracing development through time. The timeline helps you see how the stories fit into linear time, both historically and in terms of your own life. You may want to make several timelines, one for your parents and grandparents, one for your own life, and another for your memoir, which may include only a portion of your life. Some memoirs cover decades and several generations; some memoirs tell the story of just a week or a month of real time.

Your timelines will help you keep track of what happened to you, to other members of your family, and to the community. We do not exist in a vacuum. Our lives and memories are tied to events in the larger world. In my generation, for example, a frequently asked question was: Where were you when President Kennedy was killed? Most people were acutely aware of where they were and what they were doing when they heard the news. Time seemed to stop. The story of a nation's tragedy was linked to everyone's personal vignette of that day. September 11, 2001 is another such day.

Large historical events intersect with our lives. You can use your timelines to chart those events as well as things that happened to a sister or brother, parent or grandparents, and use them as marking points from which other events flow.

You can use the timeline on page 191 as a model for making your own. Write in dates and your age; label events in circles.

Before you make large timelines, say 18 by 24 inches, you might want to draw rough sketches of them on an 8½ by 11 sheet so that you will have an idea of how much time each will cover. That will help you figure out what size paper you'll need for the actual timelines. For the timelines themselves, you can tape several sheets of paper together or buy a pad of large paper from an art supply or stationery store. Remember that you might want to make one timeline for your entire life and another that covers a particularly significant year or two.

Draw a long horizontal line to represent linear time. Bold vertical lines demarcate segments of one, two, five, or ten years, depending on the nature of the particular timeline and how many details you want to include. Experiment. Use pencil so you can erase.

Vertical lines descending from the horizontal connect to the circles in which you will write a word or phrase to identify important

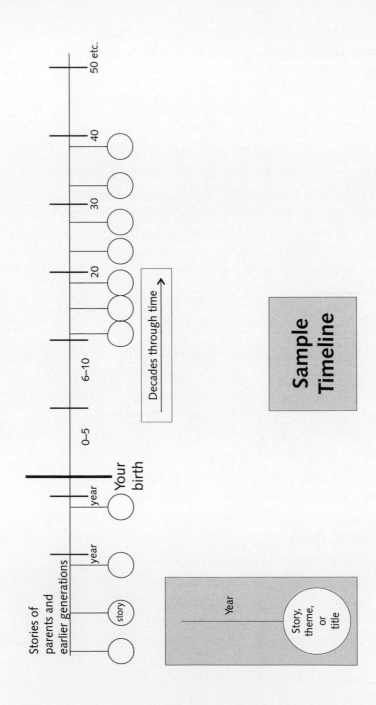

events. Place a check mark or colored dot next to all the circles that name dark stories, the ones that would be painful to write.

Writing from Your Timelines

The words or phrases you've put in the circles are the working titles of your stories. Each one provides a shortcut to the core of a story. Each designates an important or memorable occasion, perhaps a turning point or change in your life or the life of your family.

From those working titles create a list of the stories you want to write. For each story, name the characters, the location, the date or an indicator of time, the significance of the story in your family's history, and the family dynamics you want to show or explore. Here's an example:

First Move

1. *Age 3, Dad lost his job*
2. *Moved from farm to city*
3. *Turmoil in family*
4. *Memories not clear, feeling of sadness*
5. *See bars of crib? Mother crying, soft light*
6. *Empty feeling, hungry, can't stop crying*

Pace yourself. Begin with several positive stories to build up your writing muscles and emotional strength. When you are ready, dive into one of the painful stories. Remember that now you are an adult capturing the child's experience. As a narrator you have some distance from which to witness the child that you were. After writing a painful story, return to the present and nurture yourself, as described in Chapter 5.

Here's another way you can write from your timeline. Randomly choose one of the circles, set a stopwatch or timer for fifteen minutes, and freewrite nonstop about the event named in the chosen circle. Let the words flow, and keep the critic at bay. When time is up, choose another circle, and write that story for fifteen minutes. Repeat the process for a third circle.

At the end of forty-five minutes you will have the beginnings of three new stories. Often, beginnings are the most difficult parts to write. Writing will be easier to continue because you already have the beginnings. Your memoir will grow more quickly than you could have imagined.

Hooks to Hang Your Stories On

For now we see through a glass darkly, then face to face

—J Corinthians 13:12

*M*emories conjure up people, places, and things that are meaningful and carry energy. A sight, smell, or sound can propel us back in time. As a writer you can use these guideposts to the past to trigger the vignettes and longer stories that will compose your memoir.

Your Childhood Home

The house where we grew up or the place where our childhood imagination finds solace lives within us. The placement of closets, windows, and doors; the smells of gardenias and roses, wood smoke and fried chicken; the sounds of creaking floors and windows mark us for life. Thousands of memories of the house are registered within our very cells as we grow up. Our memories are located here, in this place of identity, and it is to this place that we return.

In *The Poetics of Space* Paul Bachelard, the French philosopher, says: "The house we were born in is physically inscribed in us." (1994, 14) Bachelard speaks in poetic cadences of the power of childhood spaces, how they define us and enter us, and how we return in dream and reverie to these worlds.

Writing our memories means to enter this childhood dream space. During the first annual Body and Soul Retreat I created and held in Calistoga, California, I asked students to draw and write about a house that was important to them in their childhood. One person wrote about his grandparents' apartment. We could see how important it was to him as a boy, and how it has become a part of his dream space. Another person wrote about the car that took her and her sister to and from visitations with their parents. The car was the symbol of home, a space that shapes autobiography.

During my early childhood, my grandmother and I spent most weekends with her best friends, whom I called Aunt Helen and Uncle Maj. In their house on the other side of town I would find relief from poisonous cigarette smoke and depression. The house had green shingles and red trim, and was surrounded by hundreds of roses. It stood beside Boggy Creek, which flooded so many times that they had to raise the house. In summer the windows were always open; soft breezes carried the scent of roses, and sucked the lace curtains in and out of the screens. Aunt Helen's bedroom gave the aroma of her perfumes and powders on her vanity table, and sheets dried in the sun. Every weekend she made delicious homemade bread and soup, Southern fried chicken and gravy. This was for me the house of comfort and nurturing, love and generosity. Aunt Helen's belly laugh lifted me from worries about my grandmother, giving me hope that happiness and warmth existed in the world.

I still dream of this house, long gone, moved from where it once reigned over beauty and roses and sweet summer nights. Aunt Helen, Uncle Maj, and the house are alive only inside of me, until I share them with others through my writing. This poem arose from a dream I had, in half-sleep, about the power and wisdom in old houses.

House of Memory

The house hovers alone in the forest
  shrugging off leaves and spores.
It has been in the forest a very long time.

We must be careful—it is replete with memory.
Every plank of wood, painting,
  brass fitting has a story to tell.

The house whispers in a language
  we do not understand.
It possesses a wisdom
  we need to survive.

We sit on couches that
  embraced other bodies now vanished,
taking everything they knew with them.

The house knows everything:
  how the sun rises, warms kitchen walls.
It has seen the movements of planets, seasons,
  how the years unfold like daffodils,
opening, releasing seeds of new life,
  withering, dying

The house inhales our dreams,
our words, screams and cries in the night.
Everything is etched in walls,
  runes that scramble, scuttle.
You believe it is the sound of mysterious
  insects, but it is words trying to be heard.

Who understands the wounds,
  the emptiness
when you were flooded with
  too much grief

when your child died,
when your parents refused to love you,
when your lover left you for someone else.

The house stands in the woods.
You stand beside it, tilting your head toward

creaking in the wind.
It is empty now, waiting for you to put your
  hand on the dusty dented door knob.

Open it carefully
as you would a present
wrapped in gold foil.
Be prepared
  to listen.

Exercises—Your Childhood Home

1.   Draw a house that was important to you in your childhood.
     Use colorful children's markers on large paper. Tell a friend
     or write in your journal about what you drew, describing the
     house and the memories it evokes.
2.   Write a portrait of this house and your room in it, using
     sensual details such as color, sound, smell, texture, and taste.
3.   Write a vignette or story about what made the house feel
     good or what was scary about it.
4.   If you dream about the houses of your childhood, write
     about those dreams. How often do they occur? What
     triggers them?

Nature

When we are children, the world presents itself to us as a place of
wonder and magic. We do not understand the logical world of adults,
and so we turn to the world of nature, which invites us into its mists
and leaves and clouds, scents and rustly grasses, moonlight and landscapes of beauty. The world of animals and nature captures us in its
seasons and rhythms, and reminds us of our own animal wisdom.

    When I was young, the natural world around me was so powerful
it took my breath away—the smell of the air in the morning, the liquid
warmth of summer. Birds calling out from telephone poles in the middle of the Great Plains lifted my heart. The dramatic thunderstorms

and great panoramas of clouds made me feel comforted when things were sharp and unpleasant at home. All I had to do was go outdoors, and the wind would whisper its comfort to me. The sweeping seas of golden wheat told me that there was indeed a God who had created such wonders. When I was sixteen and wracked with grief over a friend's suicide, I gathered to my heart comfort from a minuscule violet flower and its fuzzy green leaves. Its natural simplicity calmed my confusion and outrage.

Nature draws us to its eternal world of flowering, decaying, and seasonal cycling as the human stories unfold within it. To go deeper into the world of nature, to be uplifted and inspired by mountains, ocean, and forest—these are healing opportunities. We can listen to nature, even take dictation from it, listing its colors and flavors, writing about our sensual experience within its embrace. One of my students, Clare Cooper Marcus, writes extensively about this healing aspect of nature in her memoir. She writes of how she used to take refuge in nature when her family was trying to escape the bombs of London during the war, immersing herself in the scent of loam and the way light played upon the grasses and plants. She says about such a setting, "The troubles of the world disappeared."

Exercises—Nature

1. Use sensual details to describe the scenes of your early experiences of wonder and awe in nature.
2. Write about your feelings and your thoughts during those experiences. Were you alone? Did you feel alone?
3. Write a story about one of those experiences. How old were you? How did you get to the place? Why did you go there? Who was with you?

Mentors

As Alice Miller has said, when we have compassionate, helping witnesses in our lives, we are given a chance to flower and develop in ways that we might have missed without them. A mentor sees and appreciates us for who we are, and helps us recognize our talents, our creativity, and our real self—the one who shines out in spite of any pain we may be suffering. My mentor was Mr. Brauninger, my cello teacher. His warmth and gentle kindness, the caress of his voice, and the way his blue eyes gazed into mine helped me survive several difficult years with my grandmother. I still carry his image and memory within me.

Mr. Brauninger swept into my life on a fall morning in 1954. He gathered Mrs. Rockwell's fourth grade class into a Pied Piper trance with his violin under his chin, his red hair falling across his forehead, and his smile. I was hooked, and I signed up to play the cello. But more than teaching me how to play the cello, Mr. Brauninger saw the real me.

His hands danced a ballet as he conducted the Youth Symphony each Saturday morning. He introduced the magic of Haydn, Vivaldi, Bach, and Beethoven to us young musicians. He'd sweep us up and excitedly call out, "Give it to me, yes, yes." And the music would gather energy, and we'd rush through millions of notes, half unplayed, stopping breathless at the end, laughing, at one with the music.

I'd do anything to please him, to get that sweet smile to bloom. His blue eyes looked into my soul. With him, I was not just a nothing, an abandoned girl whose parents didn't want her. At Symphony, all the shadows were driven away.

He met his future wife, Eva, over the conductor's baton during his second year, and all of us in Symphony watched them fall in love. They left to teach in a college in Washington when I was thirteen years old. We lost touch for many years, but they lived in my dreams. Thirty-five years later, when we were reunited in Des Moines, it seemed like a dream come true. Mr. Brauninger's hair was white, but his blue eyes shone as they always did, and he and Eva both embraced me as if no time had passed.

I asked him what he thought of me when I was a child. He said, "I used to look in your face and see God. I saw God in the eyes of all my young students."

He'd carefully take out a CD of a Bach Brandenburg Concerto and play it on his special hi-fi, as he called his sophisticated music system. He'd sit, hands folded on his lap, in the lamplight in the geodesic dome house he'd built with his own hands, a content, beatific look on his face. When our eyes met, we were together again in that wind-blown little town of my childhood. He was conducting; I was struggling over the cello part.

During his last illness, he held my hand and whispered, "Yes, I must have been like a father to you." Tears formed in my eyes as he spoke what neither of us had put into words before—my need for a father, the emptiness in my life that Mr. Brauninger had filled. Our eyes locked, and my chest filled with the ache of knowing that I was going to lose him again.

His ability to see the real me had given me something, everything, to hold on to. When I hear strains of Beethoven and Bach, Vivaldi and Mozart, I return to the Youth Symphony on a Saturday morning. Mr. Brauninger gathers the music into his graceful hands and releases it. The melodies sweep over us in waves, healing secret wounds.

Exercises—Mentors

1. Describe a mentor or teacher who influenced you or changed your life. Write about his or her physical attributes, energy, attitudes, spiritual self.
2. Write about what else was going on in your life when your mentor appeared.
3. How did your mentor make a difference in your life? Be specific about actions, subtle undertones, or subtext.
4. How would your life have been different without your mentor?

Photographs

Photographs represent a moment of time captured and held in permanent chemical suspension; lives were going on before and after the photo was taken. Do you ever wonder what happened just before a particular photo, or just after? People in motion are caught for a split second, with an attitude, feelings, expression, and mood locked into the frame forever. Photographs can be powerful triggers for your own memories; they can stimulate your imagination about ancestors you've never met. Within the photographs you find hints about a mood, the historical time, customs, and personalities of the people in the picture. Photos give you information about the attitude and carriage of family members as you pull back the layers of meaning and subtle cues found in them.

I invite my therapy clients to bring into sessions the casual photos that are in most family albums. In the photos I look for clues about the family's closeness, distance, carriage, and demeanor. One woman brought in a snapshot of herself at the age of two; later that week she had a flashback about sexual abuse that changed the course of the therapy. Photos contain powerful messages and clues, if you know how to look for them.

For several years I tried to uncover the lives of my mother and father, both of whom were strangers to me, by gathering all the photos I could find and making copies of the images from long ago. I made a huge photo etching of my father from birth to death to try to understand his life. I copied photos of him as a young boy on cloth and quilted them—a way for me to be with him, to spend the time with him we never had while he was alive. Perhaps it was a way of mourning him. I made copies of photos of my mother and grandmother and blew up old photos, trying to extricate the story of a time and place I never knew as a way to write a photo-biography of them, a way to stand in their shoes and see life in the times in which they lived. My first biographies and autobiography took place through art, paintings, and drawings from photographs as I searched for answers embedded in those captured moments. I began to write alongside the images and then realized that I needed to use words to capture the whole story. This eventually led to my memoir.

The family photos you inherit are a treasure to be mined. Look deep into the sepia images, the black and white snapshots, and the old Kodak color photos. Look for the story within the images.

Exercises—Photographs

1. Select several photographs that stimulate your memories.
2. Freewrite about the emotional appeal or message of the photographs. How do they make you feel?
3. Write about the memories that are linked with the photographs. Tell about gestures people used, the scent of Aunt Iris's perfume, or how the crimson roses grew against the house.
4. Describe the atmosphere of the setting—the house, barn, city, or country.

Symbols

Objects in the world carry energy. They are part of our history, speaking to us as silent witnesses. Objects that seem ordinary—a book, a cup, a curtain—are part of our memory tapestry. Some spiritual beliefs hold that all inanimate objects are imbued with energy; all we need to do is to tune into them. One such symbol for me is my great-grandmother Blanche's cookstove. It was the hub of the house, where the fire burned in summer and winter, where she cooked, baked, and boiled water for coffee and dishes and sponge baths. The wood cookstove sang and clanked as she moved the iron lids with a special tool that hooked into small square slots in the lids. She threw in the wood, her face glowing an orange-red, sweat pouring from her, muttering to the stove, "Burn, burn you dang thing." The fire was alive; it roared and cackled, snapped and whistled. When it was cracking hot, she'd bake an apple pie. She'd let me roll up newspapers to start the fire, add the kindling. When I want to think of comfort, I think of the stove, how alive it made the kitchen and how exciting it was to hear its song and feel its warmth. And most of all, I can still taste the hot cinnamon in those pies.

Some families pass down heirlooms, such as jewelry, furniture, tools, and clothing, that are symbols of the past. Often these symbols or objects were gifts from long-loved relatives or friends, and they represent the relationship and its meaning. These symbols may tell a whole story—even the history of the family.

When the pioneers came across the plains they brought with them their most cherished items—tables, crocheted tablecloths, bric-a-brac—that represented the world they left behind. Once they reached rough country, they discovered that they could not continue with their wagons so overloaded. Imagine how difficult it was for them to leave their precious objects along the side of the trail, to let go of the symbols of their old life as they moved toward an uncertain future.

Think about the meaningful objects in your life and what they symbolize to you. Take an inventory of the symbolic objects in your house and how you came to acquire them. They may represent whole stories just waiting for you to discover them.

Exercises—Symbols

1. Write a portrait about an object you love or have loved.
2. Describe how this object came to have significance, the story behind it, your associations with it, and what meaning it has for you.
3. Write about the memories you associate with this object.
4. If this object has been a point of contention in the family— for example, disagreement about who would get the object when its owner dies—write about that.

Main Characters

Written portraits of the important people in your life, those who will be the main characters in your memoir, can help you to focus your thoughts and emotions about them. A portrait is a quick verbal sketch of personality, attitude, physical movement, and energy. A portrait gives the reader a sense of the character's beliefs, feelings, traits, sayings, activities, and hobbies; it shows who the person is or was and what he or she meant to you, as well as how he or she looked and sounded.

A photograph may help to inspire your writing. Even if you didn't know the person, you can use your imagination to write a well-rounded character portrait.

That's what I did with my great-grandfather Lewis, the young man who died a month after he conceived my grandmother in the cold Iowa winter of 1894. He looks out of the one photograph I have of him as the boy he was, less than twenty-two years old, with large, soft, brown eyes. His hair is shorn, and his lips are full and sensual. His cheekbones, the shape of his face, and those soft eyes mirror back to me my own face and the face of my mother and grandmother. It seems that Lewis's gift to us was his face that lived on through three genera-tions. Only Blanche knew him, and she has been dead for forty-five years. I dialogued with him once as I looked at his photograph, talked with him about the generations of our family, the tragedies, and the losses. I told him how a part of him lived in all of us. I wrote stories about his wedding to Blanche, and I found their wedding certificate in courthouse records. There they were, these young people, and there were their signatures.

Inspired, I looked for his grave again. My grandmother and Blanche and I had looked for it when I was nine years old. As our shoes sank in the soft grass, Blanche kept muttering, "I know he was buried around here somewhere," as if willing the graves to reveal the man who had died so long ago. We never found Lewis that day, and I wanted to find him for Blanche and to claim him for myself.

I looked up the date and place of his death on microfilm in the library and willed myself to find the grave. I drove to the Letts Cemetery and wandered trance-like toward a cedar tree. I turned around—and there he was: Lewis Garrett, the man who had given us his face and his genes.

All this was inspired by his photograph and my written portrait. Writing about him and to him made him real to me, so I was able to claim his blood and heritage.

Exercises—Main Characters

1. Before writing a portrait of a person, it is important to bring him or her fully to mind. Looking at photographs can help you do that. Another method is to close your eyes and picture the person in his usual environment, doing the usual activities you remember him doing.

2. Write a portrait of someone who will be a main character in your memoir. Remember to use sensual details, including color, scent, sound, and feel. Use metaphors: He looked like Cary Grant. She moved like Marilyn Monroe.

   a. *Body language* How would you describe the person's body movements? Quick, slow, jerky, bulky, sensuous, lilting, blocky? Did a shoulder rise under stress? Did her face wrinkle up in laughter or confusion?

   b. *The feel, color, and look of emotion.* How did the person's face and posture change when sad, angry, joyful, hopeful, disappointed?

3. Now write a story about the person you portrayed.

4. If this person affected or changed your life significantly, write about that.

5. What might your life have been like without this person in it? (Think about the premise in the classic film *It's A Wonderful Life*).

6. Write a portrait of a grandmother, grandfather, or any family member you have never met. Try to imagine him or her living and breathing, walking and talking. If you have a photograph of this person, write about the story behind it.

Themes to Unify Your Stories

The future enters into us, in order to transform itself in us, long before it happens.

—Rainer Maria Rilke

Once you have created a series of stories, you may find that they are built around one or more themes that run through your life. Some or all of your stories may be linked to themes such as abuse, religion, a mother or father's courage, war, or music. A memoir can be tied together by geographic location or landscape or the healing power of animals and trees or a pivotal event. This chapter provides some suggestions about possible themes. Your memoir's theme will become clear when you answer the question: What is this story about?

The why and the how of your story elucidate its meaning. The theme shows the underlining message, a philosophy of life, a point of view or lens through which the story is viewed. In his book *Turning Memories into Memoirs*, Denis Ledoux says, "The theme is dependent on your insights." (1991, 114)

Turning Points

Many different events can become turning points, moments of change or transformation, in our lives: meeting someone for the first time, spiritual experiences, joyous events such as birth and marriage, and events such as the death of someone important to us. As with crisis and opportunity, turning points can be seen as wholly positive or as a mixture of positive and negative.

Turning points change us and cause us to view life through a different lens. Eventually we integrate that new view into our sense of self as we make life changes because of it. When a turning point occurs we may not be able to make sense of what is happening to us and may even resist change. Nonetheless, a turning point is a time of power and energy, a doorway into the next chapter of our lives. Some of the most momentous turning points will be discussed here.

Illness: An illness or accident, a traumatic event—all these experiences have the potential to change our lives forever. When we become physically or mentally ill, our world is suddenly, irrevocably changed. Illness forces us reorder what is most important to us. Illness reminds us of the fragility of life, and the limitations of the body and mind. Having a serious illness can be like traveling through a dark, disordered world where we don't know the landmarks and every step is frightening. Medical memoirs, like *Immune Dysfunction: Winning My Battle Against Toxins, Illness & the Medical Establishment*, by Judith Lopez, focus on such experiences.

Even a brief illness like the flu forces us to rest and to take time to heal our bodies. This shift in our regular routine can give us the needed perspective to re-assess our lives. Illness can be a great teacher, a painful experience that may bring up ancient forgotten wounds. Writing our way through it helps us to center ourselves anew as we give voice to our fears, hopes, pain, and frustration. In our journal we capture the daily story, and in our memoir, we track the arc of the experience, from diagnosis to treatment and recovery. In his book *A Whole New Life*, Reynolds Price writes about his spinal cancer, paralysis, coming to terms with the spiritual in his life, and how to have hope when there seems to be nothing to hope for. There is a whole genre of memoirs about illness and recovery. These true stories help those who are confronted with similar traumatic experiences to learn how to keeping going, to survive and cope with events that at first seem to be without hope or the potential for growth.

Illness can become a metaphor for the journey through life, and our ability to find ourselves and our center as we pass through its stages. As in the hero's journey, we encounter dark forests, wraiths, and frightening monsters; but guides come to help us, and unexpected witnesses assist us along the way.

Death and Loss: One of the most emotionally wrenching turning points in our lives is the death of someone we love. The death of a person, or even a pet, close to us creates a permanent change and a heart-rending sense of loss. We know that life will never be the same.

Whether the death is preceded by a long, painful illness or is sudden and unexpected, the effect is devastating and traumatic. The people we love are woven throughout the tapestry of our lives and our identity. Letting go of them means letting go of a part of us. We go through loss in stages—shock, anger, sadness, and layers of complex emotions based on the kind of relationship we had with the person. After a long illness and vigil, the actual death can feel like a relief, which in turn can create guilt. And regardless of the circumstances, death can cause depression in the survivors.

Writing has been proven to help resolve depression. Because the same symptoms—tiredness, lethargy, a sense of hopelessness and helplessness—accompany both depression and mourning, writing will no doubt help mourners as well. Journal writing in particular can be useful in recording the changes and feelings that accompany loss.

Many stories can be told about the dying process, from the beginning diagnosis through treatment and the progression toward death. During that process, new relationships are forged and old ones let go of. Sometimes needed resolutions to problems come during the dying process. It is a time of potential healing for all, but the healing does not always occur. The old patterns may persist, and the family must come to terms with that as well. The shared stories of the family provide a powerful way to learn to let go.

Writing character sketches helps to preserve the person's memory and to show the nature of your relationship with him. Memories of the one you just lost may come in rapid flashbacks, a normal part of the grieving process. Although it may be painful to write down the exact details about your loved one or about the dying process you've just witnessed, the natural release of feelings during this kind of writing helps to heal a bruised and aching heart and shepherds you into the next stage of your own life.

Birth: Each baby comes into the world and into his family in the middle of a story in progress. His arrival creates a turning point for everyone, changes the family, and forges new relationships in the community. Each child figures out his role in the family and his place in the community, and learns the stories that he becomes a part of. The birth of any child into a family and community sends roots and shoots in all directions, from childcare workers to neighbors and teachers to anyone the child comes in contact with.

When we create new life, our own lives are changed forever. Most of us look into the baby's eyes and see ourselves as we imagine a happy future together. The birth of a child is most often a joyous event. But in some families a child may be unwelcome because it puts a burden on finances; or there might be questions about parentage. And in some families there is the question of whether to keep the baby or give it up for adoption, a difficult issue to resolve with the happiness and best interests of all in mind.

Because birth occurs in the context of community and family, birth practices (home or hospital birth, doctor, nurse, midwife, doula) are part of every birth story. To write the story of your own birth, you'll need to ask how you came into the world and what birthing traditions accompanied your entrance. Or perhaps you already know about your birth from family stories or other sources. When I was grown, my grandmother's best friend told me that my grandmother had not wanted to take on that role. She was a young 51 and was irritated to hear that her identity would change. She threw down the telegram and said, "So, the little brat is born." It would have been hard to guess then that she would start raising me herself when I was five. But the pattern of being an unwilling grandmother continued in her daughter, my mother, so that she saw my children only twice in their lives, for half an hour. She raged against being a grandmother and refused to participate. I understood that something was wrong with her, but it was painful to have her reject not only me but my children as well.

Our society equates birth with happiness and normalcy. But many families don't live up to this expectation of society, and their birth stories stay buried out of shame and pain. No one wants to hear about a mother who rejected her children; no one wants to know about this dark side of human nature. But for the family members, these stories cause wounds that are hard to heal, and they must be told to help release the grip they have on the soul. Birth stories range from those of beauty and great love to those of rejection and pain. Think about how you want to tell your story.

Give yourself permission to write about your journey through one or more major turning points in your life. You can be a compassionate witness to your own story.

Exercises—Turning Points

1. List the various positive and negative turning points in your life.
2. Choose one turning point and write a story describing the event, the people involved, your immediate and long lasting reaction to it, and how your life would have been different if the event had not happened.
3. Write about a time when you were sick as a child or as an adult. How did your body feel? How did your family deal with your illness?
4. If you have had a serious illness, consider writing about your life before, during, and now. In terms of your healing, what did you hope for? What disappointments did you have?

What were the positive aspects of your illness? What have you learned because of it? How has it changed you?

5. Choose a loved person or pet who died or a loved object that you lost. Write about the first time you met, describing your thoughts and feelings about the relationship at the time.

6. Write a character sketch of a loved person who died, describing him at several different moments in time, including turning points in your relationship.

7. Write about how your life would have been different without this person.

8. Describe how you were changed by the person's life and death.

9. Write the stories you know about your own birth. Include information about how you learned these stories. If you know about birth practices during your mother's or grandmother's generation, write about them also.

10. If you are a father, write about your child's birth, how you got to know your child, how the experience of fatherhood differed or was the same as you thought it would be, and how life changed after the child's arrival.

11. If you are a woman, write about how you came to know about conception and the birth process.

12. If you are a mother, write about your pregnancies and deliveries, and the similarities or differences between them. Describe the story that was already in progress when each of your children was born.

Rituals

Rituals are a way of saying hello and good-bye, announcing intentions, and making changes. Rituals mark a transition from one state to another—a state of consciousness or shift in identity. Public holidays, such as Thanksgiving, take on ritual status, as do graduations and private holidays, such as birthdays or anniversaries. Cooking and feasting can be a big part of the celebration, and food is an important aspect of family life. Whole memoirs can be written about food, such as *Tender at the Bone: Growing Up at the Table* by Ruth Reichl.

Rituals are at the heart of most religious celebrations. When Hitler wanted to deny the identity and rights of the Jewish people, he took away their ability to celebrate holy days by forbidding the purchase of wine, matzo, and ritual food for Passover. Food is often used for comfort; food rituals soothe family dynamics. When the weekly homemade bread or cake or pot roast is missing, that means something is wrong in the family.

Rituals may be as simple as lighting candles, watering plants, brushing the cat. Walking a dog twice a day can be a pleasant way to release the cares of the day. Meditation and yearly vacations, revisiting beautiful landscapes such as Yosemite or the desert can all become rituals. Vision quests and retreats are a part of renewal rituals for many people, in which a part of the self is let go and another part is invited forward. Ceremonies such as a christening, bris, baptism, bar mitzvah, and marriage are all ways to ritualize progress through life's stages. Many modern rituals derive from ancient pagan ceremonies; some are even celebrated today, such as midsummer at Stonehenge.

Exercises—Rituals

1. Write about your favorite ritual, or one that is unique to your family, or the one you most closely identify with your family.
2. Describe any rituals that you don't like or that make you feel uncomfortable or angry.
3. Write about the family rituals you hope your children will continue to observe after they leave home. Why do those rituals have special significance for you?

Love and Friendship

Our lives are threaded with love stories—romantic love, friendship, love of family, love of pets. Students in my memoir classes frequently tell their stories of first love. This story of awakening takes us past the threshold of family love and into the larger world.

Most people have a special place in their hearts for first love. We always remember the first time our pulse raced at the sight of someone who made the world look brighter and better. A first love shines in our mind forever, like a bright star, imbued with the yearning and dreams of our younger selves.

Mature or maturing love is like good wine that needs time to ferment into its full flavor. As we mature, we come to understand that feelings, emotions, and attachments rise and fall like the seasons. Whole books are written about one relationship, how it began, how it progressed through peaks and valleys, and how love bursts out of its boundaries in surprising ways. You might write such a memoir.

Writing about our best friends or the friendships we have had in our lives makes us remember the joy of discovery, of getting to know a person, letting go of expectations and clichés, sharing and laughing and crying together during upheavals and triumphs. Friends help us figure out who we are, and offer their love and witnessing. As you consider love and friendship in your life, think about the time you first realized the importance of friends, and think about what kind of friend you are to others.

The old phrase "blood is thicker than water" comes to mind. But some people don't have blood relations they can count on; instead, they discover that their friends are their "real" family. Many people come from fractured families and homes in which abuse, violence, and lack of safety dominate. When homes are unsafe, young people go out into the world to find comfort, protection, and a new identity. Each year thousands of abused children run away to a new "family" on the street. Through the years, abused children who have survived into adulthood have searched for and found family in new friends, often "adopting" them and being adopted into the newfound family.

Anais Nin says, "Each friend represents a world in us, a world possibly not born until they arrive, and it is only by this meeting that a new world is born." (1967)

Exercises—Love and Friendship

1. Describe meeting your first love for the first time. Include sensual details and show how you felt during and after this first meeting.
2. If your first love was also your first dating or sexual experience, write about how you think this has affected your ongoing romantic relationships.
3. Explain what you have learned about maturing love and how a maturing love relationship has shifted your philosophy of life, or given you new strengths or boundaries.
4. Make a list of your friends, telling when and how you met, and why you became friends.
5. Choose a best friend or lover and write about how he or she has changed your life.

Sexuality

Sex is part of our lives, a part of being embodied and being creative human beings. But sex is often not written into a life story. Sex may be a joyous part of our lives or a part of our pain and sorrow, but it is almost always significant. Each person has a sexual history that informs choices, feelings, and decisions. Sex can cause a great deal of confusion and pain; sometimes it is fraught with shame and guilt.

We learn about sexuality from a number of different sources— from friends, family, and society. Silence often teaches us about sex; from silence we learn that something is wrong, that we are wrong and bad. Religion may teach us that sex is bad and shameful. Such lessons burn into the psyche, creating a wound that is difficult to heal. We realize that sex is full of energy and danger, that it can be ecstatic and fulfilling, or that it can draw us into darkness.

As we grow and develop, our true sexual feelings and identity may be a secret, even from ourselves. We may learn from unspoken rules as well as cruel jokes and ridicule that we must hide the truth, from ourselves as well as from others.

Writing about our sexuality tunes us in to the power to say what is true—our honest and real feelings and experiences. Most of us have been taught to use euphemisms about sex, but it is important, when writing to heal, that we give ourselves permission to use all the words, both slang and correct medical terms, to describe our experience.

Unfortunately, many stories about sex are about sexual abuse. The abused person feels shame and guilt. Writing about it can cause great psychic pain and bring the trauma back. If you have suffered sexual abuse and want to write, be sure that you have the support of a therapist or good friend. You might try writing around the incident first rather than writing about it directly. For more about writing around a painful subject, see Chapter 4. Using words to tell our true stories about sex, writing about the negative experiences along with the happy, joyous experiences, gives us a sense of empowerment.

Exercises—Sexuality

1. In your private journal, list any secret sex stories you've never told or written about.
2. Write about how and from whom you learned about sex as a child, whether by example or with words, and tell how you felt about sex then.
3. Describe your first sexual experience, remembering to include sensory details.
4. If one or more particular sexual experience changed the direction of your life, for better or worse, write about that.
5. Describe how you have felt about your sexuality throughout your life and how your sexuality has changed over the years.

Spirituality

Another possible theme for a memoir is your spiritual development, your struggle to find a religion, a religious path, or God. A spiritual autobiography is a story of healing; uniting soul and body; finding a deeper meaning that gives comfort and solace, direction and intention. Thomas Merton writes of his journey to become a priest in his spiritual autobiography *The Seven Storey Mountain*. He begins with his birth in France and talks about how he wrestled with different forces in himself and in his life to find his way to Gesthemane, a Trappist monastery in Kentucky, where he became a monk. His search for God is lyrical and passionate, later tempered by his exposure to other religions, including Buddhism. He was a prolific poet and wrote many books about his lifelong spiritual search.

In my Spiritual Autobiography class I ask students to write healing stories tracing their development through pain, darkness, and suffering from the lost self or false self into a discovery of the life-altering moments that have freed them. They write about how they made their way through these lost times into the light of understanding and healing.

The word "spirituality" comes from the Latin root "spirare," which means to breathe. We have imbued it with the meaning of breathing in or taking in God, a higher power, or an energy force that guides the universe. There is no one right way to view this force; every religion and spiritual path has its own way of defining and experiencing it. People find guidance in different ways—some through meditation and prayer, some through solitude in nature; some gradually, and others through an epiphany.

Some writers include stories about their childhood spirituality in their memoirs. If religion or spirituality played an important role in your childhood, you might want to do the same, including stories about how you first experienced God or had a sense of being a part of something larger than yourself, what your understanding of religion made you think about yourself as a person, and how you came to terms with any contradictions you may have encountered.

In his book *The Story of Your Life: Writing a Spiritual Autobiography*, Dan Wakefield says that we are changed by writing from a holistic or spiritual perspective and come to understand ourselves in a new way. "By remembering and writing down our past from a spiritual perspective . . . we can sometimes see and understand it in a way that makes it different." (1990, 22)

A spiritual autobiography invites you to write from the heart and to explore the parts of yourself and your inner voice that you might censor or that are too vulnerable and private to announce to the world. It is the story of your becoming on the deepest level, the story of your soul's journey.

Exercises—Spirituality

1. Write about your spiritual philosophy and what the word "soul" means to you.
2. Describe when and how you began to suspect that spirituality might not be the same as religion and tell your thoughts about the differences.
3. Write about what religions or spiritual paths you have explored, what you have learned, and how you apply this knowledge to your life.
4. Describe your current spiritual life and the elements it may include, such as meditation, prayer, sacred readings, religion, church, or other kinds of worship.

Using the Techniques of Fiction

Whatever you can do or dream you can, begin it.
Boldness has genius, power and magic in it. Begin it now.

—Goethe

*M*emoirs written for today's audiences read like fiction, with scenes, characters, dialogue, and description. The goal of fiction is to create a believable world, a fictive dream that a reader can enter and linger in without waking up until the dream ends. Tristine Rainer calls this style of memoir writing the "new autobiography." In her book *Your Life as Story: Discovering the "New Autobiography" and Writing Memoir as Literature,* Rainer traces the history of memoir and autobiography. Autobiography has always been social history; it used to be written in essay style, without scenes or other fictional devices. But now it incorporates those devices and, instead of being written only by the famous, is written by ordinary people. The reading public has discovered that anyone can have an interesting life; readers dive into a memoir eager for a story of how real people lived as they immerse themselves in the dream of a true story. Rainer says, "The new autobiography, having moved into the literary arena of poetry and fiction, is now concerned with the larger truths of myth and story." (1998, 28)

Your memoir will sing as you develop your writing skills and become adept at using the secrets of writing found in good fiction. To
make your story come alive, you must let readers see the characters
in action. Readers identify with the protagonist, the narrator of the
story, which is you, and they see through your eyes. Description
provides visual cues for the scene. Sensual details, such as smell,
sound, taste, and texture, bring the fictive world alive and make
readers feel the scene in their bodies and minds. It's those details
that make readers live in a story and keep them connected to it. Dialogue gives the characters voice and personality as they act and react. Conflict and plot make readers eager to see what happens next
and create a sense of forward motion in your story.

Scene, Summary, and Reflection

In a memoir, action may be presented in three ways: in a scene, in a
summary, and in a reflection. The author's reflections distinguish
memoir from fiction. A scene, through narrative, dialogue, and ex-
position of details, shows the action in real time, delineates characters, and reveals plot. Description lets the reader *see* the place and the
action; *hear* the sound of the environment—nature, wind, household
activities; and *experience* the feel of clothes on skin, the humidity, the
sun, or the dampness of fog. Include these eight elements in your
scenes:

1. Setting: Where does this moment of action takes place?
2. Characters: Who is on stage at that moment?
3. Context: What is going on emotionally; what is the point of the
   scene?
4. Action: How do people move; what happens of significance?
5. Dialogue: The way people talk shows character and point of view.
6. Conflict: Everyone wants something different; these desires
   create conflict, which can be subtle or overt.
7. Historical time: Identify the time in which the story takes place.

8. Sensual details: Descriptions of how things feel, sound, look, and smell make scenes meaningful and bring people and times alive on the page.

A summary gives an overview of the scene, compressing it into a few lines. It may include reflection as well as a literal summing up of the action, the context, and how time has passed. Several years can be summarized in a sentence: "For the next five years they lived on the farm. Then one day . . ."

Memoirs also contain reflection—the private thoughts of the narrator's inner self, a musing, retrospective voice. In this voice the narrator becomes philosophical and questioning, searching for understanding and perspective. Reflections are one of the healing aspects of memoir writing.

The following scene, summary, and reflection are from my autobiography. In the scene, notice the use of sensual detail and description, some dialogue, and a specific sense of place and time.

Scene: The heat of the July day rises up from the land. Everything smells like fresh air and earth, black and loamy. The tomatoes are ripening, round globules of green and yellow and red hanging pendulous from the vines; the red was in high contrast against so much green. Blanche snaps off a tomato and bites into it. Juice runs down the crevices of her chin. Her deep-set, wise eyes, behind gold-rimmed spectacles, gaze at me from above the red tomato.

"Mmm," she mutters, gesturing that I should pick one. I hesitate. Everything is too raw, too close to the earth. I am awe stricken and a little frightened. There are bugs and dirt everywhere. Flies buzz and ants crawl all over everything. Gnats fly in my mouth and stick in the corners of my eyes. At night there are mosquitoes who eat me, in particular, and of course lightning bugs. But right now Blanche gestures at the tomatoes. I pluck one with a satisfying snap. Everything smells of tomato—acrid and a little bitter. The skin doesn't give in to my teeth. I feel silly hesitating. Blanche is a pioneer woman, born in 1873, and she tells me to eat it.

"Come on, bite down hard."

"But it's dirty."

"You got to eat a peck o'dirt 'fore you die. Come on." She smears yellow seeds around on her chin with her sleeve. She seems unsophisticated and rough, but I feel guilty of having that thought.

"Come on. Try it. It's good for ya. Nothin' like the fruit of the earth. This is what it's all about."

My teeth pierce the skin; the juices flood my mouth and run down my throat. I choke, surprised at the instantaneous tartness, flooded with tomato, the sun on my head, the smell of earth and Blanche's sweat. Her eyes laugh behind her glasses; her mouth curls up a little.

"Good, ain't it?" she says and turns around to savagely hoe the weeds that try to take away her vegetables. Every year she has fed her children from her garden summer and fall. She taught them how to plant and reap and grow things, and how to can them for the winter. The life of the land belongs to Blanche, just as it did to the Native Americans who planted corn on this very spot. Blanche sucks in air, spits out a few seeds. They will take root next year, nurtured by soil and sun, and the deep-rooted water under the land, the Mississippi sending out its life-giving waters, part of the endless cycle of life.

Summary: The day we arrived in Iowa, my great-grandmother Blanche took me out to the garden to help her hoe weeds. She insisted that I eat a ripe tomato, and she told me about our family. That whole summer when I was seven, and all the summers of my childhood, I would learn about Blanche's history and how a pioneer woman managed to live in the 1950s.

Reflection: When I think back to those days, I realize it was then that I began to be the family historian. I absorbed those nights in the featherbed, the wood cookstove, the sepia family pictures, the hints and snapshots of the past. The past seemed more alive than the present. I was obsessed about history. It was a silent ghost beside me as I walked through the garden or peered at the moss-covered stones in the cemetery. Later, in my forties and fifties, when my cousin took out the old box of photographs, I was transported back to being a little girl looking into the faces of the old ones beside me and their youthful counterparts in the picture, seeing what was in store for me.

Point of View

You, the writer, have two roles. You are the *narrator* of the story, and you are a main character. The *first person* point of view is through the eyes of the "I" character. Every member of the family has his or her own point of view, but because you lead the reader through your eyes, you get to have the last word.

Singular		**Plural**	
First person:	*I*	First person:	*we*
Second person:	*you*	Second person:	*you*
Third person:	*he, she*	Third person:	*they*

Tone

The narrator's tone conveys subtleties, music that comes through in the text. Tone, also referred to as voice, shows mood and attitude; it can be serious or playful, intimate or reserved, cheerful or somber. It can also be angry or loving, subtle or blunt, casual or high-toned, commanding or submissive. Tone is shown through cadence and word choice. Words may be poetic or practical, hard-edged or soft. Hard words convey conflict or bleakness: cut, slashed, steel, doom, gray. Soft words convey vulnerability or kindness: whisper, murmur, sing, caress, longing.

Tell a story into a tape recorder, and listen to your own voice. Then listen to a friend's voice, and notice the differences. To understand tone or voice, observe speech patterns around you, eavesdrop in malls and coffee shops. Listen to the way people speak, how they construct their sentences, how they use words. As you read, be aware of voice; notice the way a narrator draws you in, or fails to. Think about the kinds of words, images, and moods that appeal to you.

For a good example of tone used by one of my students, see "Me and My Mom," by Pearl Saad, on page 274. Notice the way the narrator, an adolescent girl, presents her world. You can see her personality, her perceptions, and her feelings expressed authentically, the way a young girl would think and speak. Saad's piece has the voice of an adolescent girl.

Dialogue

Dialogue is often one of the more challenging fiction techniques. It takes time to learn how to capture people's speech patterns and make them sound natural. Dialogue reveals a character's attitude, feelings, background, and level of education. It also reveals place—through accent, word usage or dialect, and cadence. Dialogue needs to be natural, yet it isn't an exact translation of how people actually talk. When you write dialogue you don't include all the hesitations and errors that occur in spoken language.

Quotation marks frame direct dialogue, and, in American English, the end punctuation goes inside the mark:

> She said, "I'm leaving, I tell you, and you can't stop me."

When you need to indicate which character spoke the dialogue, it's best to use the conventional verb "said":

> "Please, please, don't go. I'll do anything . . ." he said.

If you use verbs that show emotion, such as "pleaded" or "whined" or "screamed," they detract from the dialogue. Instead of *telling* readers how the characters feel, let the characters' words *show* their emotion.

Too much direct dialogue can cause time to slow down in a scene. Too much back and forth feels like a tennis match. For variety, use indirect dialogue:

> She told me she was going to leave me. She said she
> never wanted to see me again, and she sat back in her
> seat sipping her tea.

But direct dialogue is often the most effective way to move a story along.

Most students come to me afraid to write direct dialogue. Like other writing skills, it takes practice. When I first started writing, I used no dialogue at all, but I practiced while sitting in cafés, taking dictation from those around me as I tried to learn how to write the way people spoke. I edited out the umms and ahhs so typical in regular speech. I practiced writing the different ways that people speak, and I experimented. So practice. Listen to those around you. Sharpen your ear. Read dialogue written by others and keep writing it yourself until it becomes a natural part of your writing toolbox.

Setting, Landscape, and Place

As a child, I lived on the Great Plains of Oklahoma. The land went on and on forever. I grew up under a huge blue canopy of sky; against the blue was an ever moving panorama of clouds, huge white towers that seemed to rise up to heaven. They morphed into fantastic shapes that made my imagination go wild. Weather was always on our minds. It ruled the plains with tempestuous storms and great shows of flickering heat lightning. The gathering storms made the sky go pea green and a sick purple. We were always on the watch for tornadoes. We listened for tornado warnings and sirens, and prepared our houses and ourselves for the terrible thing that might sweep down out of the sky and destroy us. There was a terrifying beauty in it all, and a thrill that coursed through my body when thunder-and-lighting storms struck. The wind tore at the house and tugged and tugged as if in the next gust it would rip it apart. The weather-stripping in the windows and doors sang like a kazoo as the wind forced its way in. The chorus of kazoo, thunder rumbles, and crashes of the wind made for a raucous summer afternoon.

The small Midwestern town of Enid, its oil refinery, its towering white grain elevators marching across the north end, one tall building topped with a red light, the air force base—all this became etched on my soul. The character of the town is as much a part of me as my own skin. Whenever I hear a dove who-who in the evening, I am there, and always my soul stands in the middle of a wheat field in spring.

Setting and place shape people and affect their lives profoundly. The location creates situations that people must react to, events that become part of their story. Every setting in the world has its own unique character, people and animals, vegetation and weather. When you write your story, think about how the weather, the land-scape—mountain, beach, desert, forest—the country and culture have affected the people you write about. Make your characters act and react in this setting. If you do not know much about a setting where your characters are depicted, then conduct research. To give a place and time verisimilitude, you need to be authentic, and this re-quires research. I did much research to make my memoir accurate when my memory failed me. Some memoirs are highly researched with dates, times, newspaper articles, and facts woven throughout as a way to guard against too much subjectivity. There isn't one right way to do a memoir, and published memoirs include a range of re-search. Most memoir writers end up doing some if not a lot. Geolog-ical history, weather events, disasters such as blizzards, floods, earthquakes, and dust storms all have an impact on the history of a place and a people.

Setting influences characterization: how people interact, what they do day-to-day, their attitudes, dress, meals, events. For exam-ple, a person on a farm gets up early, feeds the animals, and carries re-sponsibility for many other living beings; she may wear dungarees and eat her main meal in the middle of the day. An urban setting presents a different mood, lifestyle, and set of problems. Opportu-nities, routines, and duties differ depending on place. Life in a ghetto or city slum is different from life in a multicultural neighborhood or a palatial estate.

A setting in a foreign city will be unique to that place, and the description of it must reflect the flavor and taste and mood of the city at that time. The names of streets, cafés, and famous buildings can paint the picture. No city is like any other. Describe with accurate details the buildings, land, and colors; the movement, mood, and feeling in the town.

Setting determines atmosphere and mood. Think about how each of the following settings creates a different emotional sense:

- A crowded, bustling street
- A beach in moonlight
- A rundown rooming house
- A New York subway at night
- The desert in August

What pictures form in your mind when you think of these places? What kind of mood does each one suggest? Poetry? Hardship? Different feelings arise when thinking of different landscapes. One thing you can do is to write character portraits of different landscapes, the feelings they evoke in you, and your response to these different settings. The way you feel about the setting will help determine your tone and the mood you convey in your writing through choice of language.

Structure and Time

There are various ways to structure your memoir and to move back and forth in time. Because memoir explores life over time, as a memoir writer you will enter different life histories at different times in their development. The timeline, described in Chapter 18, helps you keep track of the time frame for a particular scene or story and grounds the scene in time. And presenting your stories in chronological order is one way to structure your book. Or you might decide to build the structure around characters, devoting a separate chapter or section of your book to each character and following him or her through time. You might also choose to intersperse sections of present time reflections with chapters about the past that carry the voice or tone of the past.

Tense: You can use different verb tenses to move around in time:

> Present tense refers to current time: *I drive.*
> Present progressive tense refers to ongoing current action: *I am driving.*
> Past tense refers to the recent past: *I drove.*
> Past perfect tense refers to an action beyond the recent past: *I had driven.*

So a memoirist writing from the point of view of her seven-year-old self might say:

> I *wish* I had a puppy dog. Of course I *am wishing* for any kind of pet. Last year I *wished* for a kitten, but then I changed my mind. Before that, when I was really little, I *had wished* for a goldfish.

If you are confused about using verb tenses to move through time, it will help to pay particular attention to tense in your reading and practice using the different tenses in your own writing.

Flashbacks: One way to look at the past is through flashbacks. Flashbacks work the way memory works. Let's say I return to Iowa in the summer. I am standing in the garden as an adult, and suddenly I see and hear events that happened forty years ago. I am living a flashback at that moment. When you use flashbacks in writing, you need to give your readers clues that you are moving from one time to another. The clues involve verb tenses. You can structure your flashbacks in two ways, taking care to be consistent as you go back and forth between time frames:

- Begin in the *present,* using present tense. *Flash back to the past,* using *past tense.* Return to the present, always in the present tense,

ending in the present tense. Leave two double spaces to indicate
a break between time frames.

*I look at the photograph of my mother, her dark hair curled around her
face, her dark eyes soft. Then I see her the way she was that day as she appeared at the front door, a surprise.*

*I was nine years old, and as I always did each Saturday afternoon, I
was practicing the piano. There was a knock on the door, and when I
opened it, all the blood seemed to drain into my feet. An apparition of my
mother stood there, a slight smile on her face. I knew she was real when I
heard her voice.*

I whisper to her now, an ache in my chest . . .

• Begin in the *past tense* but in *present time* frame. Flash back into the
  past in the *present tense*. This technique of using present tense for the
  past brings the reader directly into the past as if it is happening
  now, thus making it more intense. End in the *past tense* located in
  present time.

*I flipped through the dusty courthouse records, looking for the name of
my grandmother when she was twenty years old, the year her baby boy
was stillborn.*

*I see her pacing up and down the living room of the small apartment.
The pains are coming stronger now; she bends down and catches her side.
One long breath after the other as the wind forces bits of ice between the
edges of the windowpane . . .*

*The child's name was Harrison Hawkins, written in graceful cursive,
the birth and death, the same day: January 14, 1929.*

Researching the Hidden Stories

The mind is not a vessel to be filled but a fire to be kindled.

—William Butler Yeats

$\mathcal{A}$ ll my life I have been intensely curious about what came before and how people once lived. I loved hearing about earlier generations in my family and about the land that wove through conversations at the dinner table in Iowa. Every summer for forty years more than a dozen of my grandmother's brothers and sisters, their husbands and wives would gather for fried chicken dinner, my aunts in their homemade aprons decorated with rickrack and tied over generous bellies, the men's voices deep as they discussed the weather, the hayin' season, coon hunting. The Formica table would be fitted with extra leaves, and for birthdays and Christmas they'd use the good china and "silver"—actually a good stainless steel—set on freshly ironed tablecloths laid end to end. The stories made their slow way around the table, with the volume rising when one person remembered an event differently than another. After corn on the cob, mashed potatoes, and gravy scraped clean from the electric skillet, the sun would begin its slow golden glow as it set behind Eisele hill. The men retired to the living room or to lawn chairs outside to light their pipes and discuss the same things they'd talked about before dinner, while my aunts flicked each other with dishtow-els, and out of the corners of their mouths they whispered dirty jokes, their faces bright from the hot soapy water and the fun of breaking rules—that women should never talk dirty, women should always have clean minds and houses. After the dishes were washed and put away, the smell of perked coffee filled the house. Chocolate cake with chocolate frosting and peach and lemon meringue pies that I had helped create were served on dessert dishes. Around the table they all returned, and the long slow stories would unwind. "Re-member when . . . Who's Uncle Lem . . . What part of the family did they come from . . . Don't you remember the house that Edith was born in . . . the old peach orchard . . . the smoke house . . ."

Aunt Edith would bring out the box of black-and-white photos. All their stories had illustrations: model T's, horses and wagons, barns, and old-fashioned clothes and coats. They looked jaunty and young and hopeful as they stared at the camera, and around the table I could feel a wistfulness for "the old days." I learned about hard-working folks who were pleased that they'd never accepted money from the government, folks who distrusted people with money and slick talk and guile. I learned about the culture of a proud family whose history was written in the graveyards for fifty miles around. Since 1850 the family had farmed the land and raised children, and that's what life was all about—not going hungry, being proud of in-dependence no matter how many of the family myths were untrue or how much false pride may have filled the room. When I was with them, I had a history because of our blood connection, but I would find out that this was a frail thread, easily broken by breaking the rules, being too smart or intellectual, or living too far away. In the last two decades, the numbers around the table dwindled as they died one by one. I was left to make sense of this family that I was a part of and yet wasn't. Because my grandmother had a different father than her siblings, she wasn't a full blood relation, and because she had left her daughter behind and flaunted her money, she was "other," and so would I be one day because I was not part of the folks who stayed near the land, near the birthplaces.

But their history is my history, and as I became even more curious about this unspoken disapproval of my grandmother and mother, and finally me, I realized that history determines the future, and no one forgets.

When I was a child, the history of the place and the family clung to me like the fog of the Mississippi River bottom. The history of the land would come to my imagination infused with history book stories and novels about the settling of the West. I could see the moccasin tracks of Indians on the riverbank when we walked by the river, now protected by a high levee. Powerful ripples showed the muscles of one of the most important rivers in the United States, and it seemed to belong to us, to me. The river and its history and spirit had woven through the "blood dream" of generations like a spiritual father.

As an adult I followed up on child imaginings by doing research about the land, the place, and the family's history, first with my relatives, then in the local library. I wanted to know the Indian tribes who had harvested the land before the whites came; I'd heard about the Indians who came to family farms looking for food. I discovered that the land had belonged to the Sac and the Fox tribes, and that the town of Muscatine got its name from Mouscatin, another tribe of Indians from that area. Wapello, the town where my mother had been born, was named for Chief Wapello, one of Black Hawk's chiefs. Black Hawk was forced to make peace with the whites in 1837. My childhood imaginings were not that far off. Maybe the spirits of the Native Americans really were embedded in the land; maybe their spirits still roamed the banks of the Mississippi River as I'd imagined.

I couldn't write my memoir without also writing the history of my origins—the people, the land, and the culture. Questions about my own family, especially my mother and grandmother, questions about exactly when my grandmother left my mother when she was young led me to dusty county courthouses in small towns and the microfilm archives of newspapers, including the newspaper owned by my maternal grandfather's family, The Wapello Republican. For ten years I examined yellowed certificates of birth, marriage, and death to mine the dates, the when and where, the who. There weren't many clues about why or how. It was exciting to find the original signatures of Blanche and her husband Lewis, but for a while I was stuck on the questions about my mother and grandmother. Which family stories were true and which were false? It felt as if I was trying to bring my mother's childhood back to her, to knit the broken threads of the past as I did the research. Did my grandmother really leave my mother when she was a baby, as Blanche had told me? My great-aunts and uncles seemed to have no answers to these questions or didn't want to touch them because they were part of a shameful story that had trickled through the family folklore for decades. I was upsetting the applecart by asking all kinds of nosy questions. "The past is the past, and it should stay in the past," they'd say, tight-lipped as they looked away.

The Imagined Story

Research often produces more speculation than facts. But research can fill in your imagination and give you ideas about the way lives were lived, and it may help you write a story about a relative you've never met. Writing the imagined story is a way to fill in the blanks of missed history and story, and help ourselves heal. Sometimes what we imagine may be closer to the truth than we would have guessed.

One of my students, Sarah Weinberg, had always been curious about her great-grandfather, a man whose name was not even known. In her mind she began to hear the cadences of his speech and imagine his life. Research on the Internet gave her information about the town he might have come from, the customs of the town, and what it might have been that caused him to send his children to America yet not arrive there himself. No one in the family knew what had happened to him. Weinberg's story, "Imagining the Past," based on imagination and a passionate interest in her family, appears on page 277.

Information Sources

Your research may involve as little as asking family members for information or as much as sending for documents and visiting old neighborhoods and towns to find original documents and stories. Information about marriages, deaths, and births can be found on genealogical sites on the Internet, and you can research military records, the census, and professions online. Newspapers and libraries have researchable archives online as well, but some records must be found at the source, which means a research trip to the town or county where they are located. Some of my students have discovered long-hidden facts about psychiatric hospitalization; others have unearthed family stories that have been kept secret for decades, buried in lies and cover-ups because of shame.

When I decided to write the imagined story of my grandmother's elopement in 1911 and the birth of her stillborn son a year before my mother's birth, I researched the town and how life was lived at the time: the kind of clothes worn; how houses were kept warm; cooking facilities and customs; the presence or absence of electricity, telephone, and indoor plumbing. In my imagined scenario this stillbirth took place in winter during a snowstorm that delayed the doctor. I wrote the story based on my grandmother's lifelong lament that her son had died, and I gave it as much reality as I could. Later, when I found the child's birth and death certificates, I saw that they did indeed occur in winter, January 29, 1914. His death resulted from prolonged labor, during which the cord wrapped around his neck. The story I imagined was amazingly close to the real story.

I read books and stories written by local residents, reminiscences and memoirs about life during different eras in that place. Other useful resources included some Sears and Montgomery Ward catalogues still available in print. They show all kinds of goods that people used at the time and help you describe the past with authentic details.

Old photos, letters, family bibles, journals and diaries, attic trunks, old books, keys, tools, recipes—all these family items can give you clues to the stories you seek. Libraries collect local histories, biographies, and memoirs; such stories also appear online. From phone books you can put together the history of where a family member lived and worked. I found my father listed in the Louisville phone book: it gave his address and his employment. Going through several phone books, I traced his whereabouts in the decades before I was born, which helped make his life real to me thirty years after his death.

Interviews with relatives may be audio- or videotaped. Genealogists combine those tapes with written stories that provide an archive for storytellers like you.

Weaving the imagined story with facts and accurate details can be healing. By creating a story, the writer heals the torn fragments of family life as she fills in the unknown, empty places. Writing the imagined story of the stillbirth of my grandmother's first child gave me compassion for her as a young girl of twenty and helped me let go of some of the anger I felt toward her.

At the end of "Imagining the Past," Sarah Weinberg writes about how the imagined story of her great-grandfather was healing for her.

Research Steps

- As you write your first draft, keep track of the details that need to be researched. Descriptions of clothes, hairstyle, household appliances, cars, houses, and neighborhoods all need to be accurate to create verisimilitude.
- When you're resting after creating new work, you can do the research.
- Examine photos for details that you can use in your stories.
- Interview family, neighbors, and community members for stories, details, and history.
- Use public resources such as libraries, newspapers, and court records to trace your family's history and immigration background.

- Once you have gathered all the details, you can complete an imagined story of an unknown ancestor or a family member you knew but want to understand better.

Bringing Your Memoir into the World

Hope is the memory of the future.

—Gabriel Marcel

Bringing your memoir into the world means traversing that invisible line that protected you all along as you wrote your stories. Then you simply wrote, listened to your inner voice, and healed, as your first draft evolved. You completed the first four stages of writing your memoir, described in Chapter 17: beginning, developing, focusing, and quilting. Now, after months or perhaps years of writing, the snippets and journal entries and vignettes and stories have become transformed into a larger story with the arc of narrative structure and themes. Now you have the makings of a book.

First assess the risk. Imagine strangers and acquaintances and friends reading the intimate details you've written about your life. If you feel that your story is too personal to make public or that doing so would make you too vulnerable, then you may not want to share it or publish it. That is fine. You do not have to do anything else with your accumulated writings, though you may want to go through at least the next stage just for your own satisfaction.

The rest of this chapter is addressed to those who do want to get their book out into the world. It takes you through the last two stages of creative writing: smoothing and presenting.

Smoothing

Smoothing means rewriting—and rewriting some more. You will certainly create a second draft; you may complete a third; a few of you may even write a fourth. Begin by reading your first draft, considering it as an entity instead of a series of small pieces, thinking about the issues below, and making notes about how to proceed. A writing group or coach can help you go through this process of discovery and rediscovery. Get yourself and your will out of the way. Listen to the book, to what it tells you it needs to become whole.

Genre: For the purpose of healing, you have written the first draft as a memoir. Now it's time to decide whether your final version will be straight memoir or some combination of memoir, fiction, or poetry. Many novels are actually thinly disguised autobiography: *The Prince of Tides* by Pat Conroy, *The Joy Luck Club* by Amy Tan, *The House of the Spirits* by Isabel Allende, *Rumors of Peace* by Ella Leffland, *To the Lighthouse* by Virginia Woolf, and *Bastard Out of Carolina* by Dorothy Allison.

You may choose to fictionalize your memoir to protect your family, your friends, or yourself. You may choose to treat your story as fiction for ethical or legal reasons. As I said in Chapter 14, you must be certain that you do not defame anyone's character or invade the privacy of others. You must avoid libel. To prevent problems, consult an attorney who specializes in publishing law. An attorney can vet your manuscript (read it and note potential legal problems) and suggest ways to avert trouble.

If you do write a fictionalized version of your memoir, to avoid confusion in your own mind don't change characters' names until the final draft. Also, you must understand that memoir and fiction are critiqued and presented differently. For instance, the literal truth does not matter when considering plot, characters, and actions for fiction.

In fact, the unbelievable aspects of real life must be changed when presented as fiction. The genre does not fare well with coincidence, bizarrely convenient events, or characters whose motivations are hard to understand. In memoirs, however, as in real life, such things happen all the time and can be justified by the statement, "This is hard to believe, but it is in fact true, and I stand behind its veracity."

If you decide to stay with pure memoir, then you should show your second or third draft to the people named in it and obtain their written consent before putting it in print. If you receive negative feedback, take it seriously. You may find it necessary to disguise someone's identity or even remove that character from the story. Again, consult an attorney to be safe.

Creating the Second Draft: As you read through your first draft, you may find that it is too long, shaggy, fragmented, or overburdened with emotions, such as rage or resentment. Do not despair. You will smooth over all those problems in the second or third draft.

Consider your protagonist's voice. Does he or she sound angry, grudging, or resentful? If the voice resonates with unresolved emotion, readers will find it more difficult to enter the story and stay with it. To solve this problem, write the raw story several times. The more you write it, the easier it will be for you to stand back from it and present it objectively, from a perspective that embraces all the characters. This is healing, as well as good writing. Your goal is a protagonist or narrator who sounds resolved or positive or neutral.

Consider the characters in your book. The narrator and at least some of the other characters must appear sympathetic enough for readers to identify with. Readers need to feel they can step into the narrator's shoes and empathize with his or her actions and motivations even if they don't agree with them.

Consider how your story moves through time. If you find holes, you may need to add scenes to fill them in; or you may need to add a paragraph here and there to smooth out transitions between scenes. If the story still feels incomplete, you may decide to begin or end it at a different time.

Where you begin and end can also depend on the size of your manuscript. Most books contain between twenty thousand and eighty thousand words. For practical reasons related to publishing costs, you may decide to shorten or lengthen your manuscript. But the integrity of your story should take precedence over practical matters. Consider your book's pace. Does the rate of movement in each scene fit the mood? Remember that you can speed up the pace through rapid bursts of dialogue, action, and quick movement from one incident to another. To slow down, use more description and narration (in which you tell rather than show what happened).

Consider the theme that ties your book together. Your reflections and summaries should present a unified philosophy that readers can identify and understand.

As you complete the second draft, you may feel overwhelmed and worried about continuing. Ask for support from your writing group and your writing coach. This is not a time to quit! Keep rewriting, chapter by chapter. It may take you a few months, but it gets done, one chapter at a time. As one of my students, Denise Roessle, wrote:

> Joining a writing group was one of the best things I've done during this process. Writing is such a solitary pursuit. After a while it's as if you're working in a vacuum. You don't know if what you've written is good or bad or makes any sense at all, or if anyone else is going to be the least bit interested in what you have to say. We all need feedback, especially from other writers, and most especially from those who are also working on personal stories. It's scary at first, reading to a group of strangers. But in the end, it's the only way to learn what you're doing well, what could be improved, and how to grow as a writer.
>
> Encouragement is just as important. So many times I've been sick to death of my own words, wondering why the hell I ever thought I could write. Reading aloud to other writers on a regular basis and hearing their appreciation for what I've done makes all the difference. Sharing our struggles and solutions is

invaluable. I come away from every session with renewed momentum to keep going.

Roessle learned how to listen to her book, how to hear its wisdom and needs. Most of all, she had perseverance.

Throughout this smoothing, rewriting stage, entertain yourself by imagining the cover of your book and creating a list of possible titles. When you reach the next stage, you can learn about what makes a title and cover a winner in terms of the marketplace. For now, just have fun with it and dream about it.

Presenting

At last the second draft is complete, and you are ready to prepare your book for the world. This stage has a steep learning curve, but it is also fun.

Editors: The most important aspect of bringing your book into the world is to present your prose, your ideas, and your story in the best possible way; this means hiring an editor. Before you decide how you would prefer to publish your book, before you look for an agent or write a proposal or approach a publisher, before you think about the design of your book or any other production matters, you should allow a professional editor to guide you through the process of smoothing your manuscript into a marketable product. Engage the services of an experienced book editor who performs both developmental (or substantive) editing and copyediting. Look for someone with whom you feel comfortable—even though, in this computer age, you may never meet in person; someone who understands how to maintain your voice despite any changes he or she may make; and someone who provides a contract that stipulates the editing will be performed on a work-for-hire basis, with all rights retained by you. Remember that it is your editor's job to tell you about problems in the manuscript, to point out or correct errors, and to make suggestions for improvement. A good editor makes you feel good about the changes being made.

Learning about Publishing: Many books can help you learn about the publishing world. Here are a few to get you started. Many have been revised; be sure to consult the most recent editions:

- *The Prepublishing Handbook: What you should know before you publish your first book.* Patricia J. Bell, Cat's-paw Press
- *The Self-Publishing Manual: How to Write, Print and Sell Your Own Book.* Dan Poynter, Para Publishing
- *The Writer's Legal Companion.* Brad Bunnin and Peter Beren, Perseus Press
- *1001 Ways to Market Your Books.* John Kremer, Open Horizons.
- *Literary Agents: What They Do, How They Do It, and How to Find and Work with the Right One for You.* Michael Larsen, Wiley Books
- *How to Write a Book Proposal.* Michael Larsen, Writer's Digest Books
- *Write the Perfect Book Proposal: 10 Proposals That Sold and Why.* Jeff Herman and Deborah M. Adams, John Wiley & Sons
- *Formatting & Submitting Your Manuscript.* Jack Neff, Glenda Neff, Don Prues, Writer's Digest Books

Other ways to become informed about the publishing business include taking courses, attending conferences, and joining organizations and e-mail discussion lists. Use your favorite search engine to find a list of lists; then join all those that relate to publishing. For the first few weeks just read the messages you receive; after you have a sense of the differences among the lists you can choose to drop one or continue them all, and you can begin asking questions. The e-mail and online publishing community is one of the friendliest and most helpful there is. The two organizations for independent publishers, Publishers Marketing Association (PMA) and Small Publishers Association of North America (SPAN), both offer excellent newsletters and learning opportunities. In many areas around the country affiliated groups meet monthly and provide education and support for new publishers.

Remember, however, that it's best not to focus on publishing matters until you have finished your second draft. I've found that students tend to get caught up in publishing too easily even though their writing may be blocked. Complete the major writing first.

Publishing Options: The publishing world is highly competitive, and certain genres have ups and downs like the stock market. One year memoir may be in, another year It Is not. Nonetheless, every month you may notice newly published memoirs.

Time, money, and business experience factor into the decision about how to publish. Many people turn to independent publishing partly because modern technology makes it possible. You can establish your own publishing company, produce your own book, and get it out into the world more easily, more quickly, and less expensively than ever before. And you need not depend on the whims of an acquisitions editor or get involved with the politics of a large corporation. Of course you pay for all this freedom by footing the bills and taking the risks yourself. On the other hand, you also reap all the profits.

Many people want to be published by a large commercial company or a small literary house because they want to receive an advance, and they think they can count on promotion by an established company. Of course the advance offered to first-time authors with no claim to fame is generally small; it can be as little as five hundred dollars to about fifteen thousand. *Writer's Market,* a yearly publication of Writer's Digest Books, lists publishers of all sizes and provides information about whether they accept manuscripts from first-time writers or from those who don't have agents, the amounts of advances and royalties offered, and the amount of time between acceptance and publication (which can be from twelve to eighteen months).

Most first-time authors do not receive the royal-road-to-fame treatment. Furthermore, regardless of whether a large New York house publishes your book or you publish it independently, you will have to publicize and promote it yourself. Think about it. Why do you suppose famous authors appear at your local bookstore? Their publishers expect them to participate in selling their books. Book tours, signings, and television interviews can be grueling; but they are an integral part of marketing to bookstores and the general reading public.

One alternative to finding a commercial or literary publisher is to engage a so-called POD (print-on-demand) company that, for a fee, will publish your book and print as few or as many copies as you need; however, not all book distributors and retail outlets look favorably on such books or accept them for sale because many POD publishers exercise no editorial quality control; as a result you may find it more difficult to sell your book.

If you choose to join the growing ranks of independent publishers, you can follow a less traditional route and produce an e-book, which will have a limited distribution and readership, or you can produce a regular book in hard cover or paperback. If you go that traditional route, you can ask a printing company that uses digital technology to print a small number of books (PQN or print quantity needed). You may want only 25 or 250 copies at first. Of course each copy will cost more than if you have a few thousand printed on a regular printing press.

Each of the many publishing options has advantages and disadvantages. Once you complete your writing and take the time to learn about the publishing world, you will know which option is best for you.

Endings and Beginnings

You deserve a pat on the back and congratulations for many reasons. You have taken the brave journey through the dark forest and have arrived at a new place. When you write a healing memoir, one that probes the depth and breadth of your identity and sense of self, you will find yourself at a place different from where you began—and you will know the place for the first time. Take pride in your perseverance and courage, your discipline and determination to heal and to learn to tell the stories that are important to you, stories that may have saved you. The journey no doubt took you to places within yourself that you did not plan to visit, and it may have caused you to stumble along the way. But you kept going, and marched through the darkness and into the light.

> *What we call the beginning is often the end*
> *And to make an end is to make a beginning.*
> *The end is where we start from.*
>   —T.S. Eliot, *Four Quartets*

There is more to your story, and more stories yet to come. But you have given yourself the permission to hear your own voice, and in that process to become whole.

Appendix A:
More Student Stories

In "Nesting," Linda Kitahara writes about a turning point, the birth of a child, while living with her Japanese husband in Kawasaki.

Nesting

By Linda Kitahara

When I returned to Japan from my yearly visit to America I compared the houses and lifestyles. Kawasaki did not have well-appointed houses with well-kept yards but a hodgepodge of buildings—factories, apartments, and stores—co-existing in supposed harmony, if one didn't mind their diverse characters or the racket coming from the factory at night. My apartment looked out over run-down houses where laborers came and went. During the last two years that my husband and I have lived here, I have spent many hours in the early evening standing on our balcony watching these men. They'd stand there in their long underwear smoking cigarettes. On hot days, they wiped their faces and bare arms with wet cloths. On some of these evenings I felt more isolated than usual, and found myself looking forward to watching them. For some absurd reason they made me feel less alone, as if we had something in common—perhaps a mutual feeling of homelessness.

My apartment was one room, with a small adjacent kitchen. None of the furniture matched; our bed occupied most of the room. We still needed to buy a crib for the baby. I would be changing my baby on the bed, and he or she would be sleeping with me. As I looked around our apartment that first day back from America, I idly thought about fixing up my apartment for the baby, but soon I had to accept the futility of it. A few outfits that I had received at a baby shower were the only evidence, besides my size, that proved there would be a baby soon. I realized that I needed to go shopping.

I went to Komiya, a department store in downtown Kawasaki, where I bought diapers, diaper covers, baby T-shirts, bottles, and of course a maternity bra. I stood in the dressing room looking at breasts that nine months ago I did not have. I put my hands under them and lifted them; they were heavy. So this is how it feels to have breasts, I thought. Soon they would become bigger, filling with milk. I tried to imagine opening the flap of this strange size-C bra and offering my baby my breast, but I could hardly imagine what she or he would look like; would she or he have brown wavy hair like mine or straight black hair like Ken's? Would her eyes be large, her nose long? Would she look Japanese or Caucasian? I could not evoke any image.

On the morning of October 5 when the doctor checked me, he told me I was a few centimeters open and to go into the hospital.

During the five-minute drive Ken said, "So this is it."

"I guess so." I looked at him, wondering what he was feeling, wondering why I wasn't feeling excited or nervous. I felt as if I was going to a hotel rather than a hospital to have a baby.

When we got there and were led to my room, I asked Ken to talk to the nurses about him being present during labor. I didn't want to be left alone.

I heard what I had feared. "Eie, Eie," they said. No, no. "Shinai . . . can't be done. No one does that."

"Sensei wa . . . the doctor . . ." I started but could not finish, so I asked Ken to explain to them that my doctor had already agreed. I thought about my doctor, a short pudgy man who prided himself on his horrid English and the fact that he'd had one other *gaijin* (foreigner) patient before me. His consent for my husband to be present was meaningless, I realized. Perhaps they were only words used to impress his gaijin patient of his liberal ways. By the way these nurses were standing their ground, I understood that it was the nurses who ruled the roost; the doctors were only visitors.

"They said they can't do it. I can't be there, but I can during delivery."

"During delivery?" That made no sense at all. A lump grew in my throat. I could feel tears building. I was about to cry in front of these stern, rigid women, in front of other mothers-to-be lying in beds around me. I muttered something, my voice high, hysterical.

The nurses shook their heads. They were enforcers of the rules, a tradition that could not be broken.

"Tell them to talk to the doctor," I told Ken. His voice was apologetic, as if he was apologizing for me, his hysterical gaijin wife. I tried to excuse him, reminding myself that it is the Japanese way of asking favors (and to them this was a favor), always starting the request with the equivalent of "I'm sorry to burden you, but. . . ." I reminded myself that he was not raised with the concept that the husband is a part of the birth. But I was not raised to be stoic or to do this alone. Once again I felt our cultures clashing. Once again I was reminded how far away from home I was. I felt suddenly very sad, but also angry. Fifteen minutes after our arrival, the answer was still no. I would be doing this alone, no exceptions. For once, my gaijin status would not give me any benefit.

I finally said good-bye to Ken, who promised to come back later. I looked around the ivory maternity room—six beds, and three were occupied. Two of the women were talking quietly. The other seemed to be sleeping. I looked out the window at the Kawasaki station across the street, wishing I were taking the train somewhere, wanting to be anywhere but here. I looked again at the two chatting women. They had no husband, but it didn't seem to bother them. Why should it bother me? I decided that I would be as strong as any of these women. I would prove to them that American women could be as strong as they were.

For the next twenty-four hours I lay in the hospital bed, roamed the hallways, and watched women go into the labor room and come out. I never heard a sound. At eleven the next evening, I was progressing, but I didn't feel much pain. I was shown into a narrow room with one cot. The nurse handed me a buzzer to use whenever I needed it. I took her seriously and used it often. I am not sure exactly what I felt—if it was fear of pain more than pain itself, or that Ken was not with me—but I squirmed on the bed, unable to lie still. I began to scream and press the buzzer. After the fourth or fifth time, I lost count, the nurse told me to be quiet because I was keeping the other women awake. I tried; I wanted to be like them. I imagined them talking among themselves. "Boy, these gaijin women are weak," they'd say. "And selfish. She kept me up all night. Doesn't she have any pride at all." Then they would all sigh and say, "These gaijin," and roll their eyes.

I tried to breathe the way I'd seen in the movies, wondering why I had never taken labor classes. The pain was in my back, not my stomach. Was that okay? I had never heard of back labor. No, I could not be a good example of the American woman. I screamed and buzzed again. They finally put me into the delivery room, an extremely bright room with one huge, reclining bed in the middle.

"Am I ready?" I asked.

"No. The room is farther away. It'll be better," the nurse said and left, closing the door.

They were treating me as if I was crazy. I felt as if I was being put into a padded cell, not having a baby. I was disconnected from my body, but I tried to concentrate. "I am having a baby, I am having a baby," I chanted. After a while I added, "Soon there will be a new life." But these were only words. I could not feel the pain, I could not feel my body. It was not *my* body. Only my fear, loneliness, and humiliation were real.

Then suddenly the doctor was there, not my doctor but a young tall doctor I had never seen before. A young nurse followed him in, and a nurse then began giving me shot after shot. "Nan desu Ka? What's that," I asked.

"It'll help you," is all she said.

She straddled me and began to push down on my abdomen. What the hell was she doing? Should I push? While the nurse pushed at my abdomen, the doctor tried to vacuum my baby out. And so it went for what seemed forever: pushing, sucking, pushing, sucking, the woman's hands on me, the vacuum sucking at my baby. I imagined my baby's head being grabbed by a vacuum cleaner, pulling at it like a stuck piece of taffy. It didn't seem that I was really a part of this, with the nurse doing my job of pushing and each of them talking to each other but not to me in Japanese. I felt useless, totally unneeded. But then, a slippery feeling, and I knew my baby was out. They wrapped the pink, sticky baby in a towel. "It's a girl." A girl—I had wished for a girl. Ken was by the door. He gazed at the baby and at me. We were a family now.

The Clinic

By Robin Malby

My first day at the Gateway Clinic was a real eye-opener. The waiting room was packed. People of all ages and health conditions were sandwiched into every available chair. Some were in wheelchairs. A few had no outward physical traits to suggest what their health problems were. As I studied the many patients collected around me, apprehension built. I knew I was ill, but the reality of just how bad I was hadn't registered fully until now.

Chinese, Filipino, or Mexican women staffed the front desk. They were hospitable and efficient. Red banners and oriental flowers decorated the lobby. Large brush paintings of lakes and steep, mountainous peaks hung in a hallway. The hour wait turned into two. As I stiffly paced around, a woman nearing sixty approached my sister and they started talking. "This is Barbara," Kathy said. "She is from South Carolina, and this is her second week at the clinic."

"Actually," Barbara interrupted in a heavy southern lilt, leaning forward so her face was close to mine, "ah came here a while ago but while ah was waiting ah heard someone in the next room screaming bloody murder from the immune shots. Why honey, it scared me sooo bad ah got on a plane and flew straight home! It's taken me a year to get back here!"

"Immune shots?"

"Oh yes, honey, but don't worry, everybody has to get them their first day here. They're these big ole vitamin shots they stick in your rear. Hurt like hell at first, but you get over it. 'Mule kickers' they like to call them." She rolled her eyes grandly for emphasis.

Barbara went on to explain that it was average for new patients to wait as long as four hours to see Dr. Lee. On the days that patients came in just for IV treatment, the wait was much shorter. Some received chelation IVs, others homeopathic treatments or vitamin drips.

"Don't ask what they are giving you in those IVs," she drawled authoritatively. "I think it's better not to know. If you knew, why it would just scare you to death!" This elicited more nervous laughter from Kathy and me. "I think they should have a separate room for new arrivals," Barbara added, "this is just too much to take in all at once." She stood up and wandered off to talk to others she'd met before.

Finally, at 1:45, Dr. Lee was ready for me.

"Robeen, Robeen Malbeee!" a nurse with a thick accent called. "Follow me!"

Dr. Lee's office looked professional, with a large mahogany desk and bookshelves that held many impressive titles. Hope and anticipation begin to surge. Surely this woman would be able to help me.

While we waited for Dr. Lee to arrive we began cracking a few jokes. We were pretty punch drunk by this time, Kathy from her flight the day before and me from my tiring trip from Concord. The long morning wait hadn't helped. Any stupid pun resulted in peals of laughter. Into this gaiety marched Dr. Amy Lee.

"Whoa! Laughter!" screeched Dr. Lee, her face incredulous. "Now there's something I don't hear from patients in this place very often!" For a moment I was completely taken aback. First by her statement, second by her appearance. Was she going to be another arrogant doctor who made you prove you were ill? Would she not believe me now because she'd overheard me laughing? Let's face it, sick people aren't supposed to laugh. Dr. Lee was a tiny, wiry Chinese woman. Her black hair was piled up high in a sort of late 50s bouffant. Her face was heavily made up; her lips were painted a blazing red. Large circles of rouge emphasized her high cheekbones. Two vibrant black swooshes served as eyebrows. I was mesmerized. She wore a brightly colored blouse and was wedged into a tiny skirt. Dr. Lee challenged my image of how a doctor should look.

Dr. Lee reviewed all the previous blood work, allergy testing, and other information I'd brought. She expressed herself with great animation and energy. We discussed my concerns about my continuing back pain, chronic headaches, and inability to digest food. I showed her the test results that indicated ileitis and the presence of an amoeba. Was fibromyalgia at the root of this? Dr. Lee said she hoped not, as fibromyalgia was one condition they'd been unable to cure. She felt they could work with my other problems. I disrobed so Dr. Lee could examine me.

"Oh my goodness, you are so wasted away!" she exclaimed as she saw my protruding ribs. At ninety-two pounds I was pretty skeletal. At last! A doctor who seemed to take my thin frame seriously. "You have nice breasts. Are they real or did you have them done?" she asked. Surprised, I stammered that they were real. "You're lucky!" she exclaimed. "One doesn't usually see such large breasts on such a small woman."

Stunned by her comments, Kathy and I exchanged glances. I immediately broke out laughing. I loved the absurd directness of it. It sure beat the boring questions most doctors had. I was starting to like Dr. Lee.

She tested all my acupuncture points and examined my pulses. She said I had a highly allergic and sensitive system. She wanted additional allergy testing, blood work, and circulation tests, even an E.K.G. She wanted me to stay for twenty-one days of vitamin and homeopathic IV treatments. Twenty-one days! The cost of all this would run about ten thousand dollars for treatments I wasn't even sure would help. I found myself reeling. Dr. Lee patted my shoulder and looked at me sternly. "I don't know how you are doing this," she said. "Most people in your shape wouldn't even be able to get out of bed in the morning much less get themselves here to our clinic. Your basic constitution is good, but your gut is not. You need to build up your body. Your strong spirit has kept you going, but now you need help."

My earlier doubts about Dr. Lee believing the seriousness of my present state vanished. The validation felt wonderful. I agreed to take the tests and start vitamin IVs the next day.

The immune shots were administered in a smaller waiting room down the hall, by a Dr. Janice Flynn. "O.K. Robeeen, lay on your stomach, pull your pants down, and prepare for pain. These are gonna hurt. We don't call them mule kickers for nothing," she announced in a heavy accent, followed by laughter. Kathy sat in a chair next to the examining table. She took one look at the shots and turned green. A sympathetic medical assistant handed me a pillow to squeeze while my other hand held onto Kathy. Janice plunged the needles in. The injection didn't hurt as much as the searingly hot sensations that followed. Fighting back tears, I limped stiffly to the waiting room. Burning pain shot down both legs, and I could hardly walk. I tried to stand in line at the front desk to schedule the next day's IV treatments. I had to lean against a nearby wall, tears trickling down my cheeks. People in the waiting room stared at me, compassionate understanding registering in their eyes. I was humiliated. After enduring three years of chronic back pain that was more excruciating than those shots, I was blubbering like a child.

Out of the corner of my eye I caught sight of a man shuffling toward me. Each foot was painstakingly placed a few inches in front of the other as he slowly and tediously made his way to where I was perched. He didn't look a day over thirty, yet he moved like a ninety year old. I had no idea what ailment could disable him so completely. He stopped a few inches away from me. Huge, beautiful, brown eyes drew me in. Reaching to take my hand, he bent forward and whispered, "I had to lean against the wall all night after I had those shots. It helps if you go up and down the stairs a few times. It cuts the pain."

He nodded toward a stairway at the end of the waiting room. "Thank you," I replied. Smiling, he gave my hand a gentle squeeze.

Using the wall as support, I wobbled to the stairway. As I went up, I found myself alone and out of sight. I let my tears flow. Tears of exhaustion and frustration, relief and gratefulness. Gratefulness that Dr. Lee had felt she could help me. Gratefulness that my sister Kathy had been willing to stay with me. And gratefulness for the gift of caring from a total stranger. If he could, in all his disablement, conduct himself so elegantly, then I knew I could too. Angels come in different packages, and I'd met one that day at the Gateway clinic. His kind words let me know I wasn't the only one having a rough go. We were all in this together. He had emanated a state of grace. The instant his hand had touched mine, I'd known I was going to do O.K. I was going to handle whatever the clinic had to offer. Maybe I was even going to like it.

"The Grandmothers" is from Nothing Left Standing But the Frame, *a work in progress by Audrey Martin about anorexia during adolescence and its effect on her in later years.*

The Grandmothers

By Audrey Martin

I was a very small girl to begin with. I experienced my size early as a focal point of other people's attention. There was something about being petite and delicate that was of value to them and therefore of value to me. The women in my family were buxom and curvaceous for the most part, except for my paternal grandmother, Jo, who was thin and angular and forever fretting about her size.

My grandmother's energy was boundless. Always in motion, she would ambulate at hummingbird pace; cleaning, moving furniture, putting everything in proper order. She was a horrible cook, with a dreaded chicken paprikash, her one staple meal at our family gatherings, which we all were obliged to endure.

Mostly, my grandmother subsisted on the following: Manichewitz whole wheat matzoh, dry, one cracker sheet broken in two on her plate; green salad with dietetic dressing; and black coffee, Maxwell House, by the cupful. Fueled on this, she walked miles for her errands or simply for exercise. She didn't drive a car. She also swam the breast stroke around the periphery of the swimming pool in her apartment building, which housed primarily Jewish seniors, and showered in a stall outside so as not to wet the tile on her own bathroom walls. My grandmother unabashedly loved me.

In contrast, my maternal grandmother, Eve, moved in slow deliberation. She was an excellent cook and baker and represented the redolence of old world and new in her kitchen, with sweet and complex smells emanating from her always busy stove. Her body was my refuge. Soft and round, bones muted by tender flesh. In her arms as a little girl, I felt her powerful womanhood. At her table there was whole milk in glass jars with cream at the top; there was sweet cream butter that floated in pools over hot farina at breakfast. In almost every room of her home, of which there were many, little glass or porcelain dishes were filled with candies and nuts there for the taking. There was no sneaking. A stop in the dining room for a nonpareil, a handful of pistachios, red die stains forming in a child's sweaty palms; there were no secrets for there was nothing to hide.

We lived in a two-flat on Custer Street in Evanston, Illinois, on a busy block with a hill where mother's pushed their strollers up and down, a front entrance we were forbidden to use, and a back door where we would come and go. This with the caveat that we must pass inspection for sand and dirt that hung on our clothes like ghosts dragged home from playing at the park nearby.

My father's parents, Jo (short for Josephine) and Alex, owned our building and lived downstairs with my aunt Ceci and my cousin Adrienne, who was ten months younger than I. I lived with my parents and two younger brothers in the upper flat. My grandparents' apartment furniture—the pale beige sofa, the matching side chairs, the white skin table lamps—was covered in plastic. This was imposed by my hummingbird grandmother to enforce the need for cleanliness that ruled her. My grandfather, Alex, a slow-moving and sage old man would shake his head in wonder at my grandmother's frantic pace. He napped every day after sitting with a book. He read Thoreau. One day when I was twelve or so, he asked me whether other women moved their refrigerators each week to clean the dust behind them. At five foot two and one hundred pounds, my grandmother was a powerhouse.

At Grandma Eve's, my Grandpa Sam drank rye whisky at meals and sang loudly as we giggled. He smoked Lucky Strikes while he planted his summer garden. Most Sundays we gathered, my family, aunts and uncles and cousins, to partake in rich Jewish feasts, taking pleasure in the cornucopia of delight my grandmother had created.

It wasn't long before I began receiving attention for the amount of food I consumed. "You eat like a little fegela," I'd hear my aunt chuckle from the table. "What are you having tonight, a chicken wing and a lettuce leaf?" Everyone would laugh. My reputation as a small eater was an anomaly in my mother's family, where voracious appetites were the norm and competition for food was a playful part of family meals. I would shrug my shoulders and smile as platters of roasted chicken, beef brisket, and farfel were consumed, carrots glazed with brown sugar, steaming rolls of kishke, and iceberg lettuce salads with cherry tomatoes and cucumber slices resting on plates.

My mother's kitchen was empty compared to my Grandma Eve's and abundant in relation to Grandma Jo's. In our home, my father's whims ruled our palettes. He was absorbed by a passion for fitness; there was an emphasis on health food and an absence of sugar and junk food, which members of my extended family found amusing. Jokes about having to hunt for anything fun to eat abounded. I became interested in nutrition and in fasting, which easily segued into not eating at all for extended periods of time. I did this without paying much attention to whether it was good for me.

Death Valley Journey:
A Daughter's Search for Reconciliation

By Cindy A. Pavlinac
(A longer version of this story was published in *Earthwalking Sky Dancers*, edited by Leila Castle, Frog, Ltd., 1997)

My father died when I was 19, nine months after I ran away from home to attend college. Years later I wished to observe the anniversary of his death and shocked myself by realizing I did not remember the exact date. Searching for my copy of his death certificate, my casual inquiry became a compelling demand for action to consciously mourn and to deliberately end mourning. My personal remembrance blossomed into a self-reflective journey to honor my father's memory, reconnect with my ancestors, transform the distress of abandonment, define my role as a woman artist and healer, and proclaim myself as a daughter of this American continent.

The remembrance impulse began as an image to spend a night alone in Death Valley, fasting, praying, waiting, conjuring my father's ghost from within me to say the good-byes I'd never had a chance to say. I felt a physical need to profoundly understand my role on Earth and sought to ground myself with the teachings I had learned from American Indian medicine people. They showed me respect for the land with their sense of sacred limits, consequences, nature, and community. They taught me to focus intention and how to behave, pray, sing, thank, and giveaway. Through ceremony I touched the matrix of cosmic order and glimpsed the ancient world of ancestors and relationship to place. In the macrocosm of ancient American archetypal landscapes, the desert is the Determiner. Death Valley leapt to mind. If I could touch bottom in the lowest point in the Western Hemisphere, perhaps I could rise renewed, soaring to new heights. I also chose Death Valley because of its reputation for swallowing pilgrims.

A personal relationship to land seems fundamental to our psyche. Acting out ritual remembrance evokes deep participation and immersion in the landscape. Once I recognized my need to go to Death Valley, I trusted that a ceremony would emerge from the land itself. Transformation could come when I emptied myself and opened to being held in the land. I left for Death Valley on a May Sunday morning.

I park the car at 2 a.m., seven years to the hour of his death. The moon had passed its first quarter, like my life. With a woolen cape I had made from a rummage sale coat, a pine box of feathers, and a wooden flute, I walk out into the black cold silence to meet my father. Crossing a dry riverbed, I huddle by a talking bush half expecting it to burst into flames. There is no shelter in this harsh landscape from the wind, from the cold, from the night, from myself. Listening intently with every fiber of my longing, I realize my father is not here. He is not anywhere. He is dead. All that I would meet in the desert is that which I have brought. So I sit through the night watching stars arc overhead and think of him. Burning some sage, I remember how his five brothers hurt to see the youngest of them die first. The wind accompanied me as I played his double flute from Yugoslavia. I imagine conversation with them, the brothers, sons of immigrants, wishing them well. None of them have spoken to me since the funeral, and I am unprepared to suddenly know another brother has died. My grief includes their grief and all that we will never share, all that I will never know about who they were, all they will never tell me, all the thick silences and unspoken stories of their vanished world. Overhead, Mars crosses the dark sky as I ask for strength in my life, guidance, wisdom, grace. The Pleiades sparkle, and I think of my mother's side of the family, aunts and grandmothers. They arrive to greet me one by one and depart into thin forgetfulness. The women's threads and stories of remembrance remain strong, whirling back into the mists of time much farther than the men's, perhaps all the way back. Two long bright strands of hundreds of people who never met each other meet in me. Wanting to give an intimate offering of myself, I pull out a few strands of my long hair and let the wind take them one at a time. Staring at the stars, I am an empty watcher in the night.

The sky began to lighten hours before I expected. Dawn swallowed the eastern stars as Mars and Saturn set in the west; the young warrior and the wise old man who ate his children. As the sun broke the horizon I stiffly stood to thank the Directions and the land host. Some time in the night while dialoging with the memory of my father, we spoke of hair. I had always worn mine long and untrimmed. Any thought of cutting it brought to mind the story of Samson and his lost strength when his hair was cut, so I had refrained. The image of long blonde hair was an ideal of feminine beauty for my father, and I now saw that I had kept my hair to please him, long after he could appreciate it. To truly claim my entire self I would have to "eat my hair" to internalize my beauty and step out from behind my self-created veil. Returning to the car I drank some water and drove on into the mountains. To help focus my intention before coming to the desert I had made a prayer arrow out of a stick and shells, feathers, pebbles with holes, and trinkets all wrapped with brightly colored yarn. Climbing 5,100 feet by late afternoon, I looked for the place to plant it. The Mountaintop is the place of Giveaway. Walking up a dry wash I found a quiet rock with a commanding view. Setting down the prayer arrow laden with gifts and wishes, I gathered a fistful of bangs and severed my hair with my Boy Scout knife. Holding up the 32-inch shank of long hair in the wind, I shuddered with the irrevocability of the act. Air chilled the top of my head. Shaking, I tied the hair to the stick with bright thread and felt a resounding shock at what I had done. I had scalped myself. I had declared myself individuated, unique, visible. I cut another fistful of hair from the other side and added it to the stick. Planting the arrow in the rocky ground with sage and prayers, I became the offering. Wind lifted my hair softly and it floated around the medicine stick. It was alive and it was me, yet it was no longer mine. For a moment, I was the prayer arrow with my hair billowing in the wind on a mountain in the sunset. Yet I could stand and walk away. The last rays of the sun ignited the hovering hair, and I said good-bye.

Crown of Roses

By Andrew Pelfini

The pale yellow shades are at half-mast. I press my face against the cool windowpane. The roses that trail the fence outside are bowing to greet the sun and bend gracefully in a way that the finest ballerina cannot imitate. The ivory-pink baby roses belonging to our neighbor Marie bloom every year in May.

This Saturday I am first one up. I am excited because today my sister Linda is having her friends over to make crowns of flowers, mostly roses that we will gather from the fence. Linda was chosen this year to be the May Queen at our school. Every year we look at the statue and almost begin to believe Mary is real, right here. "Hail Holy Queen Enthroned Above. . . ." We are learning this song at school. I love this song. "Oh Maria . . ."

Being a boy of six, I can sing as high as my sisters. I am not sure what to do about this. Linda was chosen to be the May Queen because she was voted the nicest and smartest girl in the class—the one most like our Blessed Mother. My mom smiles when she tells the neighbors, a smile of subtle pride. Linda represents what my mother admires most in a child.

Around 10:30, Linda's friends arrive in shorts and plaid blouses, their bare feet in brown leather sandals. Joan Bigham (big ham, we call her behind her back) is pudgy and pink skinned. Her blond curly hair looks like Bozo the Clown's. But she is nice to me, so I never call her big ham to her face.

"Hey, Andrew, how are you, kid? Was that you singing a minute ago? It was beautiful. I heard it from the walkway, and I thought it was a record. You're good, kid." Joan cackles and pulls a chair out next to me.

My mom raises the window shades all the way up. The kitchen is a flurry of flowers on our wax-paper-covered kitchen table.

"Oh Linda, you are gonna look beautiful." Joan smiles as she plucks the stems of the baby pink roses.

"Watch for the thorns. Be careful, Andrew." My mom pats my head.

Thin strips of wire are cut in many sizes to make crowns for the girls to thread roses in. I select a wire and shove it through the green leafy stem surrounding the bud. But where is my crown? My head dances with thoughts. As I thread roses together on wire, I want to place a crown on my head, wondering why boys can't wear flowery dresses and crowns. It is simply unfair. I am alone inside my head and sad, wanting my mom to rescue me from my discontent and find me a crown of roses. Even without my crown, I am welcomed and loved at the table. My sister and her friends think I am cute, a nice little kid. I think that would change if I let my desires be known, so I am quiet about it. Silent or not, I know my sister loves me. I know by the way she takes care of me and kindly stays with me. I am safe with Linda. She is my big sister, and I know exactly where her classroom is at school. I am in room number one; she is in number eight.

I thread roses, waiting for my mother to read my thoughts, to give me permission to have my crown and to wear it in the procession. I bet if Linda knew, she would make me a crown and secretly protect me from harm, safely placing it with love upon my tiny blond head. With my crew cut, it would look like roses on straw. About my flowering interests, no one ever tells me, but I think my family tries to protect me from ridicule—not too sure if I am all boy yet. I take pleasure in the things my sisters like: Barbie dolls and their plastic shoes, jump rope, jacks, and roller skates. At school, dodge ball and four-square meet my interest along with Father Jiminez, who lets the little girls sit on his shoulders and touch his slicked-back black hair. I am silently envious of them and minimally disturbed by this injustice. No boys ride on his shoulders. I trail behind the lucky girl on his shoulders from the church to the school yard, red bricks under my feet, wondering how to get my chance.

I wandered freely in my mind, not questioning my envy of the little girls in blue plaid jumpers who got the good father's attention. And a few years later, without having a name for my kind, I discovered that little gay boys don't have rights; no one pays them any mind because they do not know what to do with them. In recent years I wonder what would happen to the Boy Scouts of America and the safety of an all-boys slumber party if gay little boys were there safe to be themselves.

Smelling roses on thin wire, I twiddle my legs under the kitchen table; my cheeks are hot. I know that I won't fit in with the Boy Scouts anyway. I refused to go to the Cub Scout orientation meeting last week. So I pick up a pale pink rose and take a good whiff.

Come 11:00 on Sunday morning, I pay careful attention to the little girls on the church steps in white piqué dresses, patent leather shoes, and lacy cotton socks. Somehow their attire fits more with my desire to love a man. To get a boy, you have to be like a girl. Six years old going on seven, I know what I want and who I like. Father Jiminez will do just fine. He is dressed in a white robe with lace on the cuffs just like the girls' lacy socks. His face is smooth and his eyes dark like his hair. I raise my head up toward his face. He begins to promenade like a show pony. We follow, walking under arches of flowers held by two girls. The red carpet is spongy under my black Buster Brown tie-up shoes.

"Ave, Ave, Ave Maria," we sing out. I raise my eyes toward the ceiling high above my head. Choral and crimson-colored patterns cover the ceiling, and amber chandeliers hang from the exposed beams. When we all get to our places, the song changes. "Hail Holy

Queen Enthroned above . . ." The organ pipes blow like trumpets—a call for the May Queen. I turn back and peer around the pew. My mom lets me sit on the end so my view is unhampered. I tug at her dress announcing my sister's arrival. Two girls march ahead of Linda in their white dresses, carrying the crown of flowers—the big one Linda made to adorn the statue of our Blessed Mother. Linda's legs shake as she reaches the statue. She climbs the tall ladder. Our Blessed Lady is about to be adorned. Linda places the crown on her head; her reach barely completes the task. Her head bends gracefully like the roses on the fence. A mere statue becomes a good lady in my eyes. The crown suits her. With my eyes on Linda and my feet dangling in the pew, I somehow know I too could be the Queen of May if I put my mind to it.

Inhaling

By Helene Redmond

This story consolidates many aspects of my childhood: the black humor in my family, addiction, Mormon influences, and my rebelliousness and need for acceptance. My upbringing in a Mormon family that didn't obey the rules formed my support of women's rights and the struggle for self-acceptance. When I write, I see that my past was difficult and I was angry. Through my writing, I can explore the anger and also see the good things, which were unknown to me when I began. I am more able to enjoy my current good fortune and appreciate my hard work. It makes me proud. It's right there on the page.

Tonight my best pal, Trini Jorgenson, is going to teach me how to inhale. I can hardly wait. Of course, I'll wear my Levi 501s. They are my uniform 'cause I wear them every day. They make my legs and butt look skinny once I get them buttoned up (which means lying down on the floor so my fat can go south). Once I get up, my tummy rolls sort of hang over the top of my pants, so to cover these unsightly things, I choose my long white tee shirt and red sweatshirt. These cover my rolls and make me look like a deer hunter. I should fit right in at church. I'm sure those Mormon men are deer killers just like Dad. To top off my outfit, I'll wear my black-and-white saddle oxfords. Pretty soon, I'm getting the two-toned tan-and-brown ones. I'll get them with my babysitting money 'cause I'm sure Mama and Dad wouldn't give me the money as long as these are still in good shape. They don't get it. These oxfords are my only attempt at being a beta. The betas are goody-goodies and cheerleaders and class officers. I don't want to be one and couldn't be one if I tried, 'cause I'm a trouble-maker and too fat, and my parents are drunks and jack Mormons, which means they don't follow the Mormon rules. The rest of my clothes make me fit in with the greasers, but I can throw everybody off with my shoes. I'm in a big hurry to learn how to smoke like the greasers. I want to fit in with them. I want them to be my people.

My heart races when I steal Mama's cigs. Especially with that crazy picture right on the kitchen table with her message about what I'm supposed to fix for dinner. Frankie drew a picture of Mama sort of as a skeleton with a skull and crossbones. Where her lungs would be, he scribbled two black blobs. Mama liked the picture so much that she drew a balloon out of her mouth on the picture and made copies to use as stationery.

I am outta here! I walk down the lane and start out on 21st East. As I pass the Arctic, I'm tempted to get a cone, but across the street are John Upton, Blaine, and Willy Greenhurst. I sure don't want them to see me eat. I don't want anybody to think I ever eat. Then maybe they won't notice how fat I am. They are definitely the bad boys. They're members of the church but never go. Hell, they don't even make it to school most of the time. They spend most of their time in detention. They sure are cute, with their 501s down around their hips, their Levi jackets, construction boots, and those great hairdos with the ducktails in front and back. I wave but I'm way too shy to go over and talk to them, and instead I stay on my side of the street and just move a little faster, keeping my mind on what I'm about to do. I wonder: if I knew how to inhale, would I join them right now?

Smoking cigs is extremely cool. It's neat and makes people look tough and in charge. Smoking hurts my throat like hell, makes me cough and choke, but the way it looks is worth all of it. I've been practicing, mostly at home by myself, trying to get it right before I show off to my friends and enemies. I pick through Mama's butts, which gives me plenty to practice on. Mama's butts are pretty long. She always has one going, sometimes a couple, in different places in the house because she forgets, and she's got to have something to shove into her mouth at all times. God forbid if she ever ran out. I'd hate to see the consequences.

I've been a good little Mormon for years now, ever since I was about four years old. I've been the only one in this family who regularly goes to church and mutual. I went to primary, testimony meeting, and every other thing that the Mormons wanted me to do. I paid my 10 percent tithing, first out of my allowance and my babysitting money. I believe in God and Jesus, but I've never thought much of the Holy Ghost. Nobody has ever explained it to me so that I can understand, and those three levels of heaven make me a little angry. I think people from other religions can be good people, but the Mormons believe that they are the only ones who can go to the top heaven. It's a little arrogant. I have been baptized for the dead 148 times and mostly I go by the Golden Rule. I'm 13 now and I haven't done anything against the church.

I have been such a good little church goer because some of the people have been sweet and fair to me, especially Joyce Spaner. I knew she cared about me, and she was always the same. She didn't change like Mama and Dad. She would always give me a hug, and I knew she was happy to see me. She would tell me, "You're doing great. I really like how you finished this project. It's beautiful. You are such a talented girl and so smart." There have been others who were good to me, too. I think Gertrude, Rozie, and Madelyn are good Christians. Some other ward members are good people. For heaven's sake, everybody I know belongs to the church. I wouldn't know anybody or have anything to do if it wasn't for the church, but I'm changing now. Now I'm starting to smoke cigarettes. I know it's wrong, and it goes against The Pearl of Great Price (which tells people they shouldn't drink alcohol, coffee, coke, or tea, or smoke cigarettes). My parents and most relatives do all of these things to excess, but not me. I've been nigh on to perfection.

So there it is. I like looking cool, hanging out with the greasers and hoods, and dabbling with nicotine. I really need to make an impression of being one of "them." The biggest reason that I want to hang out with the greasers is that they accept me. I don't have to get good grades, be a skinny little energetic cheerleader, play an instrument, sing like a bird, or have parents who are good Mormons. I can just be who I am right now—angry at my parents, getting bad grades. I'm tired of trying to be so damn good. What has it gotten me? Not a thing except feeling like I'm never good enough. With the hoods, the only things I have to do are get in trouble at school, go to detention, and learn to smoke cigarettes.

"Hi, Trini, how's everything and what's new?" I say as I slide into the seat next to her at our evening meeting at the Ward. We start out in the big meeting room where we also meet for Sunday School. The ceiling is 20 feet high and there's a platform and a podium where the choir, the organist, and the elders all sit. I'm smiling and winking at her because I know how everything is and exactly what's new, and that is that we're going to be smoking up a storm in just a few minutes. I have two brand new Raleighs in my jacket pocket and a book of matches.

"When can we split?" I say, because really, I just can't wait.

"Where should we go," whispers Trini.

"I don't know. I thought you had a plan for us," I say.

"Well, let's stick around here for a little while 'cause that will look good. When it's time for class, we'll leave," she says.

After the announcements, people stand up to go to class. Trini grabs my elbow and steers me to the front door of the church and around to the back. All of a sudden, Trini grabs my hand and stops me.

"What! You want to stop here, behind the church?" I ask, surprised. It's pitch black out here.

Trini triumphantly announces, "I think this is the perfect place for us to commit our crime!"

It's so chilly out here, I can see my breath. I give Trini one of the Raleighs and she pulls out her lighter, takes the cigarette, puts it to her lips, and lights the lighter. She puts the lighter to the cigarette and takes a long drag. I am watching closely because she does this so well. She tells me, "You see, you suck the air into your lungs just like you're taking a deep breath. Then you can leave the smoke in there and talk. The smoke will come out of your mouth and nose." As she's talking, smoke is coming out of her mouth and her nose. Incredibly cool.

Trini passes me the cigarette, I take a drag, and just like she told me, I pull the smoke into my lungs in a deep breath. All of a sudden we hear a noise to our right. Trini takes off in the opposite direction. I just stand there, dizzy as anything from this big puff, and smoke is barreling out of my nose.

"Who's out there?" comes a booming male voice. I see the small light cast by a flashlight. There are some trees back here, and it is a little spooky. I am paralyzed, terrified. As my vision adjusts and my head clears a little, this man is coming closer. I see his round, pale, pitted, and sweaty face, his balding head. I recognize his voice and his business suit at the same time. Shit! It's Bishop Potter!

"What's going on out here?" he booms. I wish I could say, "What does it look like, stupid? Smoke's barreling out of my nose, and it smells like Sunday afternoon in a Jack Mormon home," but instead I said, "Nothing, Bishop Potter."

"You can't fool me, young lady. You've been smoking!" says the brilliant observer. "Miss Larsen, who do you think you are, desecrating church property with your shenanigans?"

You'd think after all these years he'd at least know my name. I literally do not know what to say. I am dead-assed caught.

"What do you think your parents will have to say about this?" asks the Bish.

"Please don't tell my parents anything; please, they don't understand," I beg.

"I can only imagine what else you're doing with your time. Probably drinking alcohol, sleeping with boys, lots of boys. You're probably known as one of those easy girls," says the all-knowing. "Come into the office while I call your parents."

I finally have my head back together and would like to say, "Trini Jorgenson was just teaching me how to smoke; she was forcing me at gunpoint, and when she saw you, she took off," but instead I start to walk a little faster. He grabs my hand. At this point, I'm gone. I yank my hand away and start running.

"Come back here, you little tramp, come back here. You'll be sorry!" he shouts after me.

Sorry is right, I'm thinking. Sorry I've come to church every day of my life since I was four, sorry I paid my 10 percent all these years, sorry I've been a goody-two-shoes. But not sorry that this happened because now I know how they really are. The Mormons are no different from my parents, and I'm never coming back.

Flashback: Flying to Meet My Son

By Denise Roessle

I've never had a problem with flying, but today my body is twisted into one giant white knuckle. It's only been ten days since I received the call from the registry that reconnected me with my grown son. Now here I am on a plane headed from San Francisco to New Orleans to see a young man I don't even know and yet I love so much my heart feels as if it might explode.

My mind drifts on autopilot to that flight twenty-six years before, when I'd been sent away from home and into the unknown, four months pregnant but still able to wear the gray wool coatdress my mother had sewn for me to take to college the year before. Arriving in Los Angeles, I'd scanned the crowds for a stranger, the short balding attorney who held my fate, and a cardboard sign with my last name, in his hands. Later today I would be looking for a different sign, and a different stranger—the one I gave birth to. My sense of him is strong and primal, but I'm so worried I won't find him in the crowds that I asked him to bring a sign that says "Mom."

My baby had been just five days old when he boarded his first plane and flew cross-country to a better life than an unwed nineteen year old could provide. How happy his new mother must have been, cradling that tiny blanketed bundle in her arms, adoring him, thanking God for such a precious gift.

The flight attendant's voice on the loudspeaker jerks me back.

In just eight hours I will hold my son for the first time. It is a moment I've longed for, imagined again and again, then came to believe would never happen. But sitting on this plane, fighting back the tears that come and go as rhythmically as labor, I don't feel happy, cannot bring myself to be grateful. All I can think about is what I've lost.

Pearl Davies Saad wrote this next piece from the point of view of an adolescent girl and in that girl's voice. Note the character sketches of the family, the use of sensual details, and the portrayals of relationships.

Me and My Mom
By Pearl Davies Saad

My mother is the most beautiful woman in the whole world. Her hair is fluffy, almost three inches tall. Her eyebrows are thin; her eyes are big and black, her teeth, big and white. Her face is gaunt, and her skin is sallow. She tells me the hardest thing about her diets is that she immediately loses weight in her face, and then she looks so gaunt. "I look so gaunt, and it doesn't help that my skin is so sallow." That's my mom. Oh, and she has long eyelashes too. And she wears white pearl earrings and a diamond ring. She has a London Fog raincoat and a handmade dashiki in a light lavender tie-dye color. She has big breasts and a big derriere too. I know because she tells me, "I have big breasts and a big derriere. When I was your age I looked like a grown woman. I hated the way I was treated, the way I was stared at. And my mother, she was always poking me between the shoulders, telling me not to stoop, telling me to walk tall. I just wished everyone would stop staring at me. They didn't know what it was like."

I don't really know what she is talking about. She is my mom. She tells me not to stoop. She tells me that I am lucky because when she was my age she had already had her period for several years. She tells me she developed early. I don't really want to hear about it. She has given me a booklet with a horse on the cover. It has a green background and it is about getting your period. I don't quite really understand what it is all about. I mean, what is a period? What is menstruation? The booklet says I can't go swimming and I should stay away from wearing white. With my period I will become a woman. I keep the booklet in my underwear drawer and pull it out to look at it every now and then. I want to get my period, and I want to wear a bra. A real bra, not a pullover bra but one with straps that go snap when you pull them. I don't like wearing an undershirt. Everyone can tell I still wear one, and I feel embarrassed.

We shop at RockBottom's. They have Flickers for women, and Ayds. The Flicker is a new razor. It has five blades, and it is in the shape of a circle, and you use one blade until you use it up; then you push it forward and another blade pops up to take its place. I have tried that. I shave my underarms now, because of all the staining. My mom would be happy if I shaved my arms as well. I think that's gross. My friend Annetta made fun of me for shaving. She says she cuts hers. She says her sister can braid hers. She is German. Her family doesn't do everything the American way. Me, I am American. I shave my underarms, and I shave my legs too. I spend a lot of time shaving. I have to be careful not to cut myself. It hurts. I also have to remember not to put on deodorant right after shaving; that hurts too. There is so much to learn.

Ayds are chocolate-covered diet pills that look like a box of chocolates. I would really like to buy some, and I look at them every time I go in the store. You have to be eighteen to buy them, and Annetta said they give people heart attacks. She told me that if you eat them you stay up all night. I would like to try them. I think they are such a neat idea: chocolates that make you lose weight. I read in *Seventeen* magazine that if you pinch the flesh on your stomach and there is an inch of flesh, then you are fat. You can try that all over your body. I am only fat in my stomach. If I could eat the chocolate and lose weight, that would be great. I like chocolate. Also, I feel that if I eat the Ayds I will be a grown-up, I will be a real teenager, I will be sexy. The woman on the cover of the box is wearing a bikini bathing suit and she looks almost like my mom but younger; she has big breasts and long legs and a skinny stomach. She has an hourglass figure. That's what my mom told me it's called. I know because she told me, "I have an hourglass figure. Big breasts, small waist, big hips and der-riere." My mom talks about her body a lot. She embarrasses me.

When we go shopping together it is weird. My mom likes it that people can tell we are mother and daughter. I don't like it. I don't want her to be with me. Every time we go out, she says, "Oh, look at the way they are looking at us. I bet they are wondering if we are mother and daughter." Sometimes I want to yell at her. "Well of course they do; we are mother and daughter!" We look exactly alike, so it's not hard to tell we are related. I look just like her except I have small breasts, no waist, and no hips. We wear the same size of every-thing except bras. She is a 36C. I am a 34B. I am 14 and she is 42.

Imagining the Past
By Sarah Weinberg

There is no way to process the grief and loss passed from one generation to the next not only in the not knowing but in the imagining of what might have happened. Ma used to speak about her grandfather, a rabbi in Russia, who never emigrated to America. My Aunt Lillie says his son Sam tried to find him by contacting the Red Cross, but Uncle Sam had no luck. We don't even know his name.

Some questions have haunted me over the years. Why did my grandmother Esther Annie travel alone to America? Did my great-grandfather plan to join his daughter in America later? Was he too poor or too old or too sick to come? Did he have too many responsibilities as a rabbi to leave? Yet I can surmise certain things, such as the anguish of a father saying goodbye to his child not knowing if he will ever see her again.

Since a cloud of gloom is in the air whenever Ma mentions him, I decide to conjure up his presence, waiting for an answer and the secret of our family's past to be unraveled.

In the voice of my maternal great-grandfather: I live in Belarussia, in a town called Bobruisk. The weather is cold here so I often put on my black fur hat to keep the edges of my ears warm. I have boots on with leather soles to protect myself from the cold and snow. I am proud to own a pair of boots with no holes. I have a long gray beard that keeps me warm and *pehas*, long locks that come down in front of my ears, which have never been cut. I wear a black suit and a long topcoat.

My prayer book is my daily companion. I take it with me wherever I go. When a question lies heavy on my heart, I open my prayer book randomly and I lay my finger anywhere on the page for the answer.

My prayer book was given to me by my grandfather on the Sabbath of my bar mitzvah. The pages are worn and yellowed with age and daily fingering. I open it to follow the three daily services. And I just start chanting and reading the Hebrew, with my body swaying back and forth and from side to side.

I pray for my children's safety. I had four of them—two daughters and two sons. One of my sons was a published Russian poet who died of pneumonia, and so did my wife. This *Pesach* I say the *Kaddish* to honor their memory and elevate their souls. The first few words of the Kaddish prayer—*yitgadol*, will be made great; *yitkadash*, will be made holy; and *sh'meh rabah*, the name of the great one—inspired my faith in G-d.

When I say the Kaddish, I see my wife's face, the softness in her eyes, and the corner of her lips curled up in a smile. My son, he had such broad shoulders and always stood proud, with his chin up. He branched away from religious studies and acquired a general education. He had a love of literature and an interest in politics. His poetry showed his gentleness and sensitivity, describing the richness of Jewish cultural life in Bobruisk and creating an ideal society. I miss them.

There is no public place for me to lead services since the fire of 1902. Fifteen temples were destroyed, including my own. Over two thousand Jewish families lost their wooden homes, and some of the congregants in my own temple died. It was a surprise when the Czar came to town donating rubles to rebuild Bobruisk.

Now we meet in my home or other people's homes. We must form a *minyan*, a prayer group of ten or more men, for prayers like the Kaddish to be said out loud. In the morning when I pray, I wrap myself up in my *tallit*, a prayer shawl, a safe cocoon for me to disappear into. The *tzit tzit* dangles around me as I move in prayer; It is a fringe on the outer corners of the prayer shawl, with open threads that are not hemmed in and closed.

In biblical and post-biblical times in Israel, the edges of the fields were left unharvested by the owners for the poor. The tzit tzit at each corner reminds me of the corners of the fields left for the poor. The boundaries and borders are fuzzy, not clearly defined, which shows me that we are not separate beings, but we are all interconnected and one.

It is dangerous living here; there are rumors of pogroms coming to our town. Pogroms have already happened in many other Russian cities, such as Kisheniev, Homel, Zhitomir, and Retshitse. The rich are donating weapons, and the young are organizing a resistance movement. One could come like a lightning bolt at any moment. I hear that the Cossacks ride into towns with their brightly colored uniforms and their magnificent horses. Their hooves make the boom boom sound of a fierce and powerful drum, with a beat like crackling thunder. The Cossacks come to slaughter people, especially us Jews, for our religious beliefs. I want my children to have a better life. This is no place for a Jew. I have booked passage to the New World for my three remaining children. My son Sam and my oldest daughter have made it over there, but I keep my youngest daughter, Esther Annie, with me the longest. I used to hide my baby in the large stove oven as part of a safety drill when Cossacks were expected in our town because I heard many stories about them raping girls. Esther Annie is a teenager now, and she is too big to hide in the stove oven. These days I keep the oven door open, and Esther and I sit by it for warmth.

Last week I booked passage for Esther Annie to leave here. I am an old and sick man. I don't have the money to join my children and start a new life. But my children should have a better life. Esther will leave our beloved home soon.

The morning of Esther's departure I put on my *tefillin,* the two small leather boxes containing Torah passages written on parchment. I wind the leather bands with the boxes, one on my forehead, the other leather box tied to my arm. I make the Hebrew letter *shin,* which stands for G-d's name, on my hand with the leather straps. I have carried out this ritual each day of my adult life, yet on the day Esther is to leave my hand trembles, and my arm flinches as I bind myself to G-d.

Goose bumps form on my skin as I hug Esther Annie, my baby girl, and bid her farewell. Tears start to run down her face and mine. My mouth tastes their saltiness on my lips. I can still hear Esther's voice as she is leaving. "Daddy," she says, "please don't make me go." She is my little girl, yet I force her to go. I wave good-bye from a distance. Tears run down my cheeks and hang in droplets on my beard.

My hat falls off my head as I watch her go. I step on it accidentally and crush it to the ground. My heart tightens up in a knot. What if Esther doesn't make it to the New World, and I cannot join my children? Esther, my baby girl and my hidden delight. *Estar*, her Hebrew name, means "hidden." I hope she stays hidden and true to her namesake until she makes it safely to the New World. I hope she reveals who and what she is and is able to shine on her own.

I have sent Esther to live with my cousins in a place far away called New York. I hope they treat her well. My son Sam and my oldest daughter went to live with relatives in Chicago. May G-d bless them and protect them. May G-d shine light upon their paths and grace them with peace.

Afterthoughts: It is indeed a courageous act to send one's children away. Now I understand the choice. There is a kind of knowing in Hebrew called *yadati*, which means "I know," in the soul and heart. By becoming my great-grandfather, yadati—I know in my soul and heart the pain of my ancestor. My grandmother Esther Annie Slobodin was born in 1888 in Bobriusk, Belarussia. She died when she was seventy years old in New York City on May 7, 1958, the year of my birth. How I wish I'd had the opportunity to know her!

I have a photograph of her sitting on a large, solid, wood chair next to my grandfather, who rests at her side on a wooden rocker. Grandpa's shoulder touches hers as his body slants toward her. She does not lean into him quite as much, although her head tilts very slightly in his direction.

A part of my heritage is my Russian Jewish ancestry. When I wrote this story it made the feeling of connection stronger. I did research on life in Bobruisk during the time my great-grandfather lived there. I had a feeling that he wore *pehas*, as is customary for Hassidic Jews, yet I did not want to leave this detail in the story until I knew it was historically accurate. I was delighted to learn about the Hassidic and Yiddish-speaking Jewish communities in Bobruisk. Yes, when I conjure up my great-grandfather's presence I believe that he wore *pehas*!

I know there were pogroms in Russia. I needed to research the time frames in which they occurred to be sure the information shared in my family while I was growing up was accurate. I found out that while pogroms took place throughout the 1880s, 1890s, and early 1900s, the pogrom wave actually avoided Bobruisk because of a strong resistance movement and the fact that it was a fortress town and a base for the Russian army. The wave that flooded many cities and villages in Pale of Settlement destroyed the mood in Bobruisk, where anti-Semitism was widespread and Jews were restricted from holding certain occupations. Some Jews were rich, but many who were poor left the city in droves. And there was genuine fear about the pogroms.

In order to see my relatives living out their lives and feel connected to them, I needed to learn about everyday life in Bobruisk, what type of a town it was, and its history. Through doing the research about my past and my roots to write this story, I experienced a sense of completeness that I have never known.

Appendix B:
Developmental Questionnaire

*T*hese questions are meant to stimulate memories about your life chronologically. Think about them; write about them in your journal. They may lead to stories. If a question upsets you, move on to another one. Or you might choose to write about whatever bothered you for 15 or 20 minutes, a short writing exercise to facilitate healing. You can come back to any question at any time. You do not have to go through the questionnaire chronologically if you don't want to. If a subject grabs your interest, and you find yourself with strong memories or images, then start writing. Use the questions as guides to help you remember and think about what needs healing in your life and what scenes and memories are a part of you.

Keep in mind that at different stages a child is psychologically prepared in different ways to handle the stresses of life. If a situation appropriate for a sixteen year old confronts an eight year old, it will be developmentally difficult for the younger child to receive the information in a healthy way. For instance, although sexually inappropriate behavior with a child is never acceptable, a sixteen year old may have more tools than a younger child to deal with such an event. A sixteen year old may observe and even comment on the inappropriateness of a remark or glance, but a younger child may simply be confused. An older child can use words and a larger body to set a boundary, or even to confront the unwanted action or words. A younger child may simply feel helpless or be seduced by kind words and deeds, especially if the child is alone or lonely.

Life consists of positive and negative events and memories. Together they make us human and give shape to our lives. We all go through stages, from being small humans in a confusing world to growing up and making sense of this world and our place in it. We create our identity and our sense of self though all these experiences.

Birth

From birth onward, a child is shaped by environment and family, as well as by personality and temperament. Development in early childhood was discussed in Chapter 11. From age three to five the child goes through separation and individuation, the development of healthy autonomy achieved by the right balance of closeness and separation. D. W. Winnicott, a developmental psychologist, called a caretaker who achieved this balance a "good-enough mother," meaning that children need good-enough nurturing, not perfection.

Early Childhood, Age 1 to 5

Home and security base

Who was your major caretaker(s) during those years?
What are your first memories before the age of five?
Do you remember nature, landscape, your house, your room, your bed, a favorite toy or object, siblings, mother, father, grandparents?
Did you live in the same house or apartment, town or city as extended family members?

Social world, friends, neighborhood

Did you attend preschool or kindergarten?
Did you have friends your own age? older? younger?

What socioeconomic class did your family belong to during your early years?

What do you remember about your neighborhood or your neighbors?

How about the environment in which you grew up? What do you remember about landscape, weather, and location, such as farm, city, open space, mountains, ocean?

What about experiences with nature or with awe and wonder?

Were you exposed to any religious training, or did you have any spiritual experiences?

Family

Name the people who surrounded you from birth to age five.

What are the stories about you and who tells them?

What myths do family members tell about you? (She always . . . He never . . .)

What have you heard about your early toilet training, eating habits, first teeth?

What personality characteristic were you cherished for?

What trait that they found strange or disapproved of became part of the family lore?

Separations and disconnections

Were you separated from your family during your first five years? Why?

Did you move to a new place?

Were you or your primary caretakers seriously ill?

Were there wars or political upheavals, with relatives or parental figures going to war or leaving home?

What do you know about your parents' and grandparents' attitudes regarding separations?

The School Years, Age 5 to 12

Friends and social life

What kind of friends did you have? Were they older or younger, same or opposite sex?

What did you like most and least about your friends?

Were you accepted or a loner, shy or gregarious, a leader or follower?

What do you understand about your attitude toward people, friends, closeness?

What do you remember about yourself in relation to your peers at that time?

School days

What was your attitude toward school and learning? Did you like it or dread it? Why?

What were your favorite subjects? Do they have any bearing on your life now?

What do you remember about your teachers? Who supported you or saw you as a good learner or person?

Describe your school. What was it made of? Was it old, modern, clean, messy?

How were the grades arranged?

What techniques were used for teaching and learning?

How did school affect you emotionally?

How did what happened at school integrate with your home life?

Special training, such as music, sports, science, the arts

How and when did you begin this special interest?

Did you have a special teacher or mentor?

What are your memories of these events?

How did participating make you feel? Good, bad, or mixed?

Religious or spiritual training

Did you attend services at a place of worship?
What were you taught about a higher power?
How did these teachings affect the life of the family at home?
How did these teachings affect you privately?
If you believed in a higher power, how did this belief affect your everyday life at school, home, or alone?

Your home

What do you remember about your house?
Describe your favorite rooms and the landscape surrounding your house.
What do you remember about pets?
Describe the family routine. Did you have chores?
How were weekends different from the rest of the week?
What was your neighborhood like?

Clothes

What was your family's attitude toward appearance?
How did your parents and grandparents dress?
Did you wear what you wanted to?
Did you feel proud or ashamed of your appearance?
How do you think you looked compared to the other kids?

Discipline

How did your parents use discipline or punishment with you and with your siblings?
How were mistakes at school handled at home?
Were you whipped or spanked? How do you define these terms?
Were implements, such as spoons, belts, or switches, used to punish you?
Were you yelled at or called names?

Was humiliation used as a punishment technique?
How did you feel about any punishment you received?

Play and creativity

Were you encouraged to be a child or were you pushed to act
older than your age? Were you allowed to play and
daydream?
Describe your play. What did you imagine in your play life?
Did you keep your imaginative games a secret or share them?
Did you draw or pay attention to your dreams and daydreams?

Adolescence, Age 13 to 19

Adolescence is a time to search for and find identity, often by rebel-
ling against the norm, the family, and society. Certain aspects of the
separation-individuation process of earlier years are repeated, and
the adolescent reaches a new level of autonomy.

Sexuality and your body

What was your family's attitude toward sex and physical
closeness? Was it a healthy, open attitude or one of shame,
guilt, and repression?
Were your parents physically affectionate, or was sex re-
pressed or absent in the house?
When did you have "that talk" about sex and reproduction?
Who talked to you, and what was his or her attitude?
What did you think and feel about sex and reproduction?
Did you date? As much or less than your friends?
When you first went out on dates, how did you feel about
yourself, your body, the date?
How did you feel about your body changing? Did you feel
guilty about sex, your body, masturbation?
Did you talk about sex with your friends?
What did you learn from them?

Friendship

If you had a best friend, describe him or her.

Were you social or a loner?

Did you change your social and friendship habits from when you were younger, or did they stay the same?

Did you like to spend time with the opposite sex or same sex friends?

Did you ever feel confused about your own sexual identity?

Did you have anyone you could talk to about this?

How did your adolescent friendships help to shape you into the person you are now?

What are some of your favorite memories from that phase of life when good friends mean so much?

School days

Did your attitude toward school and learning change during adolescence?

How did your life change when you began high school?

Did you have a favorite teacher or mentor in high school? How did he or she affect your life?

How did school affect you emotionally?

How did what happened at school integrate with home life?

How did you answer the question "What do you want to be when you grow up?"

What did you think about growing up at this time in your life? Did you look forward to it, dread it, worry about it, or not think about it at all?

Special training, such as music, sports, science, the arts

What activities did you engage in and at what ages?

What kind of self-esteem issues did the activities bring up for you?

Write about your favorite memories of participating in these events.

What are your worst memories?

How did participating make you feel? Good, bad, or mixed?

Did your family support your interests? If not, why not, as you understand it now and as you understood it then.

Religious and spiritual training

Did your attendance at church or synagogue change during this period of your life? If so, how and why?

How did you discuss your religious training with your parents, friends, and teachers? Did they talk about these things casually or formally, at dinner or by appointment, awkwardly or openly? Were you lectured at or listened to? Was religious training a choice or a requirement?

Did you have mystical or inexplicable experiences, such as intuitive insights or premonitions?

How did your family view death? What did you think about it?

Had anyone in your family or circle of friends died by this point in your life?

If you attended funerals or wakes, how did they affect you?

How did you feel about cemeteries?

Clothes

Were you allowed to wear the current fashions?

How much did your parents control your clothes and style?

Did you have the means to buy your own clothes?

Could you trade with friends?

Were you allowed to express your individuality through your appearance?

For girls, how was the changing of your figure and the need for a bra or sanitary equipment handled? Who was in charge of that information and how was it delivered?

Did you feel proud or ashamed of your appearance?

How did you think you looked compared to the other kids?

Were you proud or ashamed of the appearance of your family when friends came over?

Discipline

When you were a teenager, how did your parents discipline or punish you and your siblings?

How did mistakes at school get handled at home?

Were you whipped or spanked? Were implements such as spoons, belts, or switches used? How did you feel about the punishment you received?

Were you yelled at or called names?

Was humiliation used as a punishment technique?

If you were routinely punished, did you ever rebel and refuse to allow it any more? How did this refusal change your role or status in the family?

How did you feel about this change in yourself and your relationship to your parents?

Leaving home

How and at what age did you leave home? College, marriage, work, running away?

Was your family prepared for this event? Or was there a family crisis about you or your siblings leaving home?

How did you feel about leaving home?

Family rules, roles, and myths

How did your family view itself? As rich, poor, better than others, not as good as others?

Who was closest to you in your family? Who was closest to your parents?

How was power defined in your family? Who had the most?

During stress, did one person side with another? Was this pattern consistent or did the pairings change? Under what circumstances would this pairing occur? Did it happen frequently?

How was your family like or unlike your parents' families?

Is your extended family large or small?

Adult relationship with family of origin

How were holidays handled when you left home?

How did the family respond to your long-term relationship or marriage? Did they participate, send money, become over-involved, or maintain boundaries?

How did you feel about going back home in your twenties, thirties, forties, and so forth?

What did you miss most after leaving home?

How are you like or unlike your family?

What generational patterns are you aware of?

Adult Life Stages

Courtship, partnership, marriage

How did you feel about courtship and marriage?

Why did you marry the person you married?

How did your sexual orientation or identity affect your court-ship and dating years?

Birth of children

Did you want or welcome children?

How did having children affect you, your identity, or how you lived your life?

What was the best and worst aspect of having children?

If you didn't have children but wanted them, how would your life have been different if you had had them?

If you had them but didn't really want them, how do you feel about this now?

Work life and identity

How did you answer the question "What do you want to be
  when you grow up" when you were 10, 20, 30, 40, 50?
How would you answer it now?
Who are you without work roles or work identity?
Is there passion in your work life? a sense of accomplishment?
What would you do when you got up in the morning if it were
  the last day of your life?
What does money mean to you?
If you had to choose, would you choose love over money or
  money over love?
Does money bring security for you?
If you could change your life, in what way would you do so?

Spiritual changes and development

How do you define spirituality?
How do you find spirituality in your life now?
Describe the most spiritual experience you have ever had.

Appendix C:
A Note to Therapists

The principles found in this book can help you expand and develop your therapeutic healing work with clients. Methods of using writing as a healing tool range from highly unstructured, free-form, impressionistic imagery to small, selected, specific assignments in a logical fashion. The early exercises move gradually from unthreatening positive memories to traumatic ones. Like all therapy processes, writing can help to clarify and make more conscious the material clients need to work on. And as in other therapeutic interventions, issues such as compliance, resistance, and transference may occur, thus deepening, and perhaps complicating, the work.

The research by Pennebaker, Smyth, Klein, King, and others shows that writing can heal in a variety of ways—from digging deep into previous traumas to focusing on positive future goals and a best self. You must decide which technique is best for a particular client and his or her needs.

In general, if you're in doubt, ask the client to write about the positive first; avoid digging deep until the client has shown a willingness or ability to do that kind of work. Helpful exercises include writing about current positive experiences, or writing a fictional story based on the negative memory, and making it come out "right" by creating a better ending or changing the circumstances so the trauma does not take place. Writing a fairy tale, a mythic story that begins "once upon a time," offers a way to process material on various conscious and unconscious levels.

The techniques described in this book should be used with the understanding that the more fragile the client, the more structure is needed. Writing brings chaos into form, but confronting specific details and having a grounded perception about certain traumas can be too intense for clients at early stages of the work. Using freewriting or journal writing can be too open-ended and unstructured, subjecting a fragile client to feeling overwhelmed by a flood of memories and perceptions.

Writer as Witness

Writing a memoir is powerful because it allows the writer to encounter and witness former selves, and to integrate these selves into a current view of the ego by another aspect of the self. The writer observes himself as a child, adolescent, young adult, and relives his life choices, changes, and roads not taken. As the self goes back and forth between different perceptual windows, the ego is woven into a tapestry of greater strength, confidence, and understanding. That new perspective develops further if the writer creates a lengthy work over time. Each draft creates another level of understanding. A finished memoir is a powerful testament to survival and the triumph of creativity over depression and woundedness.

Memoir as witnessing performs an important healing function. Alice Miller's work provides a context for understanding the idea of therapist as witness; memoir writing extends this witnessing into creativity, imagination, and story writing. The arts have long been understood to be a mode of healing and self-expression that transcends pain and suffering.

Writing Assignments

To ensure the best results, ask clients to write in a journal about a specific, agreed-upon topic arising from the session or selected together from the many exercises in this book. If you already know your clients well, you will be aware of topics that might trigger a strong reaction and be able to guide them into that material when they are ready for it. I have often had clients read their writing to me in session, which provides a focus and support for the writing process. Also, because compliance can be an issue with assignments, if clients expect you to ask them to read during their sessions, they are more likely to do the writing.

Before assigning a particular topic, you'll want to assess your clients to make sure they have the requisite ego strength to explore and write about trauma in depth. Therapeutic concerns about re-traumatization need to be taken into account. Pennebaker did not find this to be a problem in his early studies, but his experimental population was not clinical. In the context of ongoing depth therapy, you might find more vulnerability to regression in your clients as a result of writing about areas that are too raw. If you have any doubt about how far a client should go into uncharted traumatic territory, err on the side of caution.

You may choose to create your own writing-therapy plan with each client, beginning with simple, positive stories. To assess what kinds of stories you might assign, you will need to know the client well. The developmental questionnaire in this book can be used to help assess the level of story, or trauma, the client may not yet have reached through therapy. You will discover your client's hot spots and be able to suggest an appropriate writing plan.

Clients who are not ready to examine their own life might write about other family members or conduct genealogical research in preparation for writing about the family's history. Safe writing subjects include landscape, weather, the history of the place where the family made its home, and a chronicle of the times in which the family lived. Such clients should enter the territory of memory gradually, exploring history and digging up clues. The missing pieces of the story and unanswered questions become subjects for investigation in the search for identity and self-history. This kind of writing helps to resolve questions about the family of origin and provides a way to do family therapy with one person, a technique commonly used by family therapists.

Together, you and your client can design a special notebook or journal that designates at the top of each page or two exercises you have chosen. This way, the client knows what to expect and can be thinking about the next writing exercise. Such a planned structure helps the client use writing as a gentle healing process.

As anyone who writes knows, however, writing can "accidentally" lead into unexpected and surprising terrain. An unconscious moat is breached, and new territory opens up. As the therapist, you would either need to extend the range of therapy into this new territory or back up the work until the client is fully ready to face it. These accidental incursions help break through invisible walls. Imposing a structure lessens the possibility of accidental breakthroughs, but there is no guarantee that they won't occur.

Writing is not always an appropriate intervention, but it can be added at appropriate junctures in the therapy. Most clients do benefit from therapeutic writing. Adding bibliotherapy can create an atmosphere of open exploration into ideas, fictional worlds, and character types that help clients explore denied aspects of self or that show how other families cope with problems. Reading published poetry, fiction, biographies, autobiographies, and memoirs can have a powerful effect by giving clients the sense that they are not alone as they heal, or by allowing them to identify with others who have had similar problems. See the list of published memoirs at the end of this book.

Research showing that writing helps heal diseases such as asthma, chronic fatigue syndrome, and even heart disease provides us therapists with more support and validation for using bibliotherapy and writing therapy as part of our arsenal of tools. We do not have to be writers ourselves to offer these techniques; and we can support

clients in writing not for a result or a grade but for the joy and satisfaction of self-expression. In this way, the client's identity develops,
with old roles and patterns seen as part of another self, the old self
that is being shed, like a chrysalis, for a new one.

A Four-Tiered Approach to Therapeutic Writing

1. The Past in the Family

   a. Help the client use the timeline to sort out possible
      stories, to determine the context of his family's life,
      and to figure out which stories need to be written.
   b. Choose a small number of positive family stories.
      Ask the client to write one each week or month. The
      pace will be determined by you and the client.
   c. If the client says there are no positive stories, have
      her write about how she wishes she had lived. Ask
      her to create a fictional life with positive outcomes.
   d. Create a genogram to sort out family dynamics.
   e. Use the genogram to examine patterns in the current
      generation.
   f. Ask the client to write about the insights gained in
      the process of doing these exercises.

2. The Present Self

   a. Ask the client to keep a journal or diary to record the
      present self, writing in an unstructured, free-flowing
      manner about current states of mind, goals, and
      problems. This approach is useful for those clients
      who do not need the structure of specific exercises.
   b. Have the client explore the physical, emotional,
      intellectual, and spiritual self through writing.
   c. Ask the client to keep a dream journal.

      d. Spiritual autobiography or journeys into memory can guide the client through deep internal reflection and exploration of self.

      e. Reflective exercises, such as writing answers to the question "Who Am I," help focus on identity resolution and the development of the real self. A new "Who Am I" story could be written every week or month.

3.   The Past Self

      a. Focusing on the past self or selves deepens the work and provides the possibility of integration. The past family history, the past self, and how the current self is on the way to becoming the future self can all be written about in an ongoing memoir.

4.   The Future Self

      a. The goal is to help the client envision a new life, a healed self, and a positive way to integrate his new learning. You can structure various exercises that connect to the work the client has already completed and to the life story you have come to know. Some useful questions include:

          i.   Who am I becoming?
         ii.   Who do I want to become?
       iii.   What is the best self I can be?
       iv.   What transformations do I want to make in my life?

Writing therapy gives a client another way to express her hidden self and to reveal the beautiful person she is within. Miraculous changes can happen through writing. These changes occur slowly. And they may remain invisible in the client's psyche and in the depths of his or her soul.

To learn more about the studies on writing as healing, read *Opening Up: The Healing Power of Expressing Emotions* by James Pennebaker. *The Writing Cure*, edited by Stephen Lepore and Joshua Smyth, with a last chapter by Pennebaker, includes more recent studies and continues the work of the earlier researchers exploring such questions as whether writing affects the healing process of diseases, whether positive writing has as salutary an effect as writing about pain and trauma, and how writing affects memory. Some of the studies show that positive writing about the future is as healing as writing about trauma.

As a therapist, you can use autobiographical writing as an adjunct to your therapeutic work to create awareness of family stories, to knit together the client's fragmented story, and to strengthen the client's identity and sense of relatedness to others. The client learns that a self-history carries within it wisdom about life and family, and that story is a way to create a new future as well as to heal the past.

Appendix D: Quick Reminders for When You Think You're Stuck

- Keep writing. Writing leads to more writing.
- Freewrite in a journal even if you aren't able to write a particular story.
- Read other memoirs to learn more about the writing process, style, and language.
- Outline, edit, and tinker with other stories when you aren't in the mood to write a new one.
- Go on the Internet to look at other people's writing and sites that encourage writing.
- Get out the photos, and look at the people and times you're writing about.
- Write a one- or two-page portrait of a family member or mentor who has helped you.
- Write a quick sketch of a happy moment.
- List the blessings in your life.
- Read fiction for style, technique, plot, scene, and character development tips.
- Eavesdrop in cafés, listening to dialogue and speech cadences.
- Read poetry.
- Attend author events and readings for inspiration.

References

Adams, Kathleen. 1990. *Journal to the Self*. New York: Warner Books.

———. 1998. *The Way of the Journal*. Lutherville, MD: The Sidran Press.

———. 2000. *The Write Way to Wellness*. Lakewood, CO: Center for Journal Therapy.

Albert, Susan Wittig. 1997. *Writing from Life: Telling Your Soul's Story*. New York: Jeremy P. Tarcher/Putnam.

Allende, Isabel. 1985. *The House of the Spirits*. New York: Knopf.

Allison, Dorothy. 1992. *Bastard Out of Carolina*. New York: Dutton.

Baldwin, Christina. 1998. *Life's Companion: Journal Writing as a Spiritual Quest*. New York: Bantam Doubleday Dell.

Bachelard, Paul. 1994. Reprint. *The Poetics of Space*. Boston: Beacon Press. Original edition, New York: Orion Press, 1964.

Black, Claudia. 1981. *It Will Never Happen to Me*. New York: Ballantine Books.

Brande, Dorothea. [1943] 1981. *Becoming a Writer*. Reprint, with a foreword by John Gardner, New York: Jeremy P. Tarcher/Putnam.

Cameron, Julia. 2002. 10th anniversary edition. *The Artist's Way: A Spiritual Path to Higher Creativity*. New York: Jeremy P. Tarcher/Putnam.

Chandler, Marilyn. 1990. *A Healing Art: Regeneration Through Autobiography*. New York: Garland Publishing.

Conroy, Pat. 1986. *The Prince of Tides*. New York: Houghton Mifflin.

DeSalvo, Louise. 2000. *Writing as a Way of Healing: How Telling Our Stories Transforms Our Lives*. Boston: Beacon Press.

Dillard, Annie. 1987. To Fashion a Text. In *Inventing the Truth: The Art and Craft of Memoir*, edited and with a memoir and introduction by William Zinsser. Boston: Houghton Mifflin.

Engel, Susan. 1999. *Context is Everything: The Nature of Memory*. New York: W. H. Freeman & Co.

Fox, John. 1997. *Poetic Medicine*. New York: Jeremy P. Tarcher/Putnam.

Glickstein, Lee. 1999. *Be Heard Now! Tap into Your Inner Speaker and Communicate with Ease*. Reprint. New York: Broadway Books.

Herman, Judith. 1992. *Trauma and Recovery*. New York: Basic Books.

Hanh, Thich Nhat. 1997. *Teachings on Love*. Berkeley, CA: Parallax Press.

Hoffman, Bob. 1976. *Getting Divorced from Mom and Dad*. New York: E. P. Dutton.

King, Laurie. 2002. Gain Without Pain? Expressive Writing and Self-Regulation. In *The Writing Cure: How Expressive Writing Promotes Health and Emotional Well-Being*, eds., Stephen J. Lepore and Joshua M. Smyth. Washington, D.C.: American Psychological Association.

Lamott, Anne. 1995. *Bird by Bird: Some Instructions on Writing and Life*. New York: Pantheon Books.

Ledoux, Denis. 1991. *Turning Memories into Memoirs*. Lisbon Falls, ME: Soleil Press.

Leffland, Ella. 1985. Reprint. *Rumors of Peace*. New York: HarperCollins.

Lepore, Stephen J., and Joshua M. Smyth, eds. 2002. *The Writing Cure: How Expressive Writing Promotes Health and Emotional Well-Being*. Washington, D.C.: American Psychological Association.

Levine, Peter A. 1997. *Waking the Tiger: Healing Trauma*. Berkeley, CA: North Atlantic Books.

Lopez, Judith. 2001. *Immune Dysfunction: Winning My Battle Against Toxins, Illness & the Medical Establishment*. Mill Valley, CA: Millpond Press.

Mahler, Margaret. 1975. *The Psychological Birth of the Human Infant*. New York: Basic Books.

Masterson, James. 1988. *The Real Self*. New York: The Free Press.

Merton, Thomas. 1999. 50th anniversary edition. *The Seven Storey Mountain*. New York: Harcourt Brace.

Metzger, Deena. 1992. *Writing for Your Life*. New York: HarperCollins.

Miller, Alice, 2001. *The Truth Will Set You Free*. New York: Basic Books.

Nin, Anais. 1967. *The Diary of Anais Nin*. Vol. II (March 1937). New York: Swallow Press.

Pennebaker, James W. 1990. *Opening Up: The Healing Power of Expressing Emotions.* New York: The Guilford Press.

————. 2002. Personal conversation with author, February 4, in Austin, TX.

Pennebaker, James W., and Janel D. Seagal. 1999. Forming a Story: The Health Benefits of Narrative. *Journal of Clinical Psychology* 55(10):1243–1254.

Price, Reynolds. 1994. *A Whole New Life.* New York: Plume.

Rainer, Tristine. 1997. *The New Diary: Your Life as Story.* New York: Jeremy P. Tarcher/Putnam.

————. 1998. *Your Life as Story: Discovering the "New Autobiography" and Writing Memoir as Literature.* New York: Jeremy P. Tarcher/Putnam.

Reichl, Ruth. 1999. *Tender at the Bone: Growing Up at the Table.* New York: Broadway Books.

Rothschild, Babette. 2000. *The Body Remembers: The Psychophysiology of Trauma and Trauma Treatment.* New York: W. W. Norton & Co.

Salon.com. http://www.salon.com/books/feature/2001/12/12/lauck/print.html. Accessed 6/28/02.

Smyth, J., A. Stone, A. Hurewitz, and A. Kaell. 1999. Writing about stressful events produces symptom reduction in asthmatics and rheumatoid arthritics: a randomized trial. *Journal of the American Medical Association,* 281, 1304–1309.

Suzuki, Shunryu. 1973. *Zen Mind, Beginner's Mind.* New York: Weatherhill.

Tan, Amy. 1994. *The Joy Luck Club.* New York: Prentice Hall.

Thomas, Lewis. 1974. *The Lives of a Cell.* New York: Viking Press.

Ueland, Brenda. 1987. *If You Want to Write: A Book about Art, Independence and Spirit.* St. Paul, MN: Graywolf Press.

Wakefield, Dan. 1990. *The Story of Your Life: Writing a Spiritual Autobiography.* Boston: Beacon Press.

Woolf, Virginia. [1927] 1989. *To the Lighthouse.* New York: Harvest Books.

Recommended Published Memoirs

Allende, Isabel	*Paula*
Angelou, Maya	*I Know Why the Caged Bird Sings*
Ball, Edward	*Slaves in the Family*
Baker, Russell	*Growing Up*
Balakian, Peter	*Black Dog of Fate*
Bragg, Rick	*All Over But the Shoutin'*
Brittain, Vera	*Testament of Youth*
Chernin, Kim	*My Mother's House*
Conway, Jill Kerr	*When Memory Speaks*
————	*The Road from Coorain*
Day, Dorothy	*The Long Loneliness*
DeBeauvoir, Simone	*Memoirs of a Dutiful Daughter*
Fremont, Helen	*After Long Silence*
Gebler, Carlo	*My Father and I*
Gilmore, Mikal	*Shot in the Heart*
Gornick, Vivian	*Fierce Attachments*
Gunther, John	*Death Be Not Proud*
Harrison, Catherine	*The Kiss*
Hoffman, Eva	*Lost in Translation*
Jamison, Kay	*An Unquiet Mind*
Jung, Carl	*Memories, Dreams, Reflections*
Karr, Mary	*The Liar's Club*
————	*Cherry*
MacDonald, Michael	*All Souls: A Family Story from Southie*

Maynard, Isabelle	*China Dreams: Growing Up Jewish in Tientsin*
McBride, James	*The Color of Water: A Black Man's Tribute to His White Mother*
McCarthy, Mary	*Memories of a Catholic Girlhood*
McCourt, Frank	*Angela's Ashes*
———	*'Tis*
Mead, Margaret	*Blackberry Winter*
Neruda, Pablo	*Memoirs*
Norris, Kathleen	*Dakota: A Spiritual Geography*
———	*Cloister Walk*
O'Faolin, Nuala	*Are You Somebody?*
Perel, Solomon	*Europa, Europa*
Rhodes, Richard	*A Hole in the World*
Ryan, Terry	*The Prizewinner of Defiance, Ohio*
Sarton, May	*Journal of a Solitude*
Scott-Maxwell, Florida	*The Measure of My Days*
See, Carolyn	*Dreaming*
Weisel, Elie	*The Night Trilogy*
Wolff, Tobias	*This Boy's Life*
Woolf, Virginia	*Moments of Being*

About the Author

*L*inda Joy Myers, Ph.D., is a licensed Marriage and Family Therapist with a private practice in the San Francisco Bay Area. Her
long-standing interest in the healing power of writing led her to obtain an M.F.A. in creative writing from Mills College. Since then she
has been teaching memoir writing and offers Autobiography and
Therapeutic Healing workshops and training to therapists. Her own
memoir, *Don't Call Me Mother,* describes three generations of mothers
who abandoned their daughters. Her story "Herbert Hoover's
Birthplace" won the Jessamyn West Prize in 1995. And her essay
"Who Am I?" won first place in the 2002 annual Carol Landherr
LifeWriting Competition sponsored by Story Circle Network. Her
poetry, fiction, and memoirs have been published in *Westwind, Writing
for Our Lives,* and other literary journals.

Index

Order Form

Please send me ____ copies of *Becoming Whole* at $19.95 each

Book order: $_____

7.75% sales tax (California orders only): _____

Shipping ($2.00 per book): _____

Total: _____

❑ My check/money order for $_____ is enclosed

Please charge my credit card   ❑ Visa   ❑ MasterCard   ❑ American Express

Account Number _____

Expiration date _____

Name on card _____

Daytime phone _____

Name on card _____

Signature _____

Send to:

Name _____

Address _____

_____

City, State, zip _____

Mail to:

Silver Threads
3738 Carmel View Road
San Diego, CA 92130
858-794-1597 / 866-251-3741 (toll-free)
silverthreads@silvercat.com

Order Form

Please send me ___ copies of *Becoming Whole* at $19.95 each

Book order: $_____
7.75% sales tax (California orders only): _____
Shipping ($2.00 per book): _____

Total: _____

❏ My check/money order for $_____ is enclosed

Please charge my credit card   ❏ Visa   ❏ MasterCard   ❏ American Express

Account Number _____

Expiration date _____

Name on card _____

Daytime phone _____

Name on card _____

Signature _____

Send to:

Name _____

Address _____

_____

City, State, zip _____

Mail to:

Silver Threads
3738 Carmel View Road
San Diego, CA 92130
858-794-1597 / 866-251-3741 (toll-free)
silverthreads@silvercat.com